TELLING TALES

Intimations of the Sacred in Popular Culture

By Marybeth & David Baggett

MORAL APOLOGETICS PRESS * HOUSTON, TEXAS

Copyright © 2021 Moral Apologetics Press

All rights reserved. No part of this publication may be reproduced, distributed, or transmitted in any form or by any means, including photocopying, recording, or other electronic or mechanical methods, without the prior written permission of the publisher, except in the case of brief quotations embodied in critical reviews and certain other noncommercial uses permitted by copyright law.

For Jonathan Pruitt
in gratitude for his faithful support and service

Foreword

William Kent Kruger's *New York Times* best-selling book *This Tender Land* (2019) opens with this arresting thought:

> In the beginning, after he labored over the heavens and the earth, the light and the dark, and land and the sea and all living things that dwell therein, after he created man and woman and before he rested, I believe God gave us one final gift. Lest we forget the divine source of all that beauty, he gave us stories.

In the span of a few sentences, Kruger suggests a theology of story. Stories are a gift, like everything else, from God. As such, we should expect to see God in stories too. And I'm not just thinking about the latest "Christian" movie or novel. No, if God has gifted us stories, then we should seek his divine clues in all stories—or at least all the good ones.

Stories help us see, and they teach about deep truths—including about the true story of the world. But there is a tension today between what we might affectionately call "High Culture" and "Pop Culture." The intelligentsia tell us there is no story that is alive and inviting. The true story of the world is more mundane, more this-worldly, more secular. But that story—and those individual stories built on that story—are rather boring. However, if we pay attention to the stories we love—the ones we read and re-read, and the ones we watch and re-watch, we learn something startling: they are suggestive of something transcendent, something other-worldly, something enchanted and mysterious.

So there is a tension between what we are told by a large swath of the intelligentsia and the deepest longings of the human heart. When we think about the stories we love, our hearts long for more. Our hearts long for a story alive and inviting, a story that names us even. It seems then that we find clues about that true story of the world—"Intimations of the Sacred"—in Pop Culture, in the tales we tell.

If we pay attention, these stories we love are a kind of divine clue, awakening us and setting us on a journey of discovery. Ultimately, if faithfully followed, they point us to the heart of all good stories: Jesus. But we need guides to set us on this path. I cannot think of a better pair of guides than Marybeth and David Baggett, that dynamic duo of literature, art, story, and philosophy. You are in for a real treat. In *Telling Tales*, our faithful—and funny—guides take us on a tour through some of our most beloved stories—from Kurt Vonnegut to *Ted Lasso*, *Harry Potter* to *The Hunger Games*, pointing out along the way rich insights about faith and truth, hope and goodness, love and beauty.

I'm kind of impressed with the Baggetts. They are well-versed in television and film, but they also read a ton of great books. And they know literature, philosophy, pop culture, and theology. In this way, they are the perfect guides to help us hear hints of the divine in the text and see them on the screen. Listen, along with them, for the voice of God in story.

May you enjoy this rich book of adventure and folly, comedy and tragedy, love potions and Shadowlands, theology and philosophy, Jesus and journey. And then thank the God who gives us all things, including story, to remind us of his beauty.

– Paul Gould
Associate Professor of Philosophy of Religion
Palm Beach Atlantic University

ACKNOWLEDGMENTS

It is our pleasure and privilege to thank the many people who helped make this volume possible. Numerous of the chapters were collaborations, so we were able to reprint them only with the blessing of a variety of co-writers and presses. Collaborators who allowed their work to be reproduced here include Gregory Bassham ("Love Potion, No. 9 ¾," "How to Resist Evil"), Neil Delaney, Jr. ("Friendship, Rivalry, and Excellence"), and Mark Foreman ("Human Rights, Human Nature, and *Amistad*").

We also recognize the support and guidance of various editors we have worked with in developing and polishing these essays. From Erin Stanza and Alan Noble and others at *Christ and Pop Culture*, Bill Irwin with the Philosophy and Pop Culture series, Chris Reese with *The Worldview Bulletin*, and Melanie Cogdill at *Christian Research Journal*, these skilled editors have brought their considerable talents to bear on our words and ideas, drawing out their best and minimizing any infelicities. Special appreciation goes to our son Nathaniel Davis who proofread the volume and made possible a much cleaner version. Also, Marybeth's Apologetics students in a Fall 2021 Houston Baptist University Research and Writing class served as beta readers and offered many helpful suggestions for improving the final draft. This collection is truly collaborative in that way.

Finally, we acknowledge the work of Jonathan Pruitt, managing editor of *MoralApologetics.com* and general editor of Moral Apologetics Press. Jonathan works faithfully behind the scenes, making possible the good work of these outlets. We will forever be grateful for his gift of service, and for that reason, we dedicate this volume to him.

Table of Contents

Introduction: A Call to Look Closer 1

PART I: FAITH & TRUTH
1. Kurt Vonnegut: Unlikely Apologist 7
2. Sherlock Holmes as Epistemologist 10
3. Risking Belief: *Ted Lasso* and Faith 24
4. Magic, Muggles, and Moral Imagination 28
5. *Firefly* and Freedom 40
6. *RBG* Invites Us to Love Our Political Neighbors 54
7. His Truth Is Marching On: *Selma*'s Clarion Call 58
8. The Fault in Green's Story 61
9. More Than Mere Machine:
   The Indomitable Human Spirit of Philip K. Dick 65
10. Human Rights, Human Nature, and *Amistad* 72
11. Train Up Your Wizards in the Way They Should Go 87

PART II: HOPE & GOODNESS
12. How Do You Like Them Ethics? 99
13. *The Handmaid's Tale* Evokes a Longing for Peace
    and Justice 110
14. How to Resist Evil: Nonviolence in *The Passion
    of the Christ* 115
15. "And Death Shall Be No More": Going Beyond
    Transhumanism for Kids 126
16. *Three Billboards Outside Ebbing, Missouri* Shows Us
    a World Full of Meanness 129
17. Living in the Not Yet: *Mockingjay – Part I*
    as Microcosm of the Fall 133
18. Weighing Death in *Buffy the Vampire Slayer* 136

19. *The Man in the High Castle* and the Necessity
    of Moral Faith 140
20. Hold Fast to the Good: *Fahrenheit 451*, the Love
    of Books, and the Value of People.................................... 145
21. *Once Upon a Time* and Philosophy:
    Rumpel's Redemption 149
22. Mark Twain's Tightrope Walk:
    Caught between Despair and Hope................................... 154

PART III: LOVE & BEAUTY

23. Love Potion No. 9 ¾ 161
24. Intuiting the Beauty of the Infinite:
    Ramanujan and Hardy's Partnership 170
25. J. K. Rowling: In Praise of Imagination............................ 175
26. Rats in God's Laboratory:
    Shadowlands and The Problem of Evil............................ 178
27. *About Time*: A Romantic Comedy
    That's Actually about Love 188
28. Friendship, Rivalry, and Excellence 192
29. *Jerry before Seinfeld*: Delightfully Distinct.................... 208
30. Refusing Counterfeits: *Rear Window*
    and Our Struggle as Spectators 211
31. *Interstellar* and Partiality 215
32. The Faithful Witness of Fred Rogers 219

Notes 223
General Index... 241
Scripture Index... 246
Permissions 247

A CALL TO LOOK CLOSER

The essays that follow are the culmination of two decades of writing David and I have done on popular culture. Avid consumers of pop culture ourselves, we have often found compelling the ways in which these cultural products, perhaps unwittingly, touch on important themes of flourishing, the human condition, and principled faith. And fortuitously, perhaps providentially, each of us separately have had ample opportunities to reflect more formally on these connections.

David, serendipitously enough, landed his first teaching position at King's College in Wilkes-Barre, Pennsylvania, where he met Bill Irwin, pioneer of the groundbreaking Philosophy and Pop Culture movement. It was Bill who opened David's eyes to the possibilities of drawing philosophical insights out of popular works, thereby using them as a bridge for encouraging deeper reflection on the most important questions of human existence and the nature of reality. Just as a spoonful of sugar helps the medicine go down, so, too, does a dash of Harry Potter make metaphysics palatable, if not enticing.

David also found that this work enabled him to naturally segue into questions of faith and theology. If theism, and particularly Christian theism, is true, then its fundamentals bear on all the dimensions of life—who we are as people, what we desire and what conduces to our deepest joy, what our obligations are to others, and more. As human creations, reflective of human experiences, popular culture ruminations necessarily intersect with these central existential concerns rife with philosophical and theological significance.

I, too, was privileged to discover such exciting possibilities when I started writing for *Christ and Pop Culture*. This online outlet is the brainchild of Alan Noble and Richard Clark, who shared a vision of thinking theologically about popular culture—both for the sake of the church's edification and as witness to nonbelievers. I have been involved with the site for the last seven years or so, first as writer and later as editor. Participating in that intellectually and spiritually fertile community has been a source of great satisfaction. Through that time, my appreciation for the depth and power, richness and texture of the Christian message has grown exponentially. I have seen the elasticity of Christian doctrine at work, as it organically and seamlessly takes on—and beautifully explains—unlikely writers and texts. This itself, we submit, is evidence for its truth.

Importantly, we aim in the essays that follow, not merely to treat the texts we write about as means to an educative or spiritually-removed end, but rather to respect them on their own terms. Such an approach, we hope, will lower the volume in our too-often vitriolic culture and instead emphasize common ground rather than functioning derisively and divisively as a wedge between divergent worldviews. We do have our convictions, of course, but we seek to demonstrate what has drawn us to those convictions and allow readers to come to their own conclusions. If folks cannot come together over the conclusions we draw, they can still agree on the pleasure of the pop culture piece being discussed and the importance of the questions it raises. Bridge-building and substantive conversation take primacy here over tendentious sound bites and mic-dropping diatribes.

Charles Taylor has famously written about our current Secular Age, describing our condition as contained in an "immanent frame." As he explains, the default option today is unbelief or "exclusive humanism" where people feel no need to contemplate questions of transcendence and make sense of life based on anything that isn't immediate or material.[1] And yet, as we hope these essays show, the sacred, like our cats when they want a scratch, has a pesky habit of being recalcitrant. It persists and makes itself felt even as it is being repressed or resisted. This little volume asks readers to take another and closer look, to be attentive to evidence perhaps heretofore overlooked or domesticated, and to consider carefully and in community the implications of what they discover.

A quick word about the categories by which we structured the book: they are a blend of the classical transcendentals of Truth, Goodness, and Beauty with the theological virtues of Faith, Hope, and Love. Our intent in drawing these together is two-fold: first, to highlight our own concern with juxtaposing and synthesizing philosophical and classical thinking and Christian theology while accentuating the myriad dynamic ways in which they interact. We see them less in contrast or tension and more as mutually enriching and intimately connected. Framing the essays along these lines should highlight those organic interactions.

Second, intentionally pairing these ideals generates a synergistic balance, providing a bulwark against their fragmentation when considered in isolation. Faith, for example, is sometimes thought of as fideism, divorced from reason or the need for principled evidence. Combining our consideration of faith with truth, however, underscores that they are best understood, both philosophically and biblically, as ineliminably related. Or take beauty. Divorced from love, beauty can turn grotesque, even idolatrous, and ultimately unseemly. Love keeps beauty within its proper bounds and deepens our appreciation for its value and proper enjoyment and celebration.

Our hope as you read through these essays is that you can see yet more fruitful implications and fertile applications of these ideals and their crosspollination.

– Marybeth Baggett

Part I: Faith & Truth

1

KURT VONNEGUT: UNLIKELY APOLOGIST

The late Kurt Vonnegut inspires loyalty among his readers. He's the kind of author whose fans devour book after book, reading one after another in rapid succession. Or at least I (Marybeth) did. Back in 1997 a coworker recommended Vonnegut to me, specifically *Slaughterhouse-Five*. Unable to get my hands on that novel, I checked out *Deadeye Dick*. I was hooked. By the end of the year, I'd read at least ten Vonnegut novels, only whetting my appetite for more.

Vonnegut is often thought of as cynical, edgy, and distasteful, not the most inviting qualities. This reputation is based on his role as social satirist and his liberal-leaning political stance. The winsome Vonnegut, on the other hand, is found in his letter to an English class at Xavier High School, one of the most popular *Letters of Note* posts from 2013.[1] He's charming and kind, concerned with the students' flourishing, aware of the indignities of life (his aging and its effects), yet vanquishing them with humor and grace. Reading that letter can easily instill enthusiasm for Vonnegut's work.

A Christian might feel a bit timid about her affinity for Vonnegut. The author was often conceived as tasteless, a charge getting its bite from a cursory reading of the author's irreverent and iconoclastic titles. Satirists tip sacred cows, and Vonnegut's no exception. His outspoken agnosticism further reinforced my timidity. Having flirted with both theism and atheism, Vonnegut was willing to commit to neither. He even claims that his first wife's conversion to Christianity was a key factor in their divorce. Even so, Vonnegut retained interest in scripture and Christianity, with a particular fondness for Christ himself. Closing the letter to Xavier HS "God bless you all!" is, ironically enough, vintage Vonnegut. He also once claimed, tongue in cheek perhaps, his epitaph should read, "The only proof he needed for the existence of God was music."

Vonnegut's words consistently dance with such delight, even when dealing with death and dearth—the firebombing of Dresden (*Slaughterhouse-Five*), apocalyptic nightmares (*Cat's Cradle, Galápagos*), Nazi war crimes (*Mother Night*). Yet the most salient response he elicits from readers is laughter. The humor lacing Vonnegut's letter to the high school class permeates all of his books. However heavy the subject matter, he never loses his light touch; however tragic, he retains the capacity to laugh. Vonnegut's humor exposes man's fears and limitations and invites his readers to reject human pretensions.

As he wraps up the opening chapter to *Slaughterhouse-Five*, for example, he turns the story of Sodom and Gomorrah on its head, using it as a parallel to the destruction of the Nazi-occupied city of Dresden and challenging us to reconsider the source and nature of evil and our obligations to one another:

> Those were vile people in both cities, as is well known. The world was better off without them. And Lot's wife, of course, was told not to look back where all those people and their homes had been. But she did look back, and I love her for that, because it was so human. So she was turned to a pillar of salt. So it goes.[2]

Then, poignantly: "I've finished my war book now. The next one I write is going to be fun. This one is a failure, and had to be, since it was written by a pillar of salt." The tension between loss and life, pain and joy, is felt in every line of this and many other of his books. Mingled among these jokes and laments are moving passages honoring human beings. In the aftermath of Dresden's firebombing, the main character rests in a horse-drawn wagon, appreciating the sun, rest, and full belly he'd been denied while a POW. At this moment, Vonnegut introduces two German obstetricians who care for the horse Billy and his comrades have failed to feed or groom properly.[3] Picturesque scenes like this one recur in Vonnegut's work, encouraging readers to reject easy cynicism amidst pain and tragedy.

Vonnegut is a paradox like that—a likeable curmudgeon, a pessimistic optimist, an earnest humorist. And it's his honesty about the paradoxes of life that draws readers back to him again and again. It's an honesty that, despite Vonnegut's inability to submit personally to the gospel message, brilliantly proclaims its truth. As Christian enthusiasts of popular culture realize, evidence for the truth of the gospel can appear in the unlikeliest of places. In Vonnegut recognition of fundamental gospel truth abounds, reinforcing and renewing the wisdom of John 1:1, that in the beginning was the Word, that the logos of Christ underpins reality and speaks to us all. In fact, reading Vonnegut can enliven one's understanding and practice of Christianity.

Vonnegut vividly depicts the world as it is—filled with sorrow, overwhelmed by joy, populated by valuable human beings, capable of being redeemed (if only on a small-scale in his work). There, too, is Vonnegut's inescapable paradox, a paradox resolved only by Christ: victim-perpetrators seeking salvation and absolution, powerless to save themselves. Such a world resonates with the universal human experience, and Christianity makes best sense of it. The God he denies is the One who enters into the world to save the humans Vonnegut cherishes.

2

SHERLOCK HOLMES AS EPISTEMOLOGIST

A philosopher friend of ours tends to give his waitresses a hard time, though they never seem to mind. When they ask him if there's anything else he needs, for example, he tends to reply that, now that they ask, he would like to be given the meaning of life. He's a good tipper, but not that good.

Beyond containing a skein of mysteries, life itself is a mystery, often an inscrutable one, in need of unraveling. Because omniscience for most of us, unlike Sherlock Holmes's brother Mycroft, isn't our specialization, we could use help in knowing how to go about figuring out life's answers, both big and small. Who better to ask—with Mrs. Hudson's permission, of course—than that paragon of detectives quietly smoking his black pipe in the midst of his chemistry experiments at 221B Baker Street, where tobacco smoke wafts in the air, the fire crackles, fog swirls past the window, and it's always 1892.[1]

Although it's true that the mysteries Holmes set out to solve were a bit smaller in scope than the meaning of life, he wasn't unconcerned about life's broader questions. As a character with feet of clay, Holmes, despite his great powers, was without neither weakness nor susceptibility to temptation. Sometimes saddled with angst and cognitive dissonance enough to put to shame the most ennui-afflicted existentialist, Sherlock Holmes was vulnerable to periods of dark depression and even drug-induced periods of liberation from banal commonplaces and the "insufferable fatigues of idleness."[2] There's evidence to suggest that he thought that if this life is all there is, with no afterlife in which we see ultimate justice effected, then the world is a cruel jest, for "the ways of Fate are hard to understand."[3] At another point he was "in a melancholy and philosophic mood" when he asked, "Is not all life pathetic and futile. ls not [Josiah Amberley's] story a microcosm of the whole? We reach. We grasp. And what is life in our hands at the end? A shadow, or worse than a shadow—misery."[4]

Yet despite the challenges of life, the darkness of hearts, and ubiquity of suffering, Holmes at one juncture provided a glimpse into his remaining trust in the goodness of reality. In "The Naval Treaty" he held up the drooping stalk of a moss rose, with its dainty blend of crimson and green, before saying,

> There is nothing in which deduction is so necessary as in religion. It can be built up as an exact science by the reasoner. Our highest assurance of the goodness of Providence seems to me to rest in the flowers. All other things, our powers, our desires, our food, are really necessary for the existence in the first instance. But this rose is an extra. Its smell and its color are an embellishment of life, not a condition of it. It is only goodness which gives extras, and so I say again that we have much to hope from the flowers.[5]

A remarkable and suggestive passage, even if all too brief, it won't detain us here beyond serving as evidence to suggest that Sherlock saw the power of reasoning that he employed in solving crimes as applicable to life's larger questions. The process of considering questions of what it takes to acquire knowledge, what knowledge ultimately is, and whether or not we have come to possess it is the branch of philosophy called epistemology. Here we explore the topic of Sherlock Holmes as epistemologist. Holmes was no philosopher by trade, of course, but then again, he wasn't an official detective either, despite being unparalleled as a sleuth. Early on we're told that Sherlock's knowledge of philosophy (and politics and literature) was nil although it was encyclopedic in other areas, but in Conan Doyle's second novel about Holmes, he shows knowledge of Goethe and educates Watson on philosopher Winwood Reade. Either Conan Doyle decided to flesh out his character some more, or Watson misjudged Sherlock within the fictional context, but there's a more important point behind those. Watson cast Sherlock, at the end of "The Final Problem" as "the best and the wisest man whom I have ever known."[6] Perhaps we could chalk such accolades up to eulogistic hyperbole, but if Watson's words are taken with any seriousness at all, Holmes was a man of wisdom; and philosophy, etymologically and at its best, is the love of wisdom.[7]

Logic was the forte of Sherlock Holmes, and it's also the language of philosophy. Even though Dr. Watson counted Holmes as having zero knowledge of philosophy, Sherlock's proficiency in the use of logic made him an impeccable candidate to at least do philosophy if he were so inclined, however ignorant of the history and concepts of philosophy he may have been. We won't delve inordinately into his use of logic, although we will touch on that topic. Instead, we will broaden the discussion to epistemology in general. Sherlock Holmes, by his own admission, had for his vocation knowing things that other people didn't. We will elucidate some of the reasons Holmes was able to know what he did—reasons that aren't always, or even typically, associated with the cold calculations of this mental magician. His expansive epistemological method requires an examination of a cluster of interestingly interconnected features of his character and practices if we are to understand his effectiveness as a philosophical sleuth. What we find is that many of the laudable virtues of Sherlock Holmes are generalizable as character and intellectual virtues to emulate to become better thinkers.

Examining the Premises

At the foundation of Sherlock's method was observation. In *The Sign of the Four*, Holmes identified the three qualities necessary for the ideal detective: power of observation, knowledge, and deduction. We will consider each in turn, beginning with observation. Holmes used all of his senses, even augmenting them when he could (as with a magnifying glass), to glean information about the scene of a crime and all the relevant players involved. Each piece of information would get tucked away for later use and timely retrieval, and each datum was considered clay with which to build bricks, or a symptom that a doctor can use to make a diagnosis. Without the data and evidence thus gleaned from a crime scene, he refrained from speculation and conjecture. He recognized the dangers involved in spinning theories too quickly and then, perhaps subtly and unwittingly, twisting facts to suit theories rather than constructing theories to account for the facts. Time and again Watson reports Holmes listening intently to his client's narrative, interjecting questions, his eyes riveted and his full concentration engaged. At the crime scene, Holmes, a genius for minutiae, was like a hound on a scent, darting from place to place taking measurements and collecting samples. Others could see, but they didn't observe. Holmes trained himself to take note of what others would overlook, a talent that didn't merely come naturally, but with intentionality and due diligence. Meticulous attention to detail was axiomatic for Holmes. Not content with general impressions, he concentrated himself on the details, where everything of importance could generally be found. His eyes could see the importance of sleeves, the suggestiveness of thumbnails, and the great issues that may hang from a bootlace.[8]

At the root of the task of epistemology is the challenge posed by the simple fact that appearances don't always correspond with reality. They can be deceiving. Sometimes what seems simple is deceptively complex, and sometimes what appears complicated admits of a simple explanation. The fact that we can be deceived or deluded complicates the epistemic task of finding the truth. Holmes seemed to have an acute recognition of this insight, perhaps accounting for what can be called his aversion to the obvious. Rarely was he content with what may have seemed clear cut to others. He was interested in what accounted for all the facts, not just those most at the surface. An obvious explanation in "The Beryl Coronet" case was that the son was the guilty perpetrator, appearing to have been caught red-handed. Holmes, searching for an explanation for all the observations he had made and facts in need of an account, remained skeptical. Healthy skepticism about appearances tends to be a salient feature of any credible epistemologist.

Tattoos and Typewriters

Observation gave Holmes the facts of a case. His acquaintance with the annals of crime gave him a vast reservoir of relevant background knowledge from which to draw. Such knowledge was so crucial for detective work that he said of LeVillard, the French detective with quick intuition, that he remained "deficient in the wide range of exact knowledge which is essential to the higher developments of his art."[9] Holmes had acquired knowledge of crime not just by his personal experience at solving it, but by the assiduous study he had devoted to learning about its history. He counseled the same. After discovering that a reference of Sherlock's hearkened back to a criminal from the previous century, Inspector MacDonald said, "Then he's no use to me. I'm a practical man." Holmes responded, "Mr. Mac, the most practical thing you ever did in your life would be to shut yourself up for three months and read twelve hours a day at the annals of crime."[10] Sometimes reading, Holmes realized, is the most practical course of action of all, a sentiment likely echoed by anyone who has ever had occasion to teach a philosophy course.

Because of Sherlock's expertise and knowledge, he could instantly recognize the parallels of a new case with its predecessors, detecting not just their parallels and points of similarity, but also their departures and instructive points of disconnect. He was open to their commonalities, but had also acquired a keen sense of what proved new and distinctive. This sensitized him to key points in need of special attention and focus of concentration. He would habitually refer to analogues from the history of crime, and on occasion be fairly sure of the outcome of his investigation from its outset because of its conspicuous resemblance to its precedents. In almost Wittgensteinian fashion, he was wont to note the family resemblances between crimes that could often furnish the key clues to their resolution. He described his profession to Watson in this way in *A Study in Scarlet*: "They lay all the evidence before me, and I am generally able, by the help of my knowledge of the history of crime, to set them straight. There is a strong family resemblance about misdeeds, and if you have all the details of a thousand at your finger ends, it is odd if you can't unravel the thousand and first."[11] As a rule, once Holmes heard of some slight indication in the course of events, he could guide himself "by the thousands of other similar cases" that would occur to his memory.[12] When necessary, Holmes would consult the index of cases he had compiled, not to mention his record of newsworthy persons he could readily access as needed.

Holmes had also contributed to the available knowledge by writing several monographs cataloging everything from tattoos to cigar ashes, footprints to secret signs, He had considered additional volumes on animals, the influence of trade on the form of the hand, and typewriters. The quality and breadth of his preparation were as impressive as they were effective. Moreover, his knowledge and expertise made him a better and better observer, because it enabled him to develop ever greater proficiency at noticing the right details most likely to provide the strongest clues. Watson's efforts at observation, in contrast, tended to miss the mark for ignorance of knowing where to look.

It's Abduction, Watson!

Sherlock's inferences, others have argued, were less deductive than inductive or abductive. Perhaps Conan Doyle was putting "deductive" in Sherlock's mouth but meaning it generically or colloquially. Inductive inferences are less than certain, and they trade on probabilities: Sherlock's occasional reference to something like "the balance of probability" sounds much more inductive than deductive. Abduction, then again, is an inference to the best explanation. Many logicians treat it as a distinctly third kind of inference, neither deductive nor inductive, and it is not uncommonly used in history, science, and philosophy. In a nutshell, it involves identifying a pool of explanation candidates to account for some state of affairs, then narrowing the list down by a principled set of criteria to the single best explanation, then inferring to it as the likely true explanation. The criteria by which the options get reduced include such considerations as explanatory scope, power, and conformity with other beliefs. Sherlock's consistent insistence that all the data be explained is an example of the use of the criterion of explanatory scope. The best explanation has to account not just for some of the data in question, but rather for all the relevant evidence.

In the popular imagination, Holmes's knowledge base is what most likely gets overlooked. His observational skills are legend, but his inferential powers are perhaps best known of all. It's one of the characteristics that make him such a memorable fictional character. He consistently awed Watson by his demonstrations, the careful explanations of which only mildly tempered the incredulity. Doyle, as is well known, received inspiration for the character of Holmes from his real-life teacher Dr. Bell, who exhibited qualities like those of Holmes. But it's important to emphasize that Sherlock's inferences were possible only because they were predicated on his acute observations and prior knowledge.

Another fictional example of a character who, on the basis of his previous experiences, makes impressive inferences comes from Fyodor Dostoevsky's *The Brothers Karamazov*:

> Many said of the elder that, in accepting those who had come throughout the years to entrust their souls to him, to seek his guidance and solace, he had heard so many confessions, secrets, and tales of human despair that he had finally acquired an insight so keen that he could guess, from the very first glance at a newcomer, what he would say, what he would ask him, and even what was really tormenting his conscience. Often the visitor was surprised, confounded, and even frightened on finding that the elder knew his secret before he had even uttered a word.[13]

Sherlock's inferences, though grounded in facts, could be ambitious, and he wasn't always right. Some mysteries remained unsolved. Watson writes that he doesn't chronicle those because they would be stories without endings and readers would lose patience. On occasion perhaps there wasn't enough evidence on which to base a conclusion, or perhaps there was and even Holmes missed it. At Norbury, Holmes assumed something more sinister than what was actually there. Irene Adler, of course, was the one woman who beat him, earning his undying respect in the process, and he claimed to be beaten on three other occasions by men. Watson came to expect Holmes to solve well-nigh any mystery he would confront—and for good reason in light of Sherlock's track record. Most typically, Holmes asserted, criminals make mistakes. There tends to be a flaw in the best-laid plans rendering their discovery more likely.

Here we come to an important point to emphasize. Just as Holmes was slow to weave out a theory to account for the data before he had collected all the evidence he could, he was also careful not to be too slow. This, no doubt, made many of his inferences seem presumptuous or overly ambitious, and no doubt some of them were. His being a fictional character makes this more forgivable. His willingness to give it a shot, though, is both interesting and important. It's instructive because it illustrates, at its best, an epistemic virtue. To get at the idea, consider someone racked with so many doubts about his intellectual abilities that he becomes debilitated and diffident, never or hardly ever willing to risk an inference unless he is completely sure. Some skeptics and strong evidentialists are this way, fearing failure so much they're too hesitant to risk error. The problem with this approach, as William James noticed, is that it can result in the loss of an important truth. Sometimes risk is the price we have to pay to capture the truth—or to make something true that otherwise wouldn't be. One of the most important lessons of skepticism is that we need to be skeptical even of it. So what appears to be hubris on the part of Sherlock—and numerous times Watson expresses this concern about him—may more charitably be construed as intellectual courage. Perhaps rather than being objectionably presumptuous, Sherlock often struck the right balance between intellectual cowardice on the one side and rashness on the other.

Recall how he chastised Watson on one occasion in "The Blue Carbuncle," where Watson was given the chance to infer whatever he could about the owner of a hat based on a careful observation of the hat itself. Watson claimed to see nothing, to which Sherlock replied, "On the contrary. Watson, you can see everything, You fail, however, to reason from what you see. You are too timid in drawing your inferences."[14] Holmes then went on to make a number of far-reaching inferences about the hat that prove to be accurate. Perhaps Holmes was implicitly suggesting to Watson that a greater measure of inferential confidence was possible. What might seem like Holmes's hubris may actually be intellectual courage.

Numerous times Watson wrote of what he thought to be the character flaws in Holmes of egotism and lack of humility. In their first meeting, Watson could see Holmes was clever, but he also remarked afterward that he was conceited. Indeed, Watson would later claim to be "repelled by the egotism" of Sherlock's insistence that Watson's chronicles should focus more on the logic than the story. Holmes replied by unapologetically insisting it wasn't conceit, but rather justice for his craft that motivated him. "Crime is common. Logic is rare." Later, of course, Holmes would come to see the need for narratives to make for compelling reading.[15] Likewise, Watson would come to see that Holmes stood alone in Europe both in his gifts and experience, which makes the resistance Holmes posed to Watson's analysis understandable: "I cannot agree with those who rank modesty among the virtues. To the logician all things should be seen exactly as they are, and to underestimate one's self is as much a departure from truth as to exaggerate one's own powers."[16] Sherlock freely admitted that Mycroft's powers exceeded his own, which seems to bear out his account of such matters. Even if Sherlock were mistaken in thinking that modesty required intellectual dishonesty, he made a good point in stressing that it's not necessarily immodest to acknowledge one's own gifts, any more than it would be to acknowledge those of another. Sherlock was indeed a prodigiously gifted character. If someone were truly to have such powers, objectively acknowledging them would only be honest. Humility is consistent with honesty and intellectual confidence, and epistemic humility is consistent with the intellectual courage it takes to risk being wrong in order to capture the truth.

Holmes knew when his inferences were possibly wrong, and he didn't stop once he came to his tentative conclusions. Like a good scientist, he put his ideas to the test, weighed them on the scales of balancing probabilities, and observed how well they were able to account for new evidence. He was slow to formulate his theories without adequate evidence, but once the evidence arrived, he was willing to move, formulating working hypotheses he would subject to further tests. Knowing he was liable to draw the wrong inferences, he was careful to wait for enough evidence and to await further confirmation even after formulating his account. He was acutely aware that a slight shift in perspective could radically alter the direction of the evidence. If Holmes didn't err on the side of epistemic humility, at least he didn't fall prey to a debilitating sense of intellectual cowardice and diffidence. He cared too much about finding the truth to be silenced by the possibility of error. So he moved ahead, forging and testing each link in the causal chains he envisioned in his head to account for the full range of facts and to uncover the truth.

Nor did Holmes let the intrinsic unlikelihood of some of his inferences deter him, because he realized that life itself invariably includes wild improbabilities however it plays out. Time and again he affirmed as axiomatic the idea that once the other options are excluded, what remains must be the case. This remains true even if what remains may well be otherwise thought unlikely. Finding the evidence that's actually there has to be accounted for, and on occasion can render as probable an event that, considered by itself, would be an unlikely contingency indeed. He could see, then, that the actual evidence should be followed wherever it leads, even if it's to a conclusion one wouldn't have originally expected. Certain pieces of evidence can render an otherwise unlikely explanation the best and likely true explanation after all. Inference enabled Holmes to move from the foundational facts gleaned from observation and experience to new pieces of knowledge, and he did so with refreshing boldness. Even if Holmes stands largely absolved of the charge of hubris, there's another charge that we imagine could be leveled against him, to which we now turn.

On Behalf of Irene Adler

What perhaps might strike some people as a bit strange about the phenomenon of Sherlock's unflagging popularity from the late Victorian era to today are certain features of this character that might impress readers and moviegoers alike as off-putting at best or offensive at worst. Sherlock's mistrust of women, immunity from sentiment, and aversion to emotion make him vulnerable to criticism from the ranks of feminist epistemologists—that is, those who bring to bear feminist insights in their epistemic work. Their approaches are wide-ranging and sometimes challenging and brilliant, so it's impossible to do them justice in short compass. For present purposes, it's enough to tip our hat in their direction by identifying a few of their more common concerns.[17] Such concerns arguably find suitable application when we consider the method and mentality of Sherlock Holmes. As a memorable fictional character, he exhibits some of the more extreme traits that occasionally fall within the target of feminist epistemologists. After raising such concerns, we will assess whether and how far Sherlock might be vindicated of such charges. Doing so will give us the chance to discuss additional aspects of his epistemic method that should enable us to see that he wasn't the myopic logic chopper some might think.

Contemporary analytic philosophers tend to write in the analytic spirit, respectful of science, both as a paradigm of reasonable belief and in conformity with its argumentative rigor, its clarity, and its determination to be objective. It's based in the view that knowledge is objective and impersonal, that our knowledge is of a world that exists independently of us, and that truth is what corresponds with this reality. These traditional features of Western and analytic philosophy represent some assumptions certain feminist epistemologists call into question.

Their concern is that women have their own perspective on knowledge (or perhaps several perspectives). Whereas the masculinist perspective historically led to a search for impersonal truth and absolute certitude, more feminine perspectives see truth as more personal and absolute certainty as unnecessary. It's often conjectured that the history of men subjugating women means that the experiences of those who are members of a privileged group will differ from those of someone in an underprivileged or subjugated group. The suggestion is often made that such perspectives historically were ignored or disqualified inappropriately just because they weren't the prevailing paradigms. Traditional analytic philosophy privileged impersonal and objective knowledge. So these subjugated perspectives on truth that were more personal (in the sense that the insights came about as a result of a certain kind of personal experience) and subjective (not available to those, say, doing the subjugating) were silenced. Feminist epistemology doesn't treat experience objectively and dispassionately, nor does it hold experience at arm's length. Thus it tends to be more open to the possibility of potentially veridical concrete, felt experiences.

The charge by feminist epistemologists isn't that men ignore experience in epistemology, but rather that they regard experience in a typically male way. Their reasoning about experience has been kept carefully apart from the interests and emotional involvement of people generally and women particularly. They have considered themselves justified in doing so because this was thought to be a way to ensure "objectivity," but feminists would say it's merely an illusion of objectivity. The quest for complete objectivity itself is misguided because complete objectivity, certain feminists insist, is impossible. What counts as knowledge is too tied up with different kinds of experiences, activities, and social relations.

A number of feminist epistemologists hold that there is in every experience an ineffable element—that is, an element no language can adequately describe. Analytic philosophy's reductivist, logic-chopping approach tends to be altogether inadequate to leave room for such important experiences having epistemic significance. This, however, leaves out an important aspect of deeper kinds of knowledge of which we're capable. The claim is that analytic philosophy denies the possibility of nonpropositional knowledge or merely intuitive understanding.

In the way that Sherlock Holmes privileged a scientific approach to answering questions, in his quest for complete objectivity, in his claim that reason and emotion are intrinsically and perennially at odds, his discomfort with emotion, and his generally suspicious attitude toward women, he can be thought to fall within the target of feminist epistemologists. A few illustrations should suffice to illustrate these aspects of Sherlock's approach. Take, for example, his penchant for construing mysteries as primarily intellectual puzzles rather than heart-wrenching personal tragedies, which results in his being less empathetic and sympathetic than he ought. In "The Sussex Vampire," Holmes gets chastised in this way: "It may be a mere intellectual puzzle to you, but it is life and death to me!"[18] Detection, he would insist, is an exact science and should be treated in the same cold and unemotional manner; tinging it with romanticism produces much the same effect as working a love story into the fifth proposition of Euclid.[19] Sherlock's cold reference to the death of Watson's brother stirred Watson's ire, and Sherlock had to apologize: "My dear Watson, pray accept my apologies. Viewing the matter as an abstract problem, I had forgotten how personal and painful a thing it might be for you."[20]

Perhaps the best example of all of the way that Holmes was out of touch with his emotions (an aspect of the character that Jeremy Brett admitted made playing the role oppressive for him) comes in the fascinating exchange between Holmes and Watson after they meet the woman whom Watson would later marry. Holmes denied having noticed her attractiveness after her departure, to which Watson replied, "You really are an automaton—a calculating machine! There is something positively inhuman in you at times." Holmes in reply said,

"It is of the first importance not to allow your judgment to be biased by personal qualities. A client is to me a mere unit—a factor in a problem. The emotional qualities are antagonistic to clear reasoning."[21]

After Watson proposed to her, later in the book, Sherlock couldn't congratulate him, despite admitting that she was one of the most charming young ladies he had ever met. "But love is an emotional thing, and whatever is emotional is opposed to that true cold reason which I place above all things. I should never marry myself, lest I bias my judgment."[22] Anything other than dispassionate objectivity purged of the personal was less than what Holmes aspired to. He prided himself on having no prejudices and of following docilely wherever facts may lead. This attitude permeated his whole approach to life, and as a result he admitted, "Women have seldom been an attraction to me, for my brain has always governed my heart."[23]

Vindicating Sherlock Somewhat

Although observation, inference, and experience were crucial for Holmes, they did not exhaust the resources he brought to bear in his detective work, and we run the risk of missing some of his other laudable features if we confine our attention entirely to his cold logic. For his reason, though exacting, was animated by more than logic, or perhaps by a more expansive conception of logic and rationality than one might think. Consider the passion that drove his investigations that would lead him to refrain from eating or sleeping for days on end before solving the puzzle. This is not the way of a cold, calculating machine but of a deeply passionate man who loved his work and yearned to see justice done. His eyes would shine, and his cheeks would flush at the exhilarating prospect of doing his work. Nor was his commitment to justice a legalistic one allowing for no exceptions. More than once, he allowed the guilty perpetrator to go free because of overriding moral extenuating considerations and mitigating factors. His was no impersonal, decontextualized understanding of justice of the type that feminist philosophers rightly critique.

At the risk of epistemic indulgence, he was also willing to accord significance to something like women's intuition, and instinct (and intuition in general) was something of which he seemed fond, predicting that Inspector Baynes, possessing both, would rise high in his profession. His own inferences would come so quickly that Watson characterized them as resembling intuitions; likewise, when Holmes realized that sometimes it's easier to know something than to explain the justification for it, he himself recognized the way knowledge can have features that resemble more immediate apprehendings than just the deliverances of the discursive intellect.

The artistic side of Holmes also revealed more than a logic chopper. His grandmother was the sister of a famous artist, so the idea is that art ran in his blood and happened to take the form of his particular vocation. An enthusiastic musician, he loved art for its own sake, including the art of reason. It would be worthwhile on another occasion to explore the aesthetic aspects of his epistemic approach and conception of rationality. Ostensibly averse to narrative, Holmes was a dramatist at heart by his own admission. His breadth of view, easy enjoyment of surroundings, and appreciation for the admiration of his work were all characterized by Watson as marks of his artistry.

Holmes also had to a supreme degree imagination, valuing it in others and lamenting its absence, remarking that if Inspector Gregory, a competent police officer, had but imagination he would be more successful. Imagination enabled Holmes to put himself into the shoes of others and see things from their perspective, which was a quality at least in tension with the claim that he was entirely lacking in the ability to sympathize. Imagination enabled him to sift evidence and imagine their various possible interconnections until he could come to understand how they all best fit together. He wasn't content just with facts, but with how they interlocked and related to one another. Meeting the challenge of figuring this out, especially in difficult and strange cases, appealed to his imagination and challenged his ingenuity.

Inspector Lestrade, of course, was the paradigmatic example of someone lacking such imagination, yet he and Holmes were on generally friendly terms. Holmes was moved when Lestrade expressed genuine appreciation and admiration for his work. At the end of "The Six Napoleons," Lestrade said, "We're not jealous of you at Scotland Yard. No, sir, we are very proud of you, and if you come down tomorrow, there's not a man, from the oldest inspector to the youngest constable, who wouldn't be glad to shake you by the hand."

"Thank you! said Holmes. "Thank you!" And as he turned way, we're told, it seemed to Watson that "Sherlock was more nearly moved by the softer human emotions than he had ever seen him."[24] Public notoriety meant nothing to Holmes, but the compliment of a friend meant a great deal. Perhaps this can help make sense of why, after William James finished his magnum opus *The Principles of*

Psychology, he lamented not having included a section on the importance of feeling appreciated.

Almost Human

Why Sherlock Holmes continues to captivate readers is a complex question, but humanness is likely a big part of it. Despite his almost superhuman power, he was capable of a quivering lip when he thought his best friend was hurt and of being moved by the admiration of a colleague. Holmes was not the myopic logic chopper some might imagine; he was too human for that. Yet we could, perhaps, suggest in closing that he's not entirely vindicated from the charges of the feminist epistemologists. He was at times overly cold and detached, and the dichotomy in his mind between reason and emotions was likely too artificial, though there's an impressive history of philosophical thinkers who would be inclined to agree with him. But it's likely that the psyche of human beings shouldn't be quite so fragmented—a claim that at this point must stand more as assertion than argument.

Philosophers since Plato have long realized that expertise in an area like crime can result in either a great detective or a masterful criminal. On at least four occasions either Sherlock or Watson mentioned what a great criminal Sherlock could have been, had he chosen to use his gifts in the wrong direction. Although it's hard to imagine, if anything would have tempted him to do so, it might have been the same roots that resulted in his occasional listlessness and torpor, vulnerabilities that show his humanness and perhaps, ironically enough, his need for more humanness. For when Sherlock would on occasion fail to exhibit the right balance of head and heart, or a lamentable lack of empathy, he didn't need to get more in touch with his feminine side—contra the suggestion by certain feminist epistemologists.[25] Rather, he needed to get more in touch with his humanity.[26]

3

Risking Belief: *Ted Lasso* and Faith

Given its inauspicious beginnings as a satirical NBC Sports promotion back in 2013, *Ted Lasso* surprised many who weren't expecting its charisma and quality. Premiering in August of 2020, this breakout hit has garnered numerous awards and nominations and has continued gaining fame through word of mouth. But those who have watched the show, featuring biscuits-with-the-boss and exorcisms of training rooms, will find its defiance of expectations more than fitting. Like a candy bar little Ronnie Fouch might offer you on the playground, it is so much more than meets the eye.

Ted Lasso is a comedy about a cheerful, charming, and eminently optimistic amateur American football coach (played by SNL alum Jason Sudeikis) enlisted to coach AFC Richmond, a professional soccer ("football") team in England—the land of garbage water, hazardous street crossings, boots and chips and crisps. Along with his friend and sidekick, the aptly named Coach Beard, Ted embraces the challenge with characteristic enthusiasm. The game, like the grass on the pitch, is "the same yet different."

"A metaphor?" Beard asks. "You know it, baby," Ted replies. The quip, we soon learn, has serious implications, as the show challenges viewers to look beyond surface differences and misleading appearances that too often divide or prove destructive.

For a show in so many ways easy to watch—usually light and lots of fun—*Ted Lasso* features far more nuance, depth, and philosophical resonance than one might expect. The nature of true success, sportsmanship, revenge versus justice, the importance of friendship, the imperative of respect for persons, humility, leadership, identity, virtue ethics, courage, journalistic ethics, and what love looks like: these are all topics broached by the show, and a whole lot more.

David French is particularly struck by the forgiveness motif, particularly Ted's forgiveness of team owner Rebecca—played by the enchanting and magnificently talented actress/singer Hannah Waddingham (known for her role as the Wicked Witch of the West both in London and on Broadway).[1] For Michaela Flack, a different aspect of Ted's character comes to the fore. As she puts it, Ted believes in you.[2]

This issue of belief functions as a central theme of the show, a notoriously rich philosophical concept. What exactly constitutes belief? What we honestly assent to verbally? What our actions reveal? Our dispositions? Can we believe a proposition without accepting it, or vice versa? Fine questions all, but the show usually approaches belief from the angle of "believing in" oneself or others. Ted is adamant about believing in the best of people, without being blind to corruption or cruelty. Facing much resistance, even from his own team members, Ted is undaunted. Early on, in response to Captain Roy Kent's meanspirited barbs, Ted confides in Beard, "If he's mad now, wait until we win him over." Beard offers a signature cryptic reply: "He'll be furious." The question is not if they will win the team over, but when.

Ted is an unpretentious, easy-to-underestimate coach who has a singular brilliance for building community, and he cares about more than winning. In his unorthodoxy and prodigious emotional intelligence, he refuses to think of sports as a zero-sum game. He thinks of winning in terms other than scoring more than the opponent, and sees his job as helping his players become the best versions of themselves on and off the field. His coaching style is as holistic and his personality as winsome as his character is wholesome. Watching Ted is a little like watching Mister Rogers as a soccer coach—an intentional decision by Sudeikis[3]—and how can you go wrong with that? From the first episode, the importance of believing in oneself is on full display. This took a quiet self-assurance and laudable courage in the face of chronic condescension and a chorus of derogatory epithets from "wanker" to "Ronald McDonald."

In the locker room Ted posts a sign emblazoned "BELIEVE," and when asked if he believes in ghosts, Ted immediately replies, to Rebecca's stymied response of incomprehension, "I do. But more importantly they need to believe in themselves." This playful equivocation on belief-that and belief-in brings to mind a funny exchange from our friend Jonny Walls' movie script *Couch Survivor*:

one character, hoping for a bit of affirmation, asks another, "Do you believe in me?" "Of course!" comes the gentle, sympathetic reply. "But I can also see you."[4]

Some might suppose that believing in another person, or a particular outcome, or oneself, is more a psychological matter than a philosophical one, but we suspect this is a rather false dichotomy. William James, for example, had a penchant for sharing insights with both philosophical and psychological import. In his discussion of "precursive faith," he challenged the notion that all of our beliefs need to be based on adequate prior evidence. Precursive faith, as he understood it, involves believing ahead of the evidence, which on occasion seems permissible, even important. Take social coordination cases, where a group acting in unison (and only acting in unison) can, say, stop a single terrorist (or, to use his example, train robber). Such united action requires boldly acting without the assurance of cooperation ahead of time.

Or in the logic of personal relations, we often recognize the need to function as more than strict evidentialists. Starting romantic relationships, for example, may require taking an initiative to grow a relationship before knowing for sure that our advances will be reciprocated. Such dynamics remind us of the need to qualify our accounts of belief—and what justified beliefs call for—depending on the nature of the context. This certainly has psychological implications, but it is also interesting for philosophers.

Some of the best examples of James's precursive faith come from sports. AFC Richmond's believing in themselves, that they stood a chance against Everton, despite their decades-long track record of losses against them, is just such an example. To have a chance at winning, a team may well have to believe they can do it, on at least some level or to at least some small degree—and believe before having decisive evidence that they can. This kind of "belief" will not ensure the desired result, but it may well be needed for its very possibility.

Such belief in is closely related to hope, one of the classical theological virtues, another recurring theme of the show. Rather than embracing the pessimistic mantra cynically repeated by Richmond's fans that "it's the hope that kills you"—and thus lowering expectations and expecting the worst—Ted's irrepressible optimism retains faith in faith and soaring hope, a hope that may or may not disappoint. Soccer, like life itself, involves risk, and to avoid risk by not playing is too steep a price to pay.

Those are just a few of the many rich philosophical dimensions of a show that, of all years, came out in the pandemic-ridden 2020, a rather ignominious moment, most would agree. When anti-intellectualism and public acrimony, rampant pessimism and ubiquitous grudges held sway, a show like this was just the countercultural antidote we needed.

Like Ted would say, it's like we fell through a lucky tree, hit every limb, and landed in a pile of money and Sour Patch Kids.

4

Magic, Muggles, and Moral Imagination

The vastly different attitudes toward a particular young wizard are truly remarkable. While shattering one publication record after another, the Harry Potter series also elicits angry protests, hitting number one in the American Library Association's list of the books most commonly challenged in school districts and public libraries in the United States. Some literary critics are among the series' detractors, panning it as insignificant fluff, while others hail it as a minor classic. More than one critic has written that the books leave no room for the transcendent and numinous while countless others level the charge that the books desensitize children to occult influences. Some view the books as contrary to Christian thought, while others see a deep congruence. Still others think of the story as deeply moral, while certain vocal critics accuse it of advancing a highly subjectivist moral relativism. Just as Harry is amazed to discover his fame in the wizard world, he would be amazed to discover himself in a swirl of controversy among Muggles.

The Devil Made Harry Do It

The astounding success of the Potter series, particularly among children, has without question had the salutary effect of drawing huge numbers of young people into reading. This widespread influence, however, is part of the reason many adults have such grave qualms about it. The stories are about wizards and witches, spanning several aspects of real-life occultism, from charms to numerology to ancient runes. It's no small concern that impressionable children may be unduly drawn to occultism, whether it's Wicca, Satanism, or variants of New Age theology.

Undoubtedly, many people immediately dismiss such allegations as worthy of serious consideration only by the likes of Ned Flanders, conspiracy-minded fundamentalists, and moralists. Some of the criticisms of the Potter series have indeed been humorless and contentious, as well as inadequately gracious and informed, none of which conduces to cordial debate. But neither does the condescension and dismissiveness expressed by some Potter supporters in the face of such criticisms. What's needed is not name-calling and inflammatory rhetoric, but the kind of cool-headed and respectful analysis of the allegations in a spirit of friendly discourse that Dumbledore is famous for.

Most of those issuing the accusations not only believe in the reality of the spirit world, but also believe that not all spiritual forces are benign. Those who are skeptical about the supernatural understandably find it difficult to sympathize. If someone is doubtful of God's existence, he is certainly less prone to take seriously Satan or demonic spirits, stuff thought best relegated to a pre-modern, superstitious past and a naive, unscientific view of the world.

Detractors of the series are most concerned that the stories, wildly popular with children, tend to glamorize the occult, piquing kids' curiosity about it and desensitizing them to its dangers by making it appear as harmless fun. Stirring children's curiosity in this way, it is argued, makes them vulnerable to dark spiritual forces. Again, a charitable rendering requires that we remember that such critics are neither agnostic nor skeptical about the existence of sinister supernatural influences.

It is not unduly difficult, with a little imagination, to feel the force of this objection. Children, our most valuable resource and investment, are impressionable, and are susceptible to being misguided. A healthy process of socialization is vital to their emotional well-being and social adjustment. Such a process should carefully steer clear of those influences that carry inordinate risks of doing more harm than good. The possibility of the Potter series effecting real damage, many would argue, is ample cause for serious concern. Even a minor likelihood of such damage is enough to raise suspicion, given the potential seriousness of the consequences that early interest in the occult may incur.[1]

Defenders of Potter are likely at this point to remind us that the books are, after all, fiction, not to be confused with real life. But features of the books, it has been contended, blur the line between fantasy and reality. One of those features is among the books' real virtues: their ability to engage the reader in identifying with the characters. Children's imaginations are caught up in Harry's world, identifying with his struggles, envisioning Hogwarts as real, and wishing to be part of such a place. The suggestion is that it is only a short step to believing that magic, too, is real and its resources available to the reader. Trips to most major bookstores may bolster critics' suspicions, as they peruse shelf after shelf of books on occult themes. Sections on witchcraft and magic, in fact, often now overshadow those on philosophy.

Rowling admits that about a third of the magic-based material appearing in her books are or were actual historical beliefs. Children, the argument goes, can't be expected to make the subtle distinctions between fiction and reality that more discerning adult readers can. So the (perhaps unwitting) effect of this confusion between fantasy and reality, especially among the youngest readers ill-equipped to tell the difference between what is real and what is not, could be a whetting of the appetite for the occult.

What's Wrong with Harry?

Before assessing the quality of that case, let's lay out another case that's been made against Potter, this one on moral grounds. Although some have applauded the series for the way it extols the virtues, others have lambasted it for promoting moral relativism and egoism. Richard Abanes, for example, accuses Rowling of projecting a morally ambiguous vision, in which infractions of rules often go unpunished, lying is an acceptable way to avoid trouble, and the distinction between good and evil is blurred.[2] He thinks that morality is often complex and multi-faceted, but that the Potter books do nothing to contribute to such a nuanced understanding. In articulating these concerns, Abanes represents a significant number of Potter critics who sense danger lurking.

Abanes sets out to construct a cumulative case to show the morally dubious nature of the Potter series. Examples of rule-breaking abound in the books, he reminds us. Harry is said to show an almost Slytherin-like disregard for the rules, and Harry's behavior confirms it. Harry is not legalistic when it comes to school rules or the guidelines governing the wizarding world. For example, to find out the identity of Nicolas Flamel, he sneaks into the restricted section of the library using his invisibility cloak, and he follows Professor Snape into the Forbidden Forest.

Harry's lovable friend Hagrid is also notorious for rule violations, performing spells when he isn't supposed to, and asking Harry and his friends to help smuggle his dragon out of Hogwarts.³ Hagrid had raised the dragon Nobert against the 1709 Warock's Convention law prohibiting dragon breeding in Britain.⁴

Those most concerned about the rules, Abanes points out are often the mean characters like the Dursleys, Professor Snape, or Hogwarts caretaker Argus Filch. Indeed, Harry and the readers are convinced throughout much of *Sorcerer's Stone* that Snape is completely evil. Only at the end do we find that the gentle Professor Quirell is the real villain in cahoots with Voldemort. This sort of reversal recurs when, for example, Mad-Eye Moody in *Goblet of Fire* turns out to be impersonating the real Moody or when Voldemort's minion Pettigrew turns out to have been living for twelve years in rat form as Scabbers (Ron's family pet). This distinction between appearance and reality is an object lesson in the difficult task of obtaining true knowledge, since we have to rely on appearances that may be misleading.⁵ But in a story of this nature, such reversals might be thought to blur the line between good and evil.

Violations include not only minor infractions of school rules but also significant moral rules, such as prohibitions against lying. Recall, for instance, Hermione's "downright lie" about the troll in *Sorcerer's Stone* to get the boys out of trouble. Hermione, normally the last one to violate any rules, lies and claims she has broken a rule.⁶ Or consider Dumbledore's assertion that truth is generally preferable to lies,⁷ which prompts Abanes to emphasize that this shows inadequate commitment to truth, a point he thinks is generalizable to most of the characters in the novels. Even Dumbledore himself lies to protect Harry in *Order of the Phoenix*.⁸ Harry all too often lies to conceal facts that might otherwise cause him harm. Rowling writes, "Excuses, alibis, and wild cover-up stories chased each other around Harry's brain, each more feeble than the last. He couldn't see how they were going to get out of trouble this time."⁹ In *Goblet of Fire*, Harry lies to Hermione, a house-elf, Hagrid, Snape, Trelawney, and Fudge, all without negative consequences.

In fact, Harry's infractions of the rules often go unpunished. For example, when Fudge doesn't punish Harry for inflating his aunt in *Chamber of Secrets*, or when Dumbledore doesn't punish him for finding the chamber. When Mr. Weasley finds out his sons, to rescue Harry, flew the enchanted car without permission, his first response is, "Did you really? . . . Did it go all right?"¹⁰ Indeed, sometimes misbehavior is actually rewarded, such as when McGonagall puts

Harry on the Quidditch team after he violates Hooch's directive not to fly while she is away on an errand.[11] On the same day, Harry agrees to fight Draco in a wizards' duel at midnight in the school's trophy room. Such a fight is against Hogwarts rules and would require Harry to be out of his dorm at night, a second violation of the rules, and hard to justify morally, no matter how much readers might like to see Draco get a sound drubbing,

Since Harry isn't always punished, critics think the series thereby promotes ethical relativism. Relativism makes morality a matter of preference, either of a group or of an individual. Philosophers usually call morality made subject to individual whim ethical subjectivism, and Abanes seems to focus his accusations on such subjectivism when discussing relativism. Relativism of this kind denies that there are universal moral rules and instead assigns to individuals the capacity to determine the contents of morality. Since we like Harry, the argument goes, whatever Harry does is ultimately okay. No matter how many violations of the rules, his ends justify his means. Moreover, what motivates the characters' moral choices, Abanes wishes to suggest, is crass self-interest. Whether Voldemort or Harry, the underlying motivation is the same: doing what they want to do. "Voldemort wants what he wants as does Harry. The only difference between them rests in the rules they choose to break, the lies they choose to tell, and the goals they choose to pursue."[12]

Here the actual charge isn't exactly relativism as much as egoism. As a psychological theory, egoism says that all of us are motivated by self-interest all the time. As an ethical theory, it says that self-interest ultimately should function as our only motivation. Presumably, Abanes is suggesting that Rowling depicts the characters in her novels as egoistically motivated, "good" characters and "bad" alike. Since both sides "lie when it is expedient and break rules whenever those rules do not serve their needs both sides are technically 'evil' or sinful, even though their agendas might be vastly different."[13] By endorsing such motivations, Rowling, the argument goes, is embracing and approving such ethical egoism, which contributes to the morally confused message of her books. "In short," Abanes concludes, "Rowling's moral universe is a topsy-turvy world with no firm rules of right and wrong or any godly principles by which to determine the truly good from the truly evil."[14]

Answering the Moral Charge

Let's address this charge. Starting with Harry, it's important for us to admit that he isn't perfect. He's willing to violate school rules and to lie on occasion, liable to be insensitive to the enslavement of the house-elves, and susceptible to fits of moodiness and anger. But a heroic or virtuous character need not be perfect, and occasionally will fail. Harry isn't always a moral exemplar, but he is learning as he goes, and he clearly exhibits a sort of character and integrity distinctly different from the villains. Harry, for one thing, cares about other people. He often acts to save a friend, and sometimes even an enemy, as when he saved Dudley in the beginning of *Order of the Phoenix*. Harry is willing to risk his life in order to prevent an innocent person from suffering. And none of this moral motivation is to be found in the villains. Harry is what he consistently does, Aristotle would remind us; his occasional failures don't define him.

This undermines the charge that Harry is really no better than Voldemort, since Harry breaks rules, occasionally lies, and does what he wants to do. Abanes insists that the fact that Harry and Voldemort want different things is incidental. It's what they hold in common—an essentially egoistic motivational structure—that's most important here. Surely, though, the contents of Harry's and Voldemort's desires do matter. To imply that what they want is not as important as the simple fact that they happen to pursue what they want is confused. It leaves out of the picture one of the most important morally differentiating factors of all. Consider Harry and Voldemort for a moment. Harry battles evil forces and desires to see justice prevail. Voldemort desires to crush anyone he has to on his way to achieving power. They both pursue what they want, but that hardly entails moral equivalence. The nature of a person's desires reflects the kind of person one is. What Abanes calls topsy-turvy morality may simply be a bit of genuine moral complexity. Good and virtuous characters have feet of clay, make mistakes, and may break the rules from time to time. It isn't moral subjectivism to acknowledge, as Solzhenitsyn did, that good and evil cut through each of our hearts.[15] Each of us is capable of being lured to the evil of sacrificing others at the altar of our own selfishness.

Moral complexities don't entail that everything ethical is colored gray and up for grabs. That a character like Harry may have flaws doesn't mean he's not a hero or virtuous. That a rule (such as a prohibition against lying) may admit of exceptions doesn't mean it ought not be followed. That moral dilemmas may require us to choose the lesser of two evils doesn't mean that there's no moral difference between them.

Moreover, Harry shows mercy by sparing Pettigrew's life, which eventually leads to the reemergence of Voldemort and the murder of Cedric Diggory. And Sirius inadvertently breaks Ron's leg attempting to get Harry to follow and learn the truth about Pettigrew. Abanes thinks the fact that good deeds are cast as bringing about evil results and harmful deeds as bringing about positive results further confuses the moral message of the books. However, that good consequences might come from bad actions doesn't mean that bad actions are to be generally encouraged. That bad consequences might result from good actions doesn't mean that good actions aren't to be encouraged. That moral appearances can sometimes deceive us doesn't mean we can never discern the difference between right and wrong.

It irks critics that rules are habitually broken in the Potter books, even by good characters, and that such infractions too often go unpunished. But not all violations of rules merit punishment. Sometimes violations of rules are justified, which is why Dumbledore didn't make good on his promise in *Chamber of Secrets* to expel Harry if he broke any more rules.[16] Sometimes a higher law beckons. This is why Abanes probably wants to emphasize that some of the violations in the Potter books are more serious in nature than infractions of school rules or Ministry directives that may admit of legitimate exceptions. Some of the infractions violate ethics itself, like the moral rule against lying.

Certainly truth-telling is an important virtue, and kids really do have to learn that it's not an acceptable practice to try evading responsibility or punishment by lying. Immanuel Kant was a philosopher whose ethical theory dictated that lying on all occasions is wrong. He thought that lying is motivated by a principle that can't be consistently generalized. A rule like "It's morally permissible to lie whenever doing so is in your best interest" won't work. Such a universal rule would undermine the truth-telling and promise-keeping on which we all rely when insisting we're telling the truth or that we'll keep a promise. For Kant, reason's foundation for ethics affords no exceptions to such a prohibition against lying, no matter how advantageous or beneficial a particular lie might appear. It is not the consequences of our actions that count.

Although Kant makes sense, the right moral theory needs to take into account at least some consideration of consequences on occasion, even if we have reservations about reducing morality only to a matter of consequences as the great philosopher John Stuart Mill and other utilitarians do. Although we can never fully anticipate every last consequence of our actions, there are times when we can reasonably foresee what they're likely to be, such as when protectors of Jews during the Holocaust or of slaves during the days of the Underground Railroad were asked for their whereabouts. Given the intrinsic value of life and the particular moral goods at stake on such occasions, lying seems justified, and indeed a moral responsibility! This reminds us that ethics is about more than just rigidly obeying inflexible rules. It's about the kind of person one is and the sorts of moral goods one cherishes, such as human dignity, freedom, and life. Some nonnegotiable moral rules undoubtedly hold, like the inherent wrongness of torturing children (even Draco) for fun, but lying, even if nearly always wrong, does seem to admit of legitimate exceptions.

We can at least well understand Harry's failure always to be entirely forthright with those less than trustworthy. And Harry's infractions do sometimes land him in hot water. Ironically, in *Order of the Phoenix*, Harry's commitment to telling the truth lands him in detention with Umbridge to endure a particularly unjust and painful punishment, about which, incidentally, he never complains. It was an eye-opener for Harry to learn in *Order of the Phoenix* that his dad had been far from morally perfect while at Hogwarts. That Harry's dad could grow up and improve reminds us that Harry, too, is on his way to becoming the man he's capable of being. Harry, following in his father's footsteps, is morally maturing.

Is Hogwarts a Wiccan Academy?

Critics have also leveled the charge that Rowling's books are based in the occult. They write as though fictionalized accounts of occult practices that bear a similarity to actual practices blur the distinction between real life and fantasy. Moreover, they claim, this will only confuse young people who can't be expected to maintain careful distinctions between fiction and reality. If Rowling uses examples of divination in her books, and if real-life occultism historically does so too, then occultism lies at the foundation of her books.

This argument rests on a mistake. Arguably it's the critic, not Rowling, who's blurring real life and fantasy here. Surely there's a crucial distinction between reading or writing fiction about a practice on the one hand, and engaging in the practice itself on the other. Communicating with the dead is biblically forbidden, but does that mean those who take such teaching to heart ought to decry Charles Dickens' *A Christmas Carol* because it involves a fictional tale of just such a thing? Or C. S. Lewis's *Chronicles of Narnia* because they reference astrology? Unlikely, and for good reason. Writing fiction about a practice is not engaging in the practice itself, and care needs to be taken not to use the term "occult" so freely as to encompass both.

It's true that Rowling is more susceptible to this charge because she borrows freely from real-life accounts, but she draws from a lot of sources and mythologies, from the Arthurian legends to Homer, not just the occult. What she weaves from these sources is something creative and new, even if it incorporates a range of elements drawn from history and literature. To criticize Rowling's eclecticism fails to appreciate her books on their own terms, a principle necessary for evaluating any literary work fairly (and thereby a moral requirement). Identifying elements from the stories and infusing them with significance not attributed to them by the stories themselves results in reckless leaps of logic and, potentially, an unnecessarily harsh and uncharitable spin on her work.

The Potter books do anything but glamorize evil, painting it instead in only the most negative terms. Contending that these books should be suspect on the basis of their using occult symbols is misguided. Those liable to launch such accusations typically make an exception for the sort of magic in works by traditional Christian writers such as C. S. Lewis and J. R. R. Tolkien. Indeed, Abanes questionably distinguishes the subtle differences between the magic in Lewis's *Chronicles*, for instance, and Rowling's *Potter* novels. But Abanes seems to be fighting a losing battle. On the one hand, he insists that kids who read Potter aren't sophisticated enough to distinguish real life from fiction. Yet on the other hand, he seems to think that the subtle distinctions between the magic found in Rowling and Lewis won't be lost on those very same young readers.

Imagination and Morality

Critics strategically accentuate occult connections, possible pitfalls, and macabre wit, while overlooking the potentially positive elements in the Potter books and the possibility of more constructive engagements with this incredible series. Rowling likes to describe her fictional creation as a world of the imagination—a phenomenon of which Mr. Dursley does not at all approve[17]—and a world essentially moral. At the same time, she makes it clear that it wasn't her intention to teach ethics, which reminds us of an important qualifier before we talk about her books and morality. The primary purpose of fiction isn't to make us better people. Even Tolkien rejected the view that literature is mainly about inculcating ethics. Mark Twain did as well, and put readers of *Huckleberry Finn* on notice that any persons attempting to find a moral in it are to be banished. That Tolkien's work and Twain's have been instrumental nonetheless in shaping readers' moral views doesn't change the fact that this wasn't their main intention or primary function.

There is, however, a connection between literature and morality. Philosopher Martha Nussbaum has mounted an elaborate argument for the role of literature in our moral development.[18] Good yarns, such as Rowling's, appeal to both the head and heart, eliciting from us the right sorts of emotions, and providing for us vivid moral paradigms that Aristotle thought were essential to moral education. More suggestive than dogmatic, they teach us to empathize with the sufferings of others, enhancing our capacity for seeing the world through another's eyes. As *Potter* junkie and public philosopher Tom Morris writes:

> The Golden Rule, as it is stated properly, appeals to our imaginations. It tells me to treat another person the way I would want to be treated if I were in his position. I can't be guided by it without imagining what it would feel like to be in that other person's situation, with all her morally legitimate concerns and desires. The Golden Rule directs me to use my imagination in such a way as to create empathy for others. I believe that the imagination is the single greatest natural power in human life. And so I think it's no coincidence that the greatest moral rule appeals to exactly that power.[19]

By drawing so many young people back into reading, the Potter books are igniting the imaginations of countless kids. A powerful imagination functions centrally in any commitment to morality, because so much of ethics consists in having the right kinds of emotional and intuitive responses to situations as they arise. Being truly ethical is largely about having the appropriate feelings, the proper sorts of imaginative capacities, and properly empathetic tendencies. Rowling performs a powerful service in drawing kids back into the imaginative exercise of reading.

Imagination and Faith

Some time ago a television special debunking a number of enduring mysteries, from crop circles to the Loch Ness monster, aimed at heightening the viewers' commitment to a careful examination of the evidence. On deeper reflection, though, we might suspect that it is doing more harm than good with its persistently skeptical tone. The biggest obstacle for beginning philosophy students is often their unwillingness to suspend both disbelief and skeptical doubt to exercise their imaginations. They resist engaging in thought experiments meant to stretch their creative limits and challenge their thinking to higher levels. A reluctance to imagine, cloaked as skepticism, tends to produce more arrogant cynicism than genuine wisdom. The philosopher's task is not merely to mow down superstitions. It's also to irrigate intellectual deserts.[20]

Not only is a vivid imagination crucial to morality; it is integral to religious faith. The nature of religious truth claims is not such as to appeal to the unimaginative or narrowly empirical. We are called to believe in an invisible God, battle unseen forces, and do good to those who harm us. On the face of it, this is definitely stuff that calls for a great imagination. It requires an openness to more than what the eyes can see, a willingness to believe passionately in more than the senses, a capacity to consider a broader array of evidence than a narrow scientism would admit as legitimate. Such imaginative openness to life's deeper realities may well require a cultivation of imagination: a great imagination may well prove valuable in our quest for knowledge. If the basis of one's decision about religion is just wishful thinking, following fashions, or a failure of imagination, one's rejection or acceptance is less likely to track the truth. Philosophy calls for a real and honest openness to what evidence is available, not a dogmatic assumption from the outset that one side or the other is outside the range of possibility.

Those interested in pushing the importance and legitimacy of classical religious faith should perhaps be more careful not to discourage kids from reading books like Rowling's, at least if such reading is done with discernment. Such apologists may need to think out of the box, as it were, more expansively about their task as defenders of faith, and encourage the reading of all kinds of imaginatively vivid literature. In particular, they ought to endorse the reading of morally potent fairy tales that enliven the imagination, give readers fresh eyes to see through, and open minds. Such openness is not enough, but it may well be necessary for religious hypotheses to retain plausibility and remain, in William James's phrase, a "live option."[21] Religiously motivated critics of *Potter* may wish to think twice before launching criticisms of something that may well do more for their cause than they currently imagine.

We began by talking about the widely different perspectives on Rowling's series. Aristotle had the insight that the truth often resides between the extremes, and this is likely the case with *Potter*. The books may not be suitable for six-year-olds, but that doesn't mean they're not suitable for nine-year-olds (not to mention most adults of all ages). The books may well broach moral complexities, but that doesn't mean they're morally ambiguous. They may not be the greatest literature ever written, but that doesn't mean they're not good. They remain infinitely better than many books that tout a kind of worldview that offers little encouragement to think seriously about anything at all. The *Potter* books are well-written (not to mention incredibly fun) stories that generate conversation well worth having.[22]

5
Firefly and Freedom

Take my love, take my land
Take me where I cannot stand
I don't care, I'm still free
You can't take the sky from me
Take me out to the black
Tell them I ain't comin' back
Burn the land and boil the sea
You can't take the sky from me
There's no place I can be
Since I found Serenity
But you can't take the sky from me

— "The Battle of Serenity," theme song of *Firefly*

Written by Joss Whedon and performed by Sonny Rhodes, the theme song of *Firefly* alerts readers to the central theme of this short-lived but brilliant series: freedom. It's represented in the sky, which remains a refuge and a sort of social liberation from the controlling hand of the Alliance. The result of losing the Unification War was that some, like Mal (Nathan Fillion), along with Zoe (Gina Torres), his trusted partner in the war, largely removed themselves from what they considered a corrupt society. Unwilling to cooperate with wrongful authorities or tyrannical powers, they opted out of the mainstream "civilized" society, refusing to give their tacit assent to its systemic injustices and corrupt rule of law. Having lost his faith in God and government, Mal moved to the outskirts of the solar system—the rim, or outer, planets. Forging a new community on the spaceship *Serenity*, cobbling together a living through various activities, some nefarious in the eyes of the law, Mal and his crew try to remain under the radar screen of the Alliance, even while harboring a couple of fugitives from the law.

The show's mixed genre as a Space Western adds texture to the premise. Set in the future, the series depicts the characters on *Serenity* fighting for survival on a brutal new frontier and scraping together a living, profoundly distrustful of authority. Whedon came up with the idea for the show after reading Michael Shaara's 1975 Pulitzer Prize-winning *Killer Angels*, a novel about the Battle of Gettysburg. While Whedon wasn't at all enthralled with the Confederacy's defense of slavery—though rights of self-determination (a Confederacy mantra) are thematically important in *Firefly*—it was the idea of the losers in a war that captured his attention.[1] There have been efforts at mixing the genres of science fiction and Westerns before, of course: *Gene Autry and the Phantom Empire*, *The Adventures of Brisco County, Jr.*, *Star Trek*, *The Wild Wild West*, *Battlestar Galactica*, to name a few. Ubiquitous Western vernacular, combinations of fiddles, guitar twangs, and symphonic sounds, various codes of behavior, rugged individualism, revolvers, layers of rustic western dust, muted earth tones, settlers of all kinds, boots and vests and horses, retro Wild West accents, all juxtaposed with holograms and spaceships, give *Firefly* a distinctively space-Western look and sound.[2]

This essay focuses most especially on one particular episode of the show, probably the most philosophical of them all, "Objects in Space." By Whedon's admission, this episode is his attempt to capture key ideas of the existentialist writings of Jean-Paul Sartre (and of Albert Camus' *Myth of Sisyphus*). Whedon describes Sartre's philosophical fictional work *Nausea* as "the most important book I have ever read." *Nausea* is much more about what might be labeled "metaphysical" freedom, freedom internal to each person, than political freedom (from tyranny, for example). The connection between these kinds of freedom isn't always obvious. Sartre, though a firm believer in the autonomy of the individual will, embraced a socialist view of government: whereas other strong believers in individual freedom insist that laissez-faire or free market economies are the most consistent outworking of a strong prior belief in metaphysical freedom. Whedon himself, a social progressive in many respects, has been argued by some to be committed in his work to a libertarian understanding of society.[3] This essay won't try settling which economic or political picture is most consistent with existentialist freedom. It will, however, look at Whedon's portrayal of

Sartre's account of freedom in *Nausea*, the extent to which Whedon affirms existentialist views about choice and value, and the overall adequacy of Sartre's vision.

Nausea

Nausea is a brooding novel written as the journal of Antoine Roquentin, a young historian in the throes of existential angst. Horrified by his own existence and by the vacuity of experiences, he comes to see life as devoid of any inherent significance. He's profoundly cognizant of the transitory nature of life and the unavoidable, encroaching, impending reality of death. The dilemma of the protagonist is not intended by Sartre as a commentary on or to be a function of Roquentin's idiosyncratic, antisocial, and misanthropic personality; rather, his dilemma is supposed to represent the human condition per se, the existential reality we all face, whether we realize it or not. Ordinary objects, events, and places lack any intrinsic meaning or import, so there is no meaning to be discovered, a dominant Sartrean theme, making *Nausea* an almost canonical existentialist text. Sartre considered it his greatest achievement, and it contributed to the body of work for which he was awarded the Nobel Prize for literature in 1964, though he declined the award, declaring it a product of a bourgeois institution.

Encountering the meaninglessness of life and its attendant angst and disorientation, irremediably bored by life, Roquentin feels his freedom threatened: "I am no longer free. I can no longer do what I will."[4] The "sweetish sickness" of nausea colors all he does and afflicts him to the core, depriving him of all his zest and passion for life as he desperately searches for meaning. The darkness pervades every aspect of his life, from his sexual liaisons to his historical research. He comes to see this nausea as the result of a recognition that we are here by sheer accident; that we experience bare existence and imagining anything else is an effort to avoid this fact; that meanings and values are not universal or imposed, but at most invented and freely adopted. Neither the future nor the past exists, only the present. No grand metaphysical theory or cosmic lawgiver exists to make sense of life. What determines reality is our own consciousness and ability to be aware of facts and feelings and sensations. What determines the meanings of our lives is no preexisting pattern or purpose for our being here; rather, we find ourselves existing, need to come to terms with the contingency and reality of that existence, and must forge our own meanings, unconstrained by any cosmic guide larger than our own internal consciousness.

"Objects in Space"

"Objects in Space" is the *Firefly* episode largely inspired by *Nausea*. As Rhonda Wilcox puts it, it is "a story Whedon unquestionably used for spiritual, intellectual, and philosophical exploration—non-Christian existentialism."[5] In the episode, a bounty hunter named Jubal Early (Richard Brooks) comes after River Tam (Summer Glau), a member of Mal's crew.[6] River had been abducted by the Alliance, which then treated her as a means to their corrupt ends, violating her in horrific ways, but in the process making her capture and return to the Alliance a lucrative proposition for an unprincipled bounty hunter like Early. Her experiences also left her disoriented, confused, childlike, dysfunctional, and at times bordering on pathological with a take on reality unique at best, radically skewed at worst. Her instability and potential danger to the crew, and what to do about it, preoccupy the crew members at the beginning of this episode, but by the end of the episode, River is accepted, at long last, as a full-fledged member of the crew.

Early and River share a distinctive viewpoint: they seem particularly sensitive to and aware of their surroundings. River is privy to the private, unarticulated thoughts of crew members, and both wonder about the meanings and functions of objects. Early considers features of his gun unconnected with its intended function as a weapon, such as its weight and aesthetic features, whereas River exudes a childlike wonder when considering objects. In a crucial scene, a gun appears to her as a harmless object of beauty (a branch, specifically), and she says: "It's just an object. It doesn't mean what you think." She seems aware of its bare existence, unmediated by meanings imposed by considerations of its features or functions. Early, too, has a sense, less innocent though, of the solidity and reality of objects and asks philosophical questions about what imbues objects, events, or places with meaning or significance. And he seems, as Lyle Zynda perspicaciously observes, acutely aware of arbitrariness and incongruities in human life.[7] Early, like Roquentin, seems overwhelmed at times with the absurdity of his surroundings in particular and of life in general, yet he presses on with his ignoble mission.

Consider River's perception of the gun that happens to belong to the character Jayne (Adam Baldwin). Despite that the gun's designer may have intended it to be a weapon, it need not be used as one. It could make a decoration or doorstop or paperweight. The gun is not intrinsically a weapon; it's a bare object whose meaning is malleable. River sees it as an innocent object of beauty. In her subjective experience and conscious apprehension of it, that is indeed how it appears and, in some sense, what it is. Although Early and River take their unique perspectives in different directions, each seems gripped with existential insights that would make Sartre proud.

In *Nausea*, Roquentin comes to terms with the implications of a godless, meaningless world by feeling empowered. He comes to the existentialist realization that the inherent lack of meaning in the world offers him the chance to create his own meanings by his autonomous expressions of will. Rather than allowing his nausea over the insignificance of life to lead him to undervalue the present, he decides to create what meaning he can by throwing himself into an artistic endeavor and by recognizing that the meanings he constructs and projects are the only meanings he will find. He has to invent them, though, not discover the common existentialist refrain.

Mal, too, subsequent to the loss of his faith that the good guys will win or that God will ensure that all will come out well in the end, refuses to quit. He goes on, despite his loss of faith, although he's in a dark place through much of the series and most of the film *Serenity*. It's been suggested that Shepherd Book (Ron Glass), a preacher on board Mal's ship, represents an aspect of Mal's past he lost, namely, his faith. When Book asks to pray before a meal, Mal says it's fine, as long as he doesn't do it out loud. Mal's experience in Serenity Valley made him lose faith in a reliable providence. The problem of evil, we could say, was the undoing of his religious convictions.

As a teenager, having lost his own faith, Whedon was given Sartre's book, which proved so significant because it gave him a way to come to terms with his newfound atheism. Sartre is famous for his atheism, of course, as is Camus (who also influenced Whedon), although not all existentialists have been atheists (Dostoevsky, Kierkegaard, Marcel, and Jaspers, for example, are not).[8] In Sartre's view, it's the absence of any deity that leads to the basic existential reality of our coming to exist first, our meaning and purpose coming later through our volitional choice. Since we aren't created in God's image, according to some prepackaged plan or purpose, there is no meaning to discover for our lives, only meaning to invent through passionate commitment and artistic creation.

Is Whedon an Existentialist?

And this brings us to Whedon himself, although it's with some trepidation we should broach the subject of Whedon's own views and convictions. Whedon is a purveyor of some particularly memorable pieces of popular culture, and his philosophical views are neither altogether transparent nor eminently important. By his own admission, he is neither an intellectual nor a philosopher. As William Irwin writes, "Some literature, for example, may be philosophy, and it is theoretically possible that some of popular culture could be philosophy, but to my knowledge no instance yet exists. Until and unless someone manages to create a piece of popular culture that is also philosophy (or vice versa), we must limit ourselves to interpretations that give the philosophical significance of popular culture."[9]

Even if Irwin is right, though—and plenty of philosophers would disagree with him—he concedes that works of popular culture can be philosophical, from the movies of Woody Allen to those of Alfred Hitchcock. In fact, something of a cottage industry has arisen among philosophers arguing about just how philosophical popular movies and television shows can be. Still, Whedon is usually better at asking than answering the big questions his dramatizations raise. Generally, popular culture should be used as a springboard to consider various philosophical questions rather than as a source of great philosophical insight; nonetheless, with that said, let's go ahead and at least tentatively explore whether Whedon is the existentialist he thinks he is.

Lyle Zynda's excellent piece on "Objects in Space" accentuates the existentialist influences on Whedon's story. A key theme in his analysis is the way objects in this episode are, as described earlier, imbued with meaning rather than possessing meaning on their own. Neither their existence nor their essence is necessary; without value, meaning, or function, there is no reason for a thing to be the way it is. Both Early and River, in very different ways, imbue the objects around them with meanings, either innocent or horrific. The meanings aren't intrinsic to the objects; rather, they're given to the objects by people like us, which in a real sense says something special about the kind of creatures we are. There are some limits to the meanings with which we can imbue objects, but within those limits (which Sartre refers to as their facticity), there is always a free choice about how to operate.[10] River sees the gun as a harmless branch; in patent contrast with her innocent, wide-eyed wonder at things, Early, like Roquentin, sees objects as alien and alienating, producing the sort of anguish and dread of which existentialists speak. For if value is conferred, then objects in and of themselves lack such value, and this can be profoundly disorienting and disillusioning. Existentialists often attempt to move on from there, insisting that on the other side of the disorientation and disillusionment is a range of opportunities to forge meaning and significance in bold, creative ways. Early, however, does not seem to have found a very satisfactory way of processing his insights, whereas River is beginning to be able to do so much more effectively.

An intriguing question at this juncture, however, is what the basis is for deeming River's creative impositions of form and efforts at finding meaning objectively better than Early's. Clearly (per his DVD commentary), Whedon sees River's as the better response, but does existentialism contain sufficient resources to undergird such a value judgment? Existentialists may wish to insist that it does, but consider the role of volition, or choice, in their theory. If our valuations are based on free choice, doesn't this imply that they are arbitrary—not in the sense of an individual lacking reasons for her personal preference, but in the sense of no objective fact of the matter existing? If our choices aren't merely what we happen to value but determinative of what is valuable, is there an ineliminable arbitrariness about our valuations? How can an existentialist avoid this conclusion? This is often where an appeal to an absolute standard, like God, is thought to be useful, but even here the appeal is thought susceptible to an analogous challenge. The Euthyphro Dilemma, harkening back to an early Socratic dialogue, asks if God values something because it's valuable or if it's valuable because God values it. If the former, then the value of the thing is independent of God's valuation; if the latter, then anything at all could be valuable just because God chooses to value it, leading to all sorts of arbitrariness and vacuity objections and to depictions of God as a capricious tyrant. So when the will is thought to function at the foundation of our valuations, arbitrariness seems to result. This is a potential problem for the existentialist as for the divine command theorist.

But Whedon himself, and by extension Mal, most assuredly doesn't seem to think of morality as purely subjective. Examples are legion, but consider the following: despite that Mal has lost much of his idealism and that his name, in Latin, means "bad," he retains great decency, recognizing that people aren't property, that it's morally wrong to take advantage of an innocent person who's vulnerable to exploitation or harm. He rejects the cynical moral perspective that everyone uses everyone, adamantly opposes slavery, does some things just because they're the right thing to do, and demonstrates loyalty to and love for his crew.[11] Similarly Whedon, whose work is replete with the value of love and friendship, especially when these ties are bonded by choice and camaraderie (such as Buffy and Angel).

Now, one could venture to offer an existentialist analysis of Mal's or Whedon's ethics, suggesting that this set of values has been freely chosen and, once chosen, has become in some sense binding and authoritative for them (merely because they continue to choose them). But this analysis strains credulity. The much better explanation is that such recognition of objective values is beyond what an existentialist ethic can alone justify. Consider the sheriff's words in "Train Job": "These are tough times. A man might get a job, he may not look too close at what that job is. But a man learns all the details of a situation like ours, then he has a choice." To which Mal replies, "I don't believe he does." The most straightforward explanation of such sentiment is that Mal is a firm believer that it would have been wrong, and not his moral prerogative, to refrain from returning the lifesaving drugs to the people at Paradiso, despite the potential cost to himself and his crew. Mal, like Whedon, may have lost his faith, but not his humanity, basic decency, and essential moral compass. Perhaps this is why Badger still sees in Mal, not a captain of a spaceship but a duty-bound sergeant. Just beneath the surface is the old sergeant, with his homilies and stories, glory and honor. In the desperation of his circumstances, Mal's ethics have a pragmatism about them at times, but even here he's consistent with some of the most memorable of characters from Westerns.[12] In refusing to lose himself after losing his faith (the way the Operative does in the movie *Serenity*), Mal echoes an existentialist motif, namely, that after the disillusionment of loss comes liberation and the chance for new meanings. But Mal's moral paradigm also contains leftover remnants from earlier in his life, including the recognition of objective moral truth.

If Whedon, like Mal, retains convictions about promoting justice or defending the helpless, what can we make of his commentary on "Objects in Space" on this question? Consider another way in which Whedon departs from existentialism. When Roquentin in *Nausea* comes across existing things, he feels nausea; when Whedon, as a teenager reading *Nausea*, becomes aware of the fact of existence, he feels exhilaration. Something about the objective existence of things, despite the ways in which we imbue them with meaning ourselves, enthralled him. This led Agnes Curry, with perhaps tongue partially in cheek, to ask if Whedon is becoming a Thomist. It's Aquinas who thought of existence as the central piece of a thing, and ultimately God as the "pure act of existence," and finite creatures as following from God's unlimited actuality.[13] Whedon, in his commentary, says that "what makes objects so extraordinary is the fact of them, the very fact of them. It's mind-boggling. I believe that whether to have faith or not—to think about consciousness, our ability to understand that these things exist and to think about the fact of existence." If Whedon isn't becoming a Thomist, he's at least sounding awfully non-Sartrean in his enthralled recognition of the fact of existence. For Whedon, existing things have a rapture to them; apprehending them for him was an epiphany, not crisis, as Curry points out. Again, Whedon, though moved by Sartre, goes in a rather different direction.

So what do we say of Whedon's payment of homage to Sartre? Plato argued that artists don't know their own craft very well, especially when (or perhaps how) they are doing it. So what Whedon believes he is doing and what he is actually doing need not be the same thing. Then again, though, Whedon is a highly intelligent fellow. Perhaps he was taken with the idea of being an existentialist but doesn't really believe in it thoroughly. On this account, "Objects in Space" is simply a return to the ideas by which he was initially mesmerized but now no longer fully accepts. In the end, perhaps Whedon is an existentialist about some things but not others, and demands for consistency, as mentioned earlier, are unrealistic.[14] Or maybe existentialist thinking is more tempting when it comes to physical objects (human artifacts especially) but is much less tempting when it comes to natural kinds and value theory.

So perhaps some physical objects are just that: objects, then we place meaning, value, and purpose on them. Perhaps human artifacts, unlike natural kinds, have no essences after all. In other words, tables and chairs, which are human constructions, may not inherently possess essential properties the way a molecule of water possesses the property of being H_2O, which defines it in some stronger sense.[15] So even if chairs and tables (or chair and table-shaped collections of atoms) don't exist in the same sense as an atom of gold, it doesn't follow that neither natural kinds (like the atoms making up those chairs and tables) nor human persons feature essences, defining properties of their identity.

In the case of human beings, their identity or essential nature, if they possess one, would not be reducible to their atoms arranged body-wise (unlike a chair, for example, which arguably is just a collection of atoms arranged chair-wise), but something above and beyond that. Aristotle, for example, would be inclined to understand their nature "teleologically" according to their natural telos or aim or goal: their nature, for example, as rational creatures. But Sartre, of course, was famous for denying that human beings had essences; rather, our choices alone define us. This issue of essences arises again in the next section.

A final possibility is that Whedon, when it comes to moral values, remains, like most of us, a work in progress. Like some of his most memorable characters, he seems acutely aware of the gap between the way things are and how they ought to be, but somewhat at a loss as to what to do about it. There is in him a compelling tension that often plays out on the screen, between idealism and pragmatism, between light and darkness, between right and wrong. When he creates a sinister character as loveable as Dr. Horrible with designs on using his freeze ray to stop and then rule the world with the girl with whom he can't quite muster the courage to make an audible connection—or a character as conflicted and tortured yet winsome as Mal, or when he paints a beautifully inverted picture of a companion blessing a minister, it shows how goodness and badness, saint and sinner, are often juxtaposed. It's not just the white and black hats; good and evil run through each of our hearts. And rather than seeking to resolve the tension or eliminate it altogether, he lets the tension do its work. If a foolish consistency is the hobgoblin of small minds, Whedon's mind is huge. A hero can have feet of clay; the bad guy can have charming and attractive features. Appearance can be deceiving; the prostitute can have a heart of gold, and the hero can be egomaniacal. This is far from a dogmatic insistence on seeing everything in stark black-and-white: life's often just too messy for that. This doesn't deny objective morality, but it does complexify the task of sorting it all out and makes pat answers unacceptable and a lack of epistemic humility a vice.

Freedom and Value: Human and Divine

So freedom, on an existentialist analysis, is important. It's our choice how we choose to interpret the situations in which we find ourselves, how to react to those situations, whether to remain in those situations, whom to go to for advice. But as important and legitimate as all of these existentialist points may be regarding freedom, freedom seems to have its limits in what it can accomplish. Although our choices may be able to imbue a chair or gun with meaning, they can't volitionally control whether or not atoms have essential features, human beings have a telos, or, extending the discussion to moral value, whether or not cruelty or torture are right. Choice can't make just anything at all right or acceptable or valuable. However, if Zynda is right, existentialists like Sartre indeed hold that value is merely based on free choice; therefore, value must be arbitrary on their analysis. Generalizing the point about imposing value and imbuing meaning, if value per se is merely a function of free choice, it would be our volitional prerogative and power to make something, within the general confines of facticity, mean anything at all or to make nearly any action morally right or wrong. To see more clearly why, let's delve a bit more into what freedom really is. On an existentialist analysis, it's a basic fact of our existence, something about which we can be surer than just about anything else. It's autonomy of will, something to which we can't escape, something that defines us, and something for which we are responsible.[16] Perhaps most ultimately, it's the locus of value.

But is this the only or best way to make sense of the relationship between value and freedom? Just because we can make a decision doesn't mean we're morally permitted or obligated to do so. Once more, this is one of the notorious limitations of an existentialist analysis. Likewise, just because we have the technology to do something doesn't mean it ought be done. Technological mastery too easily becomes our dominant ethos and exemplar of truth, shaping our understanding of nature, society, and the human being. The Alliance chose to cut into River's brain time and again, but their ability to do so didn't make their actions right. As we saw earlier with the Euthyphro Dilemma, it would seem that even if God himself were to choose to command child torture for fun, it wouldn't make child torture right. To think otherwise is to invest in free will more importance and significance than it's rightly thought to possess. The mistake of a certain kind of existentialist is the same as that of a certain divine command theorist: investing in volitional choice a sort of valuational authority it doesn't have.

Interestingly, though, this notion of freedom as the capacity to do or value practically just about anything at all is a relatively modern notion of freedom. There's a much more ancient understanding of freedom that paints a very different kind of picture. But harkening back to it requires a departure from both an ultravoluntarist divine command theory where divine freedom is concerned, and from an understanding of existentialism predicated on a modern conception of radical freedom. On a "premodern" conception of freedom (and of certain modern ones), some moral choices aren't really choices, but "no-brainers" that are sufficiently obvious to all rational persons. A person's doubts about the wrongness of child torture, for example, do not raise questions about the propriety of child torture as much as they raise concerns about such a person's sanity. For human nature, a deliverance of reason, or our natural telos (goal or end), makes it clear what the moral path requires.

A wholesale departure from this understanding of freedom as acting in accord with our essence raises a serious question about the trajectory of society. Once a society loses its convictions in objective moral truth and in free will constrained by who we are as human beings, what guarantee or even reason to believe is there that feeding the poor, empowering the disenfranchised, or lifting up the downtrodden will continue to be values a society extols? Just because individuals can and will continue doing so is no guarantee to suggest that societies as a whole will, for if the choice to do so is just a personal (existential) preference reflective of nothing more ultimate, then it lacks authority. Although it takes time, that loss of moral authority seeps into the fabric and plausibility structures of a culture. It hasn't always been an accepted fact that all people are equal. Many ancients rejected such a notion, and more recently Nietzsche was vociferous in his opposition to it. For a society deeply imbibing notions of freedom as liberation from constraint and coercion, while resting on the largely nonteleological moral metaphysics of modernity and jettisoning convictions about a transcendent source of the good to which the will is naturally drawn, what can be said to be inherently irrational or abominable?

The point here isn't to be alarmist, but to raise a genuine question: What is a proper locus of value? It's not uncommon nowadays to hear a segment of the population rail against old-fashioned religious conviction as the source of all manner of evil, and surely plenty of evil deeds have been done in God's name. *Serenity* features such a character in the Operative (though Whedon's epistemic humility makes him far from a Richard Dawkins). But isn't an equally interesting question what range of malicious deeds are likely to result from a rejection of traditional moral foundations, a loss of conviction about human teleology, and a view of freedom that isn't predicated on the natural ends toward which rational people are drawn? What will spare us from the logic of bioethicists who deem Down Syndrome babies or congenitally deformed infants as unfit for living, or social engineers harboring hopes for a resurgence of a eugenics movement, the sorts of horrific visions we could easily conceive the Alliance entertaining?[17] Some followers of Nietzsche, arguably, would chalk up resistance to such ideas to a "slave morality" informed by the Christian myth; Nietzsche rightly saw that a rejection of that sort of transcendently grounded understanding of morality would eventually have big implications. He would say that Mal and Whedon haven't rejected enough of their past; they should give up fighting for the weak and helpless and realize that the evolution of mankind is leaving such unfortunates behind.[18]

Ultimately, again, questions about what to do with all this are the kind Whedon is good at raising. What he, like all of us, needs to do is set about trying to take such questions with dreadful seriousness. If we have reason to think that human beings have a nature or essence or teleology after all, then it would seem that such a thing should inform our understanding of and bolster our convictions in objective morality. If God exists and has a stable nature or character—like perfect love on the classical monotheistic model—then those who think that God provides the objective foundation of morality shouldn't fear the Euthyphro Dilemma.[19] For God, as God, neither would nor could command the torture of kids for fun because it would be contrary to his nature. He could no more issue such a command than decide not to exist. And if God has such a perfect nature, or if human beings have a stable nature that defines what it means to be human after all, or both, then the existentialist account of freedom seems inadequate. For any real moral constraints on us would not be objectionable limitations on us, but, instead, ways in which to realize our highest potential.

Some philosophers, from Stoics to Kantians, would argue that moral truth in general or the essential equality and dignity of persons in particular (as encapsulated in the Universal Declaration of Human Rights, for example) is sufficiently obvious that there's little cause for concern about our society losing such convictions anytime soon. But ideas have a history and a power to them, and it's tempting to attribute to, say, intuition or some other transparent moral apprehension what, in fact, is a recognition that came about only after a protracted evolution of moral thought that included seminal, transformative ethical paradigm shifts along the way. With the rejection of a metanarrative postulating a transcendent source of moral authority, and the resultant loss of conviction in human teleology, it's not altogether clear that the modern existentialist-inspired conception of freedom will prove able either to sustain itself or to provide the bulwark against moral abuses and tyrannies that some think it will. And it's certainly far from clear that Mal's final words in *Serenity* about the primacy of love will win the day. Even if Joss does become a Thomist.

6

RBG Invites Us to Love Our Political Neighbors

The opening of *RBG*, the 2018 documentary about Associate Supreme Court Justice Ruth Bader Ginsburg, is eerily similar to 2004's contentious *Fahrenheit 9/11*. Michael Moore's propagandistic attempt to thwart George W. Bush's re-election bid was equal parts entertaining and dishonest, and when it first aired, it seemed intent on ramping up America's acrimonious partisan divide—audiences across the country were unabashed in their celebration of Moore's approach. No tactic, it seemed, was beyond the pale to stop the Dubya menace.

The opening scenes of *RBG* harkened back to the vitriol surrounding that earlier film. It starts with a solid three minutes of quotes from conservative politicians, commentators, and talk radio firebrands blaming the justice for all manner of social ill and calling her a slew of unsavory names. Not this again, the viewer might think, and especially not now. Aren't we even more desperate to find common ground, given the current cultural landscape?

Thankfully, those opening few minutes don't define the overall tone or approach of Betsy West and Julie Cohen's release. In light of the compelling story that follows, they serve to remind viewers of the need to pull back the curtain of our divisive rhetoric and to reckon more honestly with the people beyond the culture wars. In *RBG*, West and Cohen offer a welcome salve for our society's wounds, a celebration of Ginsburg as Ginsburg, irreducible to any political stance. The personal and professional facets of Ginsburg's life paint a variegated portrait of a singular figure whose virtues, values, and experiences resonate—surprisingly—with both conservatives and liberals of good faith.

Many details of Ginsburg's life are familiar to viewers: her tenure at Rutgers pioneering the field of women and the law, her work with the ACLU's Women's Rights Project, her appointment to the Supreme Court by Bill Clinton in 1993, her fiery dissents to the court's conservative faction. But fleshing out that picture of Ginsburg as feminist icon are the details the film offers of her own personal fight for standing in a legal profession bent toward men. She thrived despite these barriers, serving on law review at Harvard and tying for first in her graduating class at Columbia.

Even more impressive is that she took on these challenges while caring for an ailing husband and young toddler. For Ginsburg, though, these domestic roles were crucial to her professional success: "I think my life was more balanced. . . . I was less apprehensive than my classmates because there was something going on that was more important, frankly, than the law." Ginsburg, of course, possesses a gifted legal mind, but *RBG* shows that she has grit and grace, too, all of which is evidenced in her rich and enduring love affair with Marty, her husband of fifty-six years. Although Marty died in 2010, the film includes footage of his doting on her at public appearances and excerpts from letters he penned to her. Clearly the two were partners: her supporting him during bouts of cancer, him supporting her legal career and even advocating for her appointment to the Supreme Court. Theirs is a relationship to emulate no matter one's political persuasion.

But the film is not merely intended to inspire—though it does inspire—as much as it aims to delight, and the unexpected details from Ginsburg's life delight us most: her children's mockery of her cooking, her love for opera, her strenuous workout routine, her collection of collars to feminize her justice robes. Ginsburg comes off as relatable, with her own quirks and foibles, preferences and habits. She rarely watches television and has no patience for small talk (so says more than one interviewee). She laughed off her gaffe of falling asleep at the 2015 State of the Union address, saying she was not 100% sober, and she apologized for her inappropriate remarks (given her role on the Supreme Court and need for impartiality in matters involving the administration) critiquing candidate Donald Trump in the 2016 presidential election. With such inclusions West and Cohen defy today's great sort that requires flattening out human complexity to dub public figures either friend or foe.

Although the filmmakers nod to the cultish following that has sprung up around Ginsburg, the film itself resists the hero worship that's so tempting in our divisive times. In *RBG*, Ginsburg is neither deified nor demonized; she is instead humanized, which counterintuitively honors her more than any sort of idolization would. This is not to say that conservatives won't find in Ginsburg's story much with which they disagree; her conflation of abortion access with dignity for women, for example, deleteriously denies the dignity of unborn children. Careful viewers of the film, however, can trace this lamentable blind spot back to her fixation on women's rights; such reflection can spur pro-lifers to expand their moral imagination to work toward just solutions for all parties involved in a crisis pregnancy, child and mother included. The bottom line is that situating Ginsburg's more progressive stances within the larger context of her life and career, as *RBG* does, encourages critics of those stances to more fully understand and engage with them.

And more than anything, *RBG* presents a woman who welcomes a good debate and sees real value in it. Her affinity and acuity for the law found a worthy opponent in none other than the incomparable conservative justice Antonin Scalia. Their longtime friendship, documented in the film, stretched back well before their days on the Supreme Court and adds another wrinkle to the liberal caricature of Ginsburg some might prefer. An ACLU colleague of Ginsburg's confesses that she could never be friends with a "right-wing nut job" like Scalia. Yet Ginsburg and Scalia's friendship was genuine, evidenced by the easy rapport in joint appearances and in their sharp disagreements, which were always on points of law and never personal.

These good will disagreements, which Ginsburg truly appreciated, refined her own position, as iron sharpens iron. For example, in talking about *United States v. Virginia*, the case that required Virginia Military Institute to admit women, Ginsburg has credited Scalia's dissent with strengthening her own written opinion. She had real affection for him and deep respect for his mind and personality that was undiminished by their antithetical theories of jurisprudence: "As annoyed as you might be about his zinging dissent, he's so utterly charming, so amusing, so sometimes outrageous, you can't help but say, 'I'm glad that he's my friend or he's my colleague.'" To rejoice in the other—what a beautiful sentiment, life-giving even.

We are surely in a tough cultural moment, and it's tempting to embrace a one-dimensional distortion of those who disagree with us. *RBG* is a poignant argument for why doing so would be such a shame.

That is the film's gift to its viewers, an intimation that there's a story behind any person we may encounter, no matter how contrary or disruptive we might find them. More than that, it's a charge to remember their value and to respect their dignity.

We cannot afford to ignore that charge. We have a choice, as poet W. H. Auden so starkly put it, to love one another or die.[1] For we are, even as our hyper-partisan age denies it vociferously, inextricably bound together in a network of mutuality, our fortunes intertwined.

7

His Truth Is Marching On: *Selma*'s Clarion Call

There's a poignant scene towards the close of Ava DuVernay's new film *Selma*, a scene made all the more compelling by its prescience. John Doar, Assistant Attorney General for Civil Rights during the Kennedy and Johnson administrations, warns Martin Luther King of credible threats against his life that await him in Montgomery, the destination of the Selma march protesting barriers to African American voter registration.

Doar implores King to drive—rather than walk—into the capital and to nix the planned speech, to minimize his exposure and prevent any possible harm. "Don't you want to protect yourself?" Doar asks. King's response here is telling, as it speaks of his convictions and highlights the worldview animating the film and, more importantly, the nonviolent resistance movement whose story it portrays.

> I'm no different than anyone else. I want to live long and be happy, but I'll not be focusing on what I want today. I'm focused on what God wants. We're here for a reason, through many, many storms. But today the sun is shining, and I'm about to stand in its warmth alongside a lot of freedom-loving people who worked hard to get us here. I may not be here for all the sunny days to come, but as long as there's light ahead for them, it's worth it to me.

The specific threats of violence against King echo the egregious wrongs perpetrated throughout the film—the disenfranchisement of black citizens, the murders of innocent children and protesters, the brutality of local and state police against unarmed marchers. And yet the activists refused to be intimidated. "We go again," Dr. King says after the infamous Bloody Sunday—the brutal attacks by police and posse alike on the protesters during their first attempted march across the Edmund Pettus Bridge.

The injustice on display in *Selma* is heart-wrenching. Few will leave the theater dry-eyed after witnessing the powerful using their positions and privilege, their weapons and words, to dehumanize others. Again and again, the protesters are at the receiving end of such abuse. They suffer indignity after indignity in exercising basic human rights—registering to vote, checking in to a hotel, protesting peacefully.

The scenes projected on the screen provoke outrage and disgust. And yet, the Southern Christian Leadership Conference (SCLC) led by King rejected retaliation in kind, however tantalizing the temptation. After one particularly humiliating and damaging attack, several protesters plan to round up some guns, only to be reminded that the police and government force will always be much greater than theirs. "We have to win another way," SCLC leader Andrew Young counsels.

Resisting the logic of *lex talionis*—an eye for an eye—seems counterintuive and countercultural at best, foolhardy at worst. Achieving victory by turning the other cheek seems impossible. Conceived in secular terms, victory over subjugation requires defeating one's foes by force—be it legal, corporal, psychological, economic. But justice in *Selma* goes well beyond tactics; it points to a radical conception of reality itself. Justice in the minds of the *Selma* freedom-fighters is a metaphysical fact, a real state of affairs promised and being worked out by a good God who is setting the world aright at the incalculable cost of his own son. And driven by their Christian convictions, the SCLC embraces the privilege and responsibility of participating in this process, of co-suffering with Christ.

While the scenes of outrageous abuse will infuriate viewers, the resolve of the protesters not to multiply evil through retaliation will inspire. What Marilyn Adams writes in a different context is attested to by the protesters' courageous example: "To return horror for horror does not erase but doubles the individual's participation in horrors—first as victim, then as the one whose injury occasions another's prima facie ruin."[1] Without granting its theological foundations, King's campaign was worse than foolish. Knowingly placing himself at the mercy of those who would oppose with appalling force the truths he preached took courage, courage borne from the conviction that justice is the natural bent of the universe. The values of the kingdom of God turn those of this world on their head.

As *Selma* testifies, King understood that his real enemies weren't government officials assassinating his character, racists and segregationists who thought themselves superior, nor even the man who would eventually kill him. No, he fought instead "against the rulers, against the authorities, against the cosmic powers over this present darkness, against the spiritual forces of evil in the heavenly places" (Ephesians 6:12). And he knew that in the face of an all-powerful and all-loving God, these spiritual forces of darkness and entrenched systemic evils would not and could not stand.

Selma gives us a glimpse into how this redemption works in our own lives here and now; it's terrifying, convicting, and inspiring all at once. This process—resisting the impulse to respond to injustice in kind, to daily wait on the Lord to set wrongs right, to proclaim truth without fear, to stand in solidarity with the downtrodden—is hard. It is in fact beyond hard; it is impossible in our own strength. In our personal lives we all face indignities, abuses, and wrongs—all of which *Selma* magnifies in horrifying detail. We can thus sympathize with King's weariness, his call for support, his pleas for divine intervention, his temptation to give in and give up. In the crucible of this maelstrom, we see, too, the resurrection of hope, the power of community, the hardiness of righteousness, an enactment of the gospel. We see the church at work, Christ's body setting the world to rights little by little, through the most powerful weapons there are, and the only truly efficacious ones—faith, hope, and love.

The saga of Selma echoes its clarion call to Christ's body today to be faithful heralds of truth and justice, to live and labor in the hope of what we still can't see except in fleeting glimpses and furtive glances. It is a glorious and sober reminder that if Christ be raised we have seen manifest the first-fruits of a coming victory so resounding, and a glory so amazing, that it will dwarf and eclipse any and all of this world's sufferings. Like Dr. King, let this blessed assurance inspire us to proclaim truth with boldness, battle injustice with hope, and daily carry our cross with courage.

8
The Fault in Green's Story

John Green's *The Fault in Our Stars* is a beautiful love story, really. In this young-adult-novel-turned-film, Green crafts believable characters struggling with a tragic reality in this world: childhood cancer. Despite his grim subject matter, Green never panders to the characters or readers; his portrayal avoids both the maudlin and the callous by emphasizing the human dimension throughout—joy, pain, desire, courage, humor, anger, sadness, confusion, triumph, hope, love, and loss. He depicts his characters' afflictions without cliché, uncompromising in his descriptions of the ugliness and pain involved in their diagnoses, treatments, and relapses.

Through it all, Green's characters remain energetic and engaging. Hazel Grace Lancaster, the narrator-protagonist, is downright feisty—not what one might expect of this adolescent cancer patient. Her no-nonsense, quick-witted approach to her unspeakably terrible illness establishes her character from the opening monologue which rejects easy, sugarcoated renditions of sad stories that offer up Peter Gabriel as remedy for whatever ails you.

Worldly-wise Hazel is joined by 17-year-old Augustus (Gus) Waters—charismatic, confident, offbeat, and also riddled with cancer. In ways, Green uses this relationship to update Romeo and Juliet—the consummate young romance pitted against the universe, yet those Shakespearean star-crossed lovers have nothing on Hazel and Gus. The ill-fated stars of Green's characters have infiltrated their bodies through disease, leaving precious little time or space for the couple to experience life and love to the fullest.

In Green's romance, the fault truly is in the characters' stars and not in themselves—inverting the passage from *Julius Caesar* to which Green's title alludes. Any good in Green's story, in fact, derives solely from the human spirit, despite Cassius's contrary claims about human fallibility. Green's characters share experiences that deepen their connection, enhance their appreciation of beauty, and sharpen their delight in each other. Green himself identifies that message as one of the central purposes of his tale, which found its inspiration in his volunteer work as a chaplain at a children's hospital: "[W]hen I was writing this novel, one of the things I was thinking a lot about was how much value, how much joy and how much good there can be in a short life."[1] For Green, life is valuable, no matter how short. No matter how young its possessor, consciousness is a gift. The novel and film exquisitely promote this belief, and rightly so.

If that were the end of the story, its purpose being merely to argue for life's preciousness with Hazel and Gus's plight offered up as evidence—nothing else to it, we would cheer (and cry) right along with Green's countless fans. Unfortunately, Green's story extolling the meaning and value found amid life's threat of death smuggles in some dubious assumptions about the human condition and the nature of this world.

In an early scene Gus tells a cancer-survivor support group his primary fear is being relegated to oblivion after death; later—in the film version—we learn that primarily because of this fear, Gus maintains belief in some sort of afterlife. Despite her natural introversion, Hazel speaks up to challenge this concern:

> There will come a time when there are no human beings remaining to remember that anyone ever existed or that our species ever did anything. . . . There was a time before organisms experienced consciousness, and there will be time after. And if the inevitably of human oblivion worries you, I encourage you to ignore it. God knows that's what everyone else does.

While Gus believes a human life is meaningful only within a transcendent framework, Hazel dismisses such belief as wishful thinking and—early on at least—insists on a materialistic framework that encourages cynicism (a point even more pronounced in the book). Both Gus and Hazel compromise, however, and the couple settles on a transcendence within the finitude that is life—an existential insistence on human value despite its obvious limitations.

In a key scene late in the film, Gus alters Hazel's earlier cynical response to the inevitability of death, offering human determination and bestowal of value as the only hope available:

I'm in love with you, and I know that love is just a shout into the void, and that oblivion is inevitable, and that we're all doomed and that there will come a day when all our labor has been returned to dust, and I know the sun will swallow the only earth we'll ever have, and I am in love with you.

Green's story claims its title and tragic mode from Shakespeare, but it borrows its outlook from Albert Camus. A Sisyphus of romance is Gus; this connection is encouraged through the meta-fictionally embedded hamster whose name derives from the mythological figure doomed ceaselessly to push a boulder uphill, as it repeatedly returns to its source. Camus interprets Sisyphus' struggle against this absurdity as the source of human value.[2] As with Gus, Sisyphus' defiance of his fate, his insistence on the importance of his task provides all the meaning he needs.

Green's chaplaincy exposed him to families struggling with unspeakable tragedy, and it tested his religious vocational call to its breaking point. He tells Mark McEvoy that in the face of the suffering of children, he found religious teaching unsatisfactory and, as a result, abandoned his ministerial pursuit: "I found myself really unfulfilled by the answers that are traditionally offered to questions of why some people suffer and why others suffer so little . . . . I still go to church sometimes but I would not feel comfortable leading the services."[3]

In that same spirit, *The Fault in Our Stars* portrays spirituality, particularly Christianity, as irrelevant to the brute fact of this fast-fading world rife with sorrow. Its token Christian is Patrick, the cancer-survivor support group leader whose own bout with testicular cancer motivated his service to others, but his presence—played in the film by Mike Birbiglia—offers more comic relief than substance. Rather than take seriously Patrick's faithful commitment to the group and his Christian faith bolstering such commitment, Hazel merely mocks Patrick as "ball-less" with a "depressingly miserable life-story."

Christ's redemption of the world, his rescuing us from the fault that is most definitely within ourselves, is undercut by Patrick's inane repetition that the support group meets "in the literal heart of Jesus," referring to the garish image of Christ prominently displayed on the carpet he unfurls before each meeting. (In the book, this "heart of Jesus" refers to the intersection of crossbeams in the cross-shaped sanctuary). Problematically, the story sanctions this ridicule, a tacitly jaded response to all things spiritual cutting through the storyline.

Prayer, the story suggests, is for the weak, and pat answers too often suffice to console; those in the know merely pretend to adopt that posture for the sake of their feebler friends and family.

Yet those who would dismiss Christianity as insubstantial or disconnected from suffering haven't looked closely enough, mistaking a superficial substitute for the real thing. Trivializing the "literal heart of Jesus" obscures the truth that the cross reveals: at the center of this world is a God whose love for us requires that he share our pain in order to redeem us. Pain does demand to be felt, as Green's story rightly notes, and Christ has endured that pain, not to be overcome by it but in order to overcome. Only through Christ's death, burial, and resurrection can we claim the promise of Revelation 21:4: "He will wipe away every tear from their eyes, and death shall be no more, neither shall there be mourning, nor crying, nor pain anymore, for the former things have passed away."

"You gave me forever in the numbered days," Hazel says to Gus, a beautiful sentiment if there ever was one. Interestingly, however, whereas this is at best wishful thinking, it is at worst empty rhetoric within the stultifying confines of a naturalistic paradigm where dissolution and oblivion are indeed inevitable. In a Christian worldview—in which we can partake in eternal life even now, if only we accept His prescription for our ailment—it is neither wishful thinking nor an empty hope, but rather the remarkable truth.

9

More Than Mere Machine: The Indominable Human Spirit of Philip K. Dick

It's commonplace to consider the mythical stories of ancient world literature as concerned with elemental questions of human existence. *Enuma Elish*, Genesis, *Theogony, Works and Days, The Iliad*: these texts clearly sketch the parameters of the human condition, our origins, our nature, our ends, and help us better see (and appreciate) the beautiful, the good, and the true. Science fiction, on the other hand, has the opposite reputation. It's associated with the here-and-now, the transitory, the merely material. Understandably so, given the centrality of technology and scientific developments to the genre. Science fiction's focus on the machinery of life leads many writers, critics, and theorists to identify the whole field of science fiction as philosophically materialistic, as precluding any sincere allowance for the transcendent. In his distinction between fantasy and science fiction, author Ted Chiang captures this prevailing assumption: in fantasy, he says, the universe is understood as personal; in science fiction, impersonal.[1]

Like science itself, Chiang posits, science fiction works by observation, hypothesis, experimentation, and systematization—a detachment that bespeaks a mechanical worldview for Chiang and others like him who claim for the genre an ideological bent instead of distinguishing it primarily by its formal qualities. For groundbreaking science fiction scholar Darko Suvin, a materialistic worldview is essential to science fiction. Any work that takes spirituality seriously, then, is by definition disqualified. Such is the case Suvin makes against calling Walter Miller's *A Canticle for Leibowitz* science fiction.[2] Rather than treating religion merely as cultural material, a sociological phenomenon at the mercy of historical processes, as Suvin would prefer, in this one-of-a-kind post-apocalyptic Cold War novel, Miller makes space for and even promotes faith; for that, Suvin excludes the story from the science fiction canon.

Questions of genre sometimes seem tedious to those outside the literary discipline. What does it matter, one might ask, if Suvin identifies Miller's novel as fantasy, not science fiction? In the case of *A Canticle for Leibowitz*, probably not much. Despite being grounded in time and space, Miller's story is infused with enchantment, an enchantment impossible for readers to ignore no matter the generic label provided. With its relics and rituals, saints and icons, legends and miracles, *Canticle* offers a supernatural irruption into the presumably closed system of history. In other cases, though, the philosophical strictures of Suvin's definition can easily obscure the intricacies of the text itself and unfairly skew the resulting interpretations. Rather than illuminate the material under consideration, a faulty generic framework can blunt for readers a text's creative force.

Amid Change, What Remains

Take, for example, the work of famed science fiction author Philip K. Dick. While Miller intermingles the staples of science fiction—nuclear fallout, technological advancement, scientific discovery—with the traditions of the church, Dick is much more of a science fiction purist, populating his worlds with androids, rockets, and aliens. His characters experience alternate histories, time travel, chemical mood enhancement, dystopian regimes, and virtual realities. In this way, Dick's writing does precisely what Suvin describes as the logic of science fiction: "organiz[ing] variable spatiotemporal, biological, social, and other characteristics and constellations into specific fictional worlds and figures."[3] But, with all due respect to Suvin's considerable contributions to science fiction studies, such a literary orientation to the variables of human existence does not necessarily entail or promote a naturalistic mindset. Science fiction may be what Sheryl Vint calls "the literature of change,"[4] but paradoxically that constant change can point us more insistently to what about the human condition and human beings themselves that stubbornly remains the same. Concerns with the corporeal, in other words, need not be at the expense of belief in the spiritual and, in fact, have purchase only if undergirded by "something more." As the work of Dick encourages us to consider, attentiveness to the material conditions of human existence can and should waken us to ultimate truths and values.

Born in 1928, Philip K. Dick lived a troubled life from the outset. His twin sister Jane died little more than a month after birth, and this tragedy haunted his writing over the course of his career, surfacing in his fiction as a consistent leitmotif.[5] Dick came of age in Berkeley, California, shaped by both his parents' tumultuous marriage and the radical politics of that hotbed of the mid-century American countercultural movement. These circumstances simultaneously sharpened and challenged Dick's precocious spirit, and out of that crucible emerged a body of work almost unparalleled among science fiction writers in quantity and quality. The author of over forty novels, Dick also wrote short stories galore, publishing more than ten collections; together these works changed the face of science fiction. Perhaps more significantly, he amassed this large oeuvre before dying prematurely at sixty-three after a life-long bout with poor physical and mental health, a destructive drug habit, and a string of failed marriages.[6]

Philp K. Dick pushed the previously sacrosanct boundaries of science fiction and, while drawing on the common tropes of the genre, often subverted them and opened up new possibilities for these highly imaginative stories. In doing so, he challenged readers' expectations, created zany worlds for his characters to inhabit, and coined new words that hint at the technological innovations defining his fictional worlds. Even accounting for Dick's tremendous output, the number of his books now deemed science fiction classics is remarkable. Suvin identifies six as such,[7] including *The Man in the High Castle*,[8] *The Three Stigmata of Palmer Eldritch*,[9] and *Dr. Bloodmoney, or How We Got Along After the Bomb*.[10] In Suvin's assessment, the best of Dick's books have centered on questions of society as the ground of and force behind all human relationships, particularly the role of the Marxist concepts of alienation[11] and reification[12] and the possibilities of social renewal through radical politics.[13]

Reading Philip K. Dick as Materialist

Suvin is certainly on to something. Dick's work, following the general trend of science fiction, explores the implications of social and technological change.[14] To be sure, the modern era that spawned science fiction was replete with scientific discoveries, technical innovation, and industrial encroachment. Promise and peril accompanied such rapid, ubiquitous social change, and as Suvin notes, Dick's novels imaginatively consider both extremes. *The Man in the High Castle*, for example, depicts the "politico ethical conflict between murderous Nazi fanaticism and Japanese tolerance," ultimately judging Japanese rule the better option.[15] For Suvin, any consideration of values, truths, or moral realities within Dick's texts must be circumscribed by historical processes and material conditions. Thus, all of Suvin's interpretations reduce to consideration of power relations. *Dr. Bloodmoney* envisions the collapse of pre-existing power structures and the possibilities of a utopian communal order;[16] *Martian Time-Slip* entangles an insignificant everyman in a nightmarish web of destructive capitalistic practices;[17] and *The Three Stigmata of Palmer Eldritch* tells the tale of an "interplanetary industrialist who peddles dope to enslave the masses."[18]

Even though Dick's later novels delve into theological and cosmological territory,[19] Suvin still prefers interpretations that transpose those concerns to a "highly abstract or coded form of transitive talking about individual vs. community and other crucial matters of relationships among people in Dick's time."[20] In other words, theological material is merely symbolic of historical processes, what Suvin calls a parable of collective earthly matters."[21] Coloring Suvin's reading of any given Dick novel, then, is his assumption that "in the collective, non-individualist world of Dick, everybody, high and low, destroyer and sufferer, is in an existential situation which largely determines his or her actions."[22] For Suvin, Dick's worlds are thoroughly materialistic. Nevertheless, there is arguably much about Dick's work that resists such a reading, and only distortion of the text itself can force it into a materialist mold. Many insights Dick offers about personhood and agency, for example, are an uneasy fit in a naturalistic universe, most especially his insistence on the need for moral responsibility in an increasingly technocratic world.

Satire as Moral Guide

In Dick's *The Man Who Japed*, for example, the protagonist Allen Purcell embarks on an urgent search through which he learns that being fully human in an ever-more-automated world requires him to actively discover meaning and to appropriate it for himself. It demands that he rebel against the status quo, which offers only ready-made, easy-to-digest, one-dimensional answers to life's most pressing questions. Rather than succumb to the situation at hand and be constituted by it, as Suvin argues Dick's characters inevitably do, Purcell assesses his situation, finds it morally wanting, and undertakes to change it. Even if this undertaking ultimately falls short, the story affirms Purcell's moral judgment, which challenges Suvin's materialistic reading of Dick's work. Rather than find their locus in historical processes, the values Purcell embraces and champions, and that readers affirm through their emotional support of Purcell's actions, go beyond his political and social environment. This is not to say that Dick himself is intentionally promoting a theistic worldview in his novels; rather, his works raise crucial questions that a materialistic view can answer, if at all, only with considerable difficulty.

Morec Society, the world of *The Man Who Japed*, is regimented and controlled, with oppressive restrictions on the citizenry's reading and behavior; in it, too, the constant threat of exposure and punishment for even the smallest offense keeps people in line. As the book opens, Purcell is a pillar of his community: from his perch at Allen Purcell, Inc., he creates moral propaganda reinforcing societal norms. Purcell's initial break comes in his "japing"—or vandalizing—of a statue of Major Streiter, Morec's founder. His fear of detection along with his serendipitous meeting of Gretchen Malparto, a woman deeply dissatisfied with Morec norms, forces him to face the inconsistencies and injustice of his totalitarian world.

While Purcell has learned to adapt to his stifling, stultifying environment, he finds many aspects of it reprehensible, among them the block meetings that allow anonymous accusers to humiliate their neighbors publicly. Technology also disconnects people from each other, and constant surveillance threatens to expose every indiscretion. In spite of his society's overtly stated principles of valuing its citizens, its so-called morality is self-righteous, voyeuristic, detached, pious, uncaring, and uncompassionate. Gretchen explains this poor fit between Purcell and the society he operates in: "Yes, your ethics are very high. But they're not the ethics of this society. The block meetings you loathe them. The faceless accusers. The juveniles. The busybody prying. This senseless struggle for leases. The anxiety. The tension and strain. . . . And the overtones of guilt and suspicion."[23]

Purcell is also a misfit in his role as propagandist. For example, a propaganda "packet" he created is rejected by Sue Frost, a high-ranking Committee Secretary, because it is not clearly in line with Morec principles. Its meaning is not as obvious as it should be for its readers readily to grasp its message. His employee, Luddy, explains the concern: "It's not a moral question, Al. It's a question of clarity. The Morec of that packet doesn't come across."[24] He finds that Morec society has no allowance for personal conscience, something Purcell highly prizes. Morality is thus sacrificed at the altar of clarity, convention, and compliance.

Fear is the weapon of choice wielded to reinforce this dualistic thinking. The citizens of Morec had witnessed a nuclear holocaust and cling to Morec principles as the only means of preventing a recurrence. A minor character explaining the statue vandalization exemplifies this twisted thinking: "*The people that did this mean to overthrow Morec. They won't rest until every scrap of morality and decency has been trampled into the ground. They want to see fornication and neon signs and dope come back. They want to see waste and rapacity rule sovereign, and vainglorious man writhe in the sinkpit of his own greed*" (emphasis in original).[25] The prevailing belief system rests on this binary opposition, one that when interrogated falls apart: citizens are offered either Morec or depravity. Purcell, on the other hand, recognizes that Morec *is* depravity.

But, because Purcell is so entrenched in the system, Gretchen must clarify his position to him: "You're not a 'mutant'; you're just a balanced human being. . . . The japery, everything you've done. You're just trying to re-establish a balance in an unbalanced world."[26] Rejecting the dualistic thinking of Morec—the historically contingent, politically complicit distortion of actual truth and goodness—allows Purcell to discover and more fully embrace enduring values, and with them his essential self. While David Mackey interprets this move as Purcell "breaking out from being a passive receiver of Morec's reality structure and becoming the active shaper of his own reality,"[27] what better explains the situation is Purcell apprehending a misfit between his society's rules and nonnegotiable deliverances of authentic moral truth, and through an act of will embracing the better vision. This righteous rebellion takes place through Purcell's production and broadcasting of a satire on Morec society patterned on Jonathan Swift's "Modest Proposal."

An Inveterate Human Quality

As the allusion to Swift reminds us, satire depends on the notion of a shared morality. As the *Literary Reference Center* explains, satire is "intended to expose and ridicule vice, corruption, folly, shortsightedness, pretense, hypocrisy, and bias," aimed at communal good; it can thrive only where "there is a clear difference between expected moral behavior and duty and actual behavior."[28] If Morec—the historical situation—determined moral values, then Purcell's satire would not be able to find its mark, as it so clearly does. And readers recognize in other Dick stories the valor of moral underdogs who also buck against an unjust system, a pattern that recurs in Dick's novels, according to Dennis Weiss and Justin Nicholas.[29] Although Dick's heroes don't fit the Hollywood uber-masculine stereotype, they nonetheless "quietly refus[e] to bow to the pressures of a society and a technology that attempt to flatten and control his existence."[30] Figures such as Nobusuke Tagomi and Frank Frink in *The Man in the High Castle*, John Isidore in *Do Androids Dream of Electric Sheep?*, and Douglas Quail in the short story "We Can Remember It for You Wholesale" populate the Dickian corpus. In their stubborn resistance to authoritarianism, these characters illustrate the quintessence for Dick of a significant part of what it means to be human: an innate resistance to oppression and a tenacious insistence on an objective and universal standard of moral goodness that outlasts transient earthly powers. This is the ultimately heroic trait of ordinary people; they say no to the tyrant and they calmly take the consequences of this resistance. In essence, they cannot be compelled to be what they are not.[31]

Dick's work is marked by this inveterate human quality, whose obstinacy is matched by its authenticity. In Dick's extrapolative stories, spun by introducing to the plot what Suvin calls the novum,[32] whatever human impulses and experiences emerge intact, unchanged by the contingent factors at play, just might point to essential truth. Contra Suvin, the more variables in the mix, all the more fundamental and revelatory is what remains. That is, in fact, what one discovers while surveying literary texts that span humankind's written record. Wells and Dick, no less than Hesiod or Homer, reveal to us who we are, help us understand the weighty moral challenges we face, and emphasize the sustaining values and virtues that necessarily transcend any given cultural moment, try as some might to domesticate, deflate, or deny them.

10

Human Rights, Human Nature, and *Amistad*

After making films about aliens, sharks, and close encounters that stretched both the creative potential of special effects experts and the imaginative limits of moviegoers, Steven Spielberg, in his first film for DreamWorks, depicted an actual historical case brought before the United States Supreme Court in 1841. *Amistad* is the tale, told with a healthy dose of artistic license, of a case that figured centrally in the abolitionist cause.

In 1839, in the same decade as the death of famed English abolitionist William Wilberforce, a group of abducted Africans from Sierra Leone, led by Cinqué (whose real name was Sengbe Pieh, played in the film by Djimon Hounsou), revolted on the Spanish schooner *Amistad*, killing most of the crew and demanding their return to Africa. Sailing up the coast of the United States, they were taken into custody by US officials off Montauk, New York, and then transferred to New Haven, Connecticut, for trial on charges of murder and piracy. The mutineers were about to be delivered back to Spain, but fortunately had by then garnered strong support from antislavery groups, for whom the case represented a watershed in the fight for human and civil rights.

The ensuing legal battle culminated in the Supreme Court, where former president John Quincy Adams (played by Anthony Hopkins), a passionate antislavery advocate in the House of Representatives, argued on behalf of the Africans. The case preceded by a few decades the start of the Civil War, a conflict ostensibly fought over the extension of slavery to new territories, and one that would exact a toll so bloody it almost defies comprehension. Sixty-three years before the *Amistad* case, America had declared her independence, insisting in language borrowed from the English philosopher John Locke, that all men are created equal and endowed by their Creator with unalienable rights, among them life, liberty, and the pursuit of happiness. Yet despite such lofty rhetoric, equality had not been extended to all men (and certainly not to women). Slavery remained legal, and American slavery had devolved into a particularly brutal institution—yet an institution many insisted was essential to the American economy, particularly in the South.

In 1984, producer Debbie Allen came across two volumes of essays and articles, entitled *Amistad I* and *Amistad II*, written by African American writers, historians, and philosophers. For more than a decade she researched and developed the volumes as a film project but met with little success in generating interest among the filmmaking community. After seeing Spielberg's *Schindler's List*, she realized that "here was a filmmaker who could understand and embrace this project and help me get it done."[1] Spielberg did a great service by giving Allen this chance and drawing our attention to this important but easily neglected historical episode. It is a story that needed to be told, and it gives us the chance to learn some of its lessons and some philosophy along the way.

Legal or political freedom is the central theme of *Amistad*. The discussion of rights represents one of the most important and vexed ethical questions dominating the political landscape over the past several centuries. It raises issues of moral normativity, political expediency, cultural identity, and metaphysical reality. It has occupied the talents and energies of the acutest philosophical minds, from John Stuart Mill to Immanuel Kant, John Locke to Thomas Hobbes, Jean-Jacques Rousseau to John Rawls.

In this essay, using Spielberg's remarkable movie as a springboard, we hope to offer a plausible reading of Locke's account of natural or human rights and to identify some of its insights and vulnerabilities. We confine much of our attention to the historical context of *Amistad* to make the discussion manageable in scope. We are particularly interested in the right not to be enslaved or subjugated. By focusing on a snapshot of this debate situated in its historical setting, we can broach some of the enduring questions of this ongoing dialectic without biting off more than we can chew.

What Is the Deal with Rights?

Political philosophy has for one of its salient concerns the issue of rights, which is tied closely with the notion of justice. We live in a culture exploding with rights language. Before discussing what

Amistad says about rights, we should ask two questions: What exactly is a right, and how do we know when a right is really legitimate? A right can be defined as a justified claim that individuals or groups can make on others or on society as a whole. This needs unpacking. First, a right is a claim. It is like something a person owns or possesses. Suppose you have a DVD of the movie *Amistad*. Because it is your possession, you can determine what to do with it, and others can do with it only what you allow. Rights are like that.

Second, rights are "justified" claims, meaning that rights need to be grounded in something that justifies our being able to claim them. What kind of grounding this could be depends on what kind of right we are talking about. There are "legal" (or "civil" rights such as the right to bear arms or the right to an attorney when you are in court. These rights are grounded in legal documents (like the Constitution) and legal decisions and precedents established by the legislative and judicial branches of the government as representative of the will of the people. In *Amistad* the lawyer Roger Baldwin (Matthew McConaughey), as we will see, argues on the basis of the legality of property rights as established in property law.

There are also "moral" or "basic human" rights, which are not established in any documents or by the will of the people. It is interesting to note that whereas Baldwin argues on the basis of legal property rights, Quincy Adams, in his argument before the Supreme Court, elevates the issue to the question of moral rights. Such rights are grounded elsewhere: perhaps as divine gift; as a function of rationality or rational autonomy; as something intrinsic to and morally important in human beings themselves; as a way to maximize the greatest happiness for the greatest number, as a dictate of reason; by game-theoretic considerations and various thought experiments or presumed implicit social contracts; or by appeal to the common good. *Amistad* at various turns hints at several of these approaches.[2]

So some rights can be moral and not legal (religious freedom in communist lands), some can be legal and not moral (many might argue that prostitution in parts of Nevada is an example), some can be neither legal nor moral (the right of the team that won the toss to pass or receive), and some can be both moral and legal (free speech or freedom from slavery, such as we see in *Amistad*). Because legal rights derive from political constitutions and legislative enactments whereas moral rights exist independently of these derivations, moral rights can form a basis for justifying or criticizing legal rights. Legal rights can also be eliminated and changed by the will of the people, whereas moral rights, grounded in something above our will, cannot be eliminated in this way. Finally, although there is often a correlation and overlap between legal and moral rights, they do not require each other, nor do they require reference to each other; they can exist independently of one another.[3]

Political philosophy, with its concerns about justice and rights, is part of value theory in philosophy. It is intimately related to, and perhaps even a subset of, standard ethics with its traditional concerns about virtue, goodness, and moral obligation and permissibility. Despite the overlap between moral and political values, though, in many ways political philosophy constitutes its own distinct field of inquiry. To see why, remember that rights are justified claims we have toward others. Rights involve others, and the nature of this involvement pertains to the relationship between rights and obligations. There is a principle in rights talk called the "correlativity thesis," which basically says that all rights have correlative obligations. If I have a right, someone else has an obligation. If slaves have a right to freedom, others have an obligation to grant them that freedom. Because of the correlativity thesis, moral and legal issues can often be analyzed equally well by referencing either the obligations or the rights, since the correlativity thesis implies that one can go from one to the other and vice versa. Both the obligation and the right are grounded in and justified by the same overarching moral or legal principle—which is not, however, to deny that rights language has something distinctive to offer political discourse.

Although this thesis applies to all rights, it does not apply to all obligations. Whereas all rights have correlative obligations, not all obligations have correlative rights. John Stuart Mill, an English philosopher who happened to be at the height of his career during the *Amistad* events, drew on an important distinction between two types of obligations or duties. There are duties of "perfect obligation" and duties of "imperfect obligation." Duties of perfect obligation are duties for which there is a correlative right. An example would be Baldwin's relationship with his clients. He has an obligation to defend them competently, and they have a correlative right to be represented adequately. Shirking such a duty violates a right. Duties of imperfect obligation, in contrast, are duties with no correlative rights. These are usually general obligations involving a range of choice of how to fulfill them. An example might be that abolitionists in *Amistad*'s time may have had an obligation to fight against slavery, but not necessarily to wage battle in every abolitionist cause. They could choose when and how to fulfill this obligation. No particular person would have a claim against them even though they have this obligation. Political philosophy and justice are more concerned with perfect duties and their correlative rights than with issues of moral obligation in general, and this is Mill's way to demarcate the specific terrain of political philosophy within the broader purview of ethics in general.[4] So what might *Amistad* teach us about political philosophy, justice, and rights? More than you might imagine.

Locke and the Pursuit of Property

The opening scenes of *Amistad* depict in vivid detail how slaves in eighteenth-century America were treated with egregious inhumanity. Mercilessly packed into slave ships and taken against their will to a foreign land, a horrendous percentage of them would perish on the brutally harsh and unsanitary journey. If rations ran short or there was a perceived risk of getting caught, the abductors would routinely drown some or all of the cargo, including the Africans themselves. This happens on the slave ship in *Amistad* before the transfer to the schooner—during the infamous transatlantic "middle passage." If the captives survived the voyage, a lifetime of slavery and subjugation likely awaited them. Such treatment was thought justified because the captives' humanity was denied. They were cast as subhuman, brutes, "beasts of burden," animals, and savages, rather than as human persons deserving of respect and equal treatment and imbued with rights both legal and moral.

The dehumanization of these people led to their exploitation as property and commodity. As it happens, the *Amistad* mutineers gained eventual freedom because the claim that they were the property of the Spaniards was shown to be false. In the movie, the young real estate attorney Baldwin is the one to proffer this legal strategy. Baldwin's suggestion initially offends the sensibilities of an overtly religious abolitionist who wishes the court battle to be conducted in the exalted terms of morality and justice, the "battlefield of righteousness," rather than turned into a logic-chopping wrangle over legal minutia. Interestingly, however, an important aspect of the historical and philosophical context of the case connects property and rights more strongly than many realize. To see this, we have to delve into a little intellectual history to understand some of the philosophical context of the period.

The English thinker John Locke was perhaps the foremost political philosopher of the seventeenth century.[5] The influence of Locke's political philosophy on America's Founding Fathers is generally taken for granted, although the extent of this influence has become a vexed question among Locke scholars, a question that need not detain us here. The Founders freely incorporated many of his political ideas, like a separation of powers, the need for a system of checks and balances, and a formal institutional separation of church and state. Indeed, some of his very words found their way into their bold declarations and occasionally polemical political analysis. Among what the Founders, especially Thomas Jefferson while quilling the Declaration of Independence, appropriated from Locke's work was the right of a people to revolt against a government that fails to discharge its fundamental duties. Those duties discharged by a legitimate government include upholding certain unalienable rights, among them life, liberty, and the pursuit of happiness.

Locke, much as Bentham would later write, explicitly said that things are good or evil only in reference to pleasure or pain. We call "good," he affirmed, that which causes pleasure or reduces pain, and we call "bad" what causes pain or reduces pleasure. Such hedonism represented only one aspect of Locke's complex moral theory, which has disparate parts, not all of which easily cohere; however, the similarity to Bentham in this respect is interesting. But despite such similarity, Locke's account does not belong in the same category of rights theories as Bentham's. Instead, it belongs in that family of theories that grounds rights in a deontic way. These theories, sometimes called "choice theories" ground rights in some morally important characteristic of the bearer, from our rationality, to our status as God's creations, to our autonomy.

The Declaration's language of unalienable rights of life and liberty borrows heavily from Locke. He had written a century earlier in his *Second Treatise of Government* that government's responsibility is to safeguard certain basic human rights, especially life, liberty, and, interestingly enough, property: "Man being born, as has been proved, with a title to perfect freedom, and uncontrolled enjoyment of all the rights and privileges of the law of nature, equally with any other man, or number of men in the world, hath by nature a power, not only to preserve his property, that is, his life, liberty, and estate, against the injuries and attempts of other men; but to judge of and punish the breaches of that law in others."[6]

Jefferson altered Locke's words for the Declaration, capturing perhaps the gist of Locke's meaning of "property" by replacing it with the phrase "the pursuit of happiness." Life and liberty remained as fundamental rights of human beings, although, as Mr. Joadson (Morgan Freeman) puts it in the film, the Founding Fathers left it to their sons to finish the job of uniting the states by crushing slavery.

Endowed by Our Creator

An ineliminable aspect of the historical context of the *Amistad* case, an aspect that comes through in the movie in numerous respects, is the traditional view of rights as having been conferred on us by God. There is another strong connection with Locke here as well. Locke was a firm believer that our most fundamental rights come, ultimately, from God, and also that all of us, as God's creations, are morally equal. How Locke attributed both of these important and related principles of equality and liberty to God is interesting to see.

Locke argued that our essential equality and most basic freedoms are the gifts of God. One reason for this belief was the authority Locke thought God has by virtue of creating us. Since we are here because of the work God expended in making it happen, we are his workmanship; therefore, we are his property. As such, he has the authority, because he made us, and the desire, because he loves us, to endow each of us with the right to be free. Freedom from slavery is an important implication, because, since God owns us, we cannot be owned by anyone else, including by parents (a vital point of Locke's *First Treatise*), nor are wives the property of their husbands (an egalitarian point that in Locke's day and age was often needed). Among the implications of our being God's property, Locke thought, would be that we do not have the moral freedom to commit suicide, or to give ourselves over to slavery, or to enslave another.

Because we were all created by God, we are protected from being owned by one another, which is one important way Locke's account of natural law and God's workmanship leads to the moral equality of persons. Human beings are also invested with the capacity for autonomy and reason, another argument for human equality. Created in God's image, we have the capacity to work and exercise creative power, and through these to exercise dominion in the world, analogous to God's dominion over us. As part of God's dominion over us, he has also exercised his volition in making us all equal. He gave us the world over which to exercise dominion, provided that we not use more than we need. God's decision to make us share the world, not selfishly wasting resources though allowing for some inequalities in the distribution of resources, fundamentally demonstrates Locke's conviction that God's will played a role in our natural equality.

Religious motivation was an important part of the *Amistad* story. We catch a sense of this sort of reasoning early in the film when vocal abolitionists are shouting or holding signs that read, "You cannot own another human being" and "Emancipation: It's God's way!" We know that, historically, not everyone channeled their religious convictions against the cause of slavery; sometimes, sadly, quite to the contrary. We see an example of this voiced by a southern defender of slavery, that not just the economic survival of the South depended on slavery, but that slavery, since biblical times, has been accepted as normative.[7]

Locke's understanding of natural law distinguishes his commitment to it from the version we find in one like Aquinas, according to whom, because we have been created with certain features, there is a naturalness to our behaving in certain ways. There is a natural or even eternal law, set by nature (most ultimately God's nature, and secondarily ours), which amounts to or at least approximates God's law. By seeking what gives us real fulfillment and true happiness, we can apprehend this natural law, which exists before any manmade legislation or rules for harmonious living.

We return to this version of natural law in the next section, but for now it bears emphasis that Locke's version of natural law, plausibly read, is a little different. Locke, like many theistic ethicists, struggled with the question of whether or not God himself might be subject to an eternal law if he is not directly and volitionally responsible for its contents. One way to get around this difficulty is by suggesting that, although the moral law depends on God, thereby safeguarding his sovereignty, God is not able to completely alter its contents, making good evil or vice versa. A natural law theorist in the tradition of Aquinas has this option, cashing out divine sovereignty more in terms of dependence than control.

In departing from Thomism, however, Locke seemed to embrace a more "voluntaristic" account, privileging God's will over his nature. Whereas Aquinas rooted the authority of natural law in God's mind and character, Hugo Grotius, Samuel von Pufendorf, and Locke were more inclined to root it in God's will. Natural law, as Locke conceived it, was founded in God's freedom, *his* rights, which come from his having made us—a principle we have already seen is very important in Locke. It is through acts of autonomous making that ownership is created, which demonstrates the way Locke privileged will. As Ian Shapiro puts it, "In [Locke's] moral and political writings he came down decisively in the voluntarist, or will-centered, camp. He could not relinquish the proposition that for something to have the status of a law, it must be the product of a will."[8]

Amistad itself features ambivalence in its depiction of the religious. Note, for example, the unhappiness of the protesting abolitionists that, in a humorous scene, even the Africans notice. When prospects for victory for the *Amistad* Africans look bleak after concerted efforts against them by President Van Buren (in obsequious deference to Spain and the southern states), Mr. Tappan (Stellan Skarsgård), an outspoken Christian abolitionist, says, "This news, well of course it's bad news, but the truth is they may be more valuable to our struggle in death than in life. Martyrdom, Mr. Joadson. From the dawn of Christianity, we have seen no stronger power for change." To which Mr. Joadson, a former slave, replies, "What is true, Mr. Tappan, and believe me when I tell you I have seen this, is that there are some men whose hatred of slavery is stronger than anything except for the slave himself."

This powerful scene brings to mind the words of twentieth-century political analyst Richard John Neuhaus: "Even more perverse [than those who seek martyrdom] are those who would volunteer countless others for martyrdom. In truth, those who think 'a little totalitarianism might not be a bad thing for the church' reflect an aspect of the superficiality of American culture that they deplore. The romanticizing of persecution is only possible for those who have not taken the measure of history's horror, who have not read their church history nor their Solzhenitsyn."[9] In other words, willingness to be a martyr oneself is one thing; volunteering others for the task and glorifying it the way Tappan does is quite another.

This negative depiction of Tappan brings to mind a critique of *Amistad* offered by Gary Rosen in a fascinating and provocative essay in which he issues a harsh indictment of Spielberg's characterization of religion. Rosen accuses Spielberg of denigrating white Protestant Christianity by intentionally misrepresenting the racial relations of the events in question. For example, Tappan, in historical fact, was the prime defender of the Africans from start to finish. And "far from being indifferent to their fate as individuals, [Tappan] refused to prolong their suffering by pressing for more litigation. Far from being a closet racist, this cofounder of the American Antislavery Society was extraordinary in his day for publicly condoning marriage between blacks and whites." Moreover, whereas the heroic Joadson is a purely fictional character, Tappan was the engine behind the "*Amistad* Committee" a group of "militantly evangelical abolitionists . . . who raised money for the case, publicized it, and carried it through to its successful conclusion," although this committee makes no appearance in the movie.[10]

Locke so firmly rooted basic human rights in a theistic worldview that he has been criticized by some as having promoted a theory that, in a secular and pluralistic culture, needs reinterpretation. It has been suggested by John Dunn, for example, that the biggest ideological shift that has taken place between the context of Locke's writing and the present has been the replacement of this theistic vision of the world with more secular counterparts. For example, rather than saying that people cannot be owned by other human beings because they are owned by God, contemporary rights theories are more likely to affirm simply that human beings cannot be owned by anyone at all. We later discuss ways in which aspects of Locke's theory can be applied without assuming that rights are a function of divine whim, but perhaps dependent on God after all.

Broaching religion in public discourse is often thought of as opening a can of worms, so Spielberg deserves credit for including the religious dimension of this chapter in history so prominently. It was certainly an important aspect of the context and intellectual milieu. Moreover, since Locke was pointing to the importance of recognizing moral rights that exist prior to governmental recognition and that in fact require such legal recognition, his theory of rights, as any workable theory of rights does, requires a strong sense of underlying moral realism to retain its normative force. Historically, religion was often thought best to function in that role. Even Thomas Jefferson, whose words against slavery were excised from the Declaration by the First Continental Congress, who was a firm proponent of an institutional separation of church and state, and who was by no means a conventionally religious individual, offered the following reflections on the importance of religious belief to the issue of slavery: "And can the liberties of a nation be thought secure when we have removed their only firm basis, a conviction in the minds of the people that these liberties are the gift of God? That they are not to be violated but with his wrath."[11] Jefferson's point here pertains more to confidence in the existence of rights rather than their true philosophical explanation.

However, Jefferson's mention of divine wrath resonates with Locke in another way and also points up a potential limitation in Locke's analysis. Locke closely connected God's authority to invest us with basic freedoms with his ability to mete out rewards and punishments for obedience and disobedience, respectively, to God's law. Recall again the importance, on Locke's view, of pain and pleasure as guideposts in the construction of ethics. It has been speculated that this effort to understand God's authority as establishing moral foundations was due to Locke's empiricism (the view that all of our knowledge originates in our senses). Whereas later empiricists like Hume would argue that such an epistemology undermines confidence in many treasured convictions, like belief in God, Locke believed God's existence remained, on empiricist grounds, as sure as anything. Likewise, he argued, the principles of morality, which he suggested remained as secure as those we discover in mathematics. However, an empirical grounding for moral convictions meant he needed to resort to pain and pleasure and the power of God to dole them out, requiring Locke to appeal to traditional notions of rewards and punishments rather than less empirically accessible notions of genuine divine moral authority.[12]

One important reason, Locke argued, that God has the power to make us equal and give us our basic rights is that he created us. Work, for Locke, entitled the craftsman to his workmanship. Both by his creation of us and by his sovereign choice, God made us equal, investing us with the right not to be enslaved by any man. We are God's alone. Our shared ability to think and reason also underscores our equality, as does our creative ability (fashioned after God's) to engage in meaningful work and craftsmanship, thereby entitling us to the labor of our hands as long as we do not forget that the world is to be shared with equals. But because of the importance of Locke's workmanship model, and the primacy it accords to will, his version of natural law likely suggests, in his mind, an important voluntaristic component, which raises arbitrariness objections. And Locke's empiricism led to an inadequate account of divine authority, rooted less in morality than in prudence. *Amistad* captures both the potential and pitfalls of rooting rights in religion through its range of depictions, from the sanctimonious Tappan, to the secular Baldwin, to the pragmatic Adams, to the earnest abolitionists.

"Give Us, Us Free!"

Locke believed that, metaphysically speaking, our freedom and equality come from God; but how is it that we come to know this? This is a question of epistemology. For Locke, natural law helps here. On his view, we have been invested with reason, by which we can apprehend certain truths about ourselves. Locke was of the view, as a natural law theorist and strict empiricist, that we can know, normatively, how humans are to be treated by an empirical investigation into their behavior, and not just through special revelation. A universal and relentless desire for freedom, for example, would provide evidence for Locke that such a state is not just normal, but natural, and a deviation from it unnatural and bad.[13]

Spielberg vividly depicts the desperate human desire for freedom by capturing Cinqué's experience of something approaching a panic attack in the midst of a court procedure. The escalating internal tensions within him finally manifest by his standing to his feet and repeating, with increasing urgency, "Give us, us free!" It is a powerful scene, and one of the many ways in which the theme of freedom reverberates throughout the film. In the climactic Supreme Court scene, Adams claims that, despite its appearance as a garden-variety property case, this case is far more, concerning nothing less than who and what human beings really are. The natural state of human beings, he claims, is freedom. The philosophical significance of the scene requires that we quote his words at length:

> Yes, this is no mere property case, gentlemen. I put it to you thus: this is the most important case ever to come before this court. Because what it, in fact, concerns is the very nature of man.... This is a publication of the office of the President. It's called the Executive Review, [and it] asserts that "there has never existed a civilized society in which one segment did not thrive upon the labor of another. As far back as one chooses to look, history bears this out.... Slavery has always been with us and is neither sinful nor immoral. Rather, as war and antagonism are the natural states of man, so, too, slavery, as natural as it is inevitable."

Readers might recognize in these words an echo of the philosopher Thomas Hobbes, who, in his magnum opus *Leviathan*, characterized the state of nature for human beings as a war of all against all, a pessimistic picture of the human condition indeed. Continuing, Adams reveals that, on this score, his view is much closer to that of Locke's greater optimism: "Now, gentlemen, I must say, I differ with the keen mind of the South, and with our president, who apparently shares their views, offering that the natural state of mankind is instead, and I know this is a controversial idea, freedom. And the proof is the length to which a man, woman, or child will go to regain it, once taken. He will break loose his chains. He will decimate his enemies. He will try and try and try against all odds, against all prejudices, to get home."

This powerful scene nicely connects with a Lockean understanding of natural law. The humor, intelligence, rationality, and desire for freedom of the Africans are accentuated throughout the film—from humorous comments by the captives about the dour abolitionists to Cinqué's intelligent questions to Adams about legal jurisdiction—to highlight their humanness and their equality and rights as human beings. But a critic might insist, understandably, that just because we by nature exhibit certain characteristics, like the craving for freedom the slaves manifest, it does not necessarily follow that such a natural desire carries with it normative or moral force.

Locke himself realized the need for something else to invest such intuitions about freedom and such language of rights with determinate normative force. Earlier we mentioned his workmanship argument that, he thought, invested God with the requisite authority to give us such rights, but we suggested that such an account is, at best, incomplete. Likewise, as an empiricist Locke was limited in his resources for constructing an argument for God's authority to what could be perceived by the senses.[14] The divine workmanship theory, even joined with the divine retribution theory, does not seem quite enough.

We have hinted at a Lockean-inspired account that may avoid some of these difficulties, so now we will try to deliver. If we take some of what Locke suggests and reduce or eliminate the voluntarism, we can end up with an account of natural law closer to that of Aquinas, and perhaps in the process find a more defensible view. Locke himself emphasized that we were created by God and created in God's image, so perhaps on such a view we have been invested essentially by God with a nature that, in its healthiest, happiest state, is free. Locke's theory of morality and of rights incorporated a number of different parts, and although he attempted to synthesize them, perhaps the most defensible theory we can glean from his writings will try to separate the wheat from the chaff. Maybe, if we understand human rights as a gift from God in the sense that we were created in his (metaphysical) image of personhood, we might be able to offer a hybrid account of what grounds our basic rights. True, this downplays Locke's property-of-God premise, but it still suffices for an account of unalienable rights bestowed on us by our Creator, bestowed in the sense that God created us in a form analogous to his. It also helps capture Locke's desire to avoid arbitrariness despite his hesitancy to reject voluntarism altogether.[15] Finally, despite the challenge of accounting for the full moral reasons there are for affirming our rights to be free from slavery, most of us are firmly convinced of them. So much so, in fact, that we deem them worth fighting for if necessary.

The Last Battle of the American Revolution

Some of the final lines of the movie feature Adams following Cinqué's lead, invoking his own ancestors with these words: "We desperately need your strength and wisdom to triumph over our fears, our prejudices, ourselves. Give us the courage to do what is right. And if it means civil war, then let it come. And when it does, may it be, finally, the last battle of the American Revolution." Adams could have invoked at this juncture the words of his own famous father in whose shadow he lived: "Every measure of prudence, therefore, ought to be assumed for the eventual total extirpation of slavery from the United States. I have, throughout my whole life, held the practice of slavery in abhorrence."[16] The elder Adams had also predicted to Thomas Jefferson that a national struggle between the states over slavery "might rend this mighty fabric in twain."[17]

Abraham Lincoln, in his classic Second Inaugural Address near the end of the Civil War, would speak these immortal words: "Fondly do we hope, fervently do we pray, that this mighty scourge of war may speedily pass away. Yet, if God wills that it continue until all the wealth piled by the bondsman's two hundred and fifty years of unrequited toil shall be sunk, and until every drop of blood drawn with the lash shall be paid by another drawn with the sword, as was said three thousand years ago, so still it must be said 'the judgments of the Lord are true and righteous altogether.'"[18]

Slavery advocates continually exploited fears over the potential cost and suffering produced by a war to keep abolitionists on the defensive. Note the words of Calhoun, an outspoken southerner who happens also to have been Adams's vice president: "Ask yourself, what court wants to be responsible for the spark that ignites the firestorm? What president wants to be in office when it comes crashing down around him? Certainly no court before this one.

Certainly no president before this one. So the real determination our courts and our president must make is not whether this ragtag group of Africans raised swords against their enemy, but rather, must we?"

We earlier mentioned John Stuart Mill for whom the elimination of suffering was very important. Nonetheless, it is instructive that Mill, himself a passionate defender of human rights, wrote this of war, echoing the sentiment of Adams and Lincoln: "War is an ugly thing, but not the ugliest of things. The decayed and degraded state of moral and patriotic feeling which thinks that nothing is worth war is much worse. The person who has nothing for which he is willing to fight, nothing which is more important than his own personal safety, is a miserable creature and has no chance of being free unless made and kept so by the exertions of better men than himself."[19]

A few decades ago, around the time President Carter proposed reinstating the draft registration, a Princeton student could be seen prominently sporting a shirt that read, "Nothing is worth dying for." Socrates said the unexamined life is not worth living; one might wonder, if nothing is worth dying for, whether or not anything is worth living for. Adams, Lincoln, and Mill, great thinkers all, seemed to think that some wars, terrible and tragic as they may be, are worth fighting and dying for, because freedom and the life purposes it affords make life worth living.

11

Train Up Your Wizards in the Way They Should Go

The opening lines of Charles Dickens' *A Tale of Two Cities* are among the most recognizable passages in literature—it was the best of times, it was the worst of times. The description is simultaneously timeless and time-bound: written in Victorian England, depicting the eve of the French Revolution, but somehow no matter how much time passes, it seems that they ring perpetually true. "It was the best of times, it was the worst of times." Isn't it always?

In short compass, Dickens manages to draw from his historical moment a broader truth about the human condition: "[I]t was the season of Light, it was the season of Darkness, it was the spring of hope, it was the winter of despair."[1] We humans, it seems, are continually caught between two extremes: our promise, creative potential, and idealistic possibilities on the one side and our hubris, destructive capacities, and cynical bent on the other. A quick glimpse at your social media feed will prove this point.

Okay, yes, admittedly—we're nowhere near French-Revolution-era craziness. No one's brought out the guillotines. At least not yet. But most of us can recognize something of our current cultural moment in this iconic Dickens quote. We rally behind one another in the wake of national disasters, volunteering our time and money to restore communities; meanwhile other communities are languishing in the thrall of opioid abuse. Our technological and artistic ingenuity is at an all-time high, with brilliant new gadgets and imaginative creations released daily, while fraud and corruption, violence and ill-health run rampant across the country.

How then do we proceed? What might provide some hope in these troubled times? There are a slew of answers on offer, many of them politically focused—protest, lobby, legislate, vote, agitate. While those responses are not wrong per se, absent a personal, individual revolution of the wills and characters of those who make up society, these political maneuvers will merely widen the divide between us, and deepen the challenges we face. Dickens, concerned as he was with the state of Victorian culture and its societal tendencies that had ground many of its people down, suggests another avenue for correction. George Orwell—of all writers—found something about this vision compelling, even if he himself preferred the political: "There is no clear sign that [Dickens] wants the existing order to be overthrown," Orwell reflects, "or that he believes it would make very much difference if it were overthrown. . . . His whole 'message' is one that at first glance looks like an enormous platitude: If men would behave decently, the world would be decent."[2]

J. K. Rowling's Harry Potter series, we argue, follows this same line of thought. She has, in fact, identified Dickens as an important influence on her work. Like Dickens, Rowling is asking about the cause of our woes and what remedies are on offer and drawing similar conclusions. In the pages of her seven highly imaginative, fantastical *Harry Potter* books, we find—surprisingly enough—a realistic world much like ours, filled with characters that mirror the best and worst of us and who experience the very same joy and despair. Like us, Rowling's wizards and witches long for good to prevail over the evil they see around them and sincerely want to do the right thing. Well, most of them anyway.

But those others are just as instructive in the moral arc of Rowling's story and especially in the lessons it provides for readers. Because, let's face it, Rowling—like most great storytellers—is a master teacher. *Harry Potter* is not simply set at a school; the series itself is a school, training readers to recognize, prefer, and enact what is good and right. The venerable Roman poet Horace famously said that literature should teach and delight, and Rowling executes his charge well, as readers watch her characters navigate situations that challenge their heart and mind, identify and hone their values and beliefs, and ultimately shape their very selves in their moral choices—for good or ill.

At the center of this education, of course, is the enchanted Hogwarts School of Witchcraft and Wizardry. Each year, young wizards throughout Britain await their acceptance letters with bated breath (or for muggle-borns like Hermione, are taken by surprise by them). These spirited scholars head off each fall to the fabled Scottish castle, to take up exotic subjects like transfiguration, potions, herbology, and the daunting defense against the dark arts. Here they get initiated into the world their older siblings and parents have already been a part of—learning to fly, caring for magical creatures, and finally trying their hand at apparition. It's a fanciful world, and we'd probably all welcome our own Hogwarts invite. But as whimsically as it's described, we can't forget that the curriculum is not merely fun and games for these students. It's real, hard work. They train, practice, fail, try again. They sometimes face disagreeable and downright cruel professors yet have to learn the material despite those challenges. Those O.W.L.s and N.E.W.T.s won't pass themselves.

These magical skills are crucial to living in Harry, Hermione, and Ron's world, and the three friends have varying degrees of success mastering them. Arguably these wondrous features are what make *Harry Potter* the phenomenon it is. Readers thrill at the games of Quidditch, imagining the students aloft on their broomsticks. They cheer for Harry as he participates in the Triwizard Tournament, putting his magical training to the test. Without the children's initiation to magic, they'd have no access to Platform 9 & 3/4 or Diagon Alley, no Patronus charm to fend off the dreaded Dementors. The spells and charms and magical properties of myriad objects in *Harry Potter* enlarge the story's possibilities to be sure. Pictures move and talk, invisibility and shape-shifting are live options, as are mind reading and talking with snakes. But, even though magic is at the crux of the Hogwarts curriculum, these magical techniques do not constitute the real education the books offer—neither to the characters nor to the readers. These, in fact, are mere machinery, available to the good and bad characters alike. In fact, someone as wicked as Voldemort has magical abilities at least as strong as those of the virtuous Dumbledore, if not more so. On a smaller scale, we see this contrast play out between Harry and his friends and Draco Malfoy and his.

In *The Sorcerer's Stone* these children arrive at Hogwarts full of promise, and in many ways, both sets of friends follow the same path: taking classes, learning their spells, and growing in magical acumen. But that similarity is of little concern to the story; what matters more—what is in fact crucial—is that their paths diverge, as they learn (or reject) the deeper lessons and inculcate in themselves (or don't) the virtues of friendship and love. They—and we—learn well what

Dumbledore notes in *The Chamber of Secrets*, "It is our choices, Harry, that show what we truly are, far more than our abilities." What the contrasts between Harry's and Draco's friends show is that an education caught up in teaching only technique—encouraging children's hands and minds but not guiding their heart—is not one worthy of its name. I think we all know this, but that often doesn't translate to the dominant view of education in our own world. We don't have magic, of course, but technology seems to function similarly for us. Who hasn't, at least once, been wowed by the newest gadget? Every year we hear about new medical advances, feats of modern engineering, and manufacturing capabilities that would have been unthinkable even twenty years ago. Arthur C. Clark captures the connection well with his proverbial quip, "Any sufficiently advanced technology is indistinguishable from magic."[3]

As with those in Harry Potter, we can easily confuse (or prefer) technical expertise and training with humane education. In many higher education circles, this shift toward the technical and practical—this emphasis on vocational training over the liberal arts—is just about complete. The number of humanities majors are shrinking, and fewer state dollars are going to support the liberal arts overall, deemed too impractical to add value to communities. On one hand, this shift is understandable. People need jobs. The market is changing; demand for technical skill is on the rise. However, the danger in getting so fixated on these technological pursuits, we might become mindless technophiles, subordinating all else to what Neil Postman has identified as "the sovereignty of technique and technology."[4]

In other words, we might mistake the means of education for the end of education. But, as Postman notes, "Any education that is mainly about economic utility is far too limited to be useful, and, in any case, so diminishes the world that it mocks one's humanity."[5] The Harry Potter series knows (and shows) that, although the magic it depicts (and the technology of our world that it mimics) may mesmerize us, it is neither the cause of nor the solution to our deepest human problems. Instead, the story directs our attention to other, more fundamental concerns—the virtues that make the real differences in the characters' lives and well-being, chief among them are humility, courage, and love. These virtues are the bedrock of a good life and our full development as human beings; they nurture and grow our spirit and soul. These are the lessons taught by Rowling, learned by Harry and his friends, and inculcated in the readers' imaginations.

Humility is an apt starting point in talking about education of any kind—moral or otherwise. Without humility, a student is unteachable, thinking themselves self-sufficient or better than another. The arc of Hermione's story exemplifies both the challenges a lack of humility poses to real intellectual and moral growth and the possibilities of further moral development that can stem from embracing this important habit of heart and mind. In that way, humility truly is what Edmund Burke calls it: the "firm foundation of all virtues," making way for the full flowering of a person's spirit and soul.[6] It's important, however, to distinguish between humiliation and humility. Humility is not to think terribly of oneself, but to think rightly. It is to know one's strengths and weaknesses. As Mother Teresa once explained, "If you are humble nothing will touch you, neither praise nor disgrace, because you know what you are."[7] Humiliation, on the other hand, is debasement without respect. Hermione first tasted this humiliation in *The Chamber of Secrets*, standing out as a Muggle-born among the mostly pure-blood wizards that make up the Hogwarts student body. Draco exploits this vulnerability, angrily dismissing her defense of the Gryffindor Quidditch team with, "[n]o one asked your opinion, you filthy little Mudblood."

Understandably, as the story progresses, Hermione responds poorly to these slights, by flaunting her strengths (her book learning and firm grasp on class material). Errors come in pairs, as C. S. Lewis has noted, and Hermione swings wildly from the degradation she experienced to an outsized pride, manifested at the expense of Ron. As he struggles in class to cast the prescribed spell, Hermione presumes to lecture him: "You're saying it wrong. . . . It's Wing-gar-dium Levi-o-sa, make the 'gar' nice and long." Unsurprisingly, Ron doesn't take kindly to this condescension and later says, within Hermione's earshot, that "it's no wonder no one can stand her. . . . She's a nightmare, honestly." While this is admittedly not the best start for their relationship, the education enabled by Hermione's overcorrection and Ron's candid admission plays out well for all involved and eventually forms the beginning bonds of a strong and life-giving friendship.

We know the details—Hermione, hurt, isolates herself in the girl's bathroom. When a troll gets loose in the castle, Ron and Harry take off to find her and, after many missteps, rescue her from the troll's rampage. Through this experience, Hermione modulates her view of herself and others. Friedrich Nietzsche may have thought humility a vice, a trait unworthy of the "overman" because it keeps one beholden to others, but the Harry Potter series, through scenes like this one, demonstrates humanity's interdependence and the importance of recognizing and honoring our interconnections. The value of humility is highlighted by Hermione's acknowledgment of the debt she owes to Harry and Ron: "I'm not as good as you," Harry tells her. To which Hermione responds: "Me! . . . Books! And cleverness! There are more important things—friendship and bravery." Hermione has learned well the essential lessons of humility, which Flannery O'Connor has captured in this insight: "To know oneself is, above all, to know what one lacks. It is to measure oneself against Truth, and not the other way around. The first product of self-knowledge is humility."

And upon the humility Hermione develops in *The Sorcerer's Stone* is built much good work. Her advocacy for the house elves, who have historically been poorly treated and ill-thought-of, stems from her own self-acceptance and humble service. Rather than rejecting her precarious social position as a Mudblood on the margins, Hermione embraces it and finds solidarity with others who find themselves similarly maligned. Out of that solidarity, S.P.E.W. (the Society for the Promotion of Elfish Welfare) is born, a gesture reminiscent of the kindly acts of Hagrid toward magical creatures, especially those unwanted or perceived dangerous. Humility, these stories teach us, breeds compassion and empathy, essential components of a strong community.

Two things are important to keep in mind here: First, humility does not come upon a person unbidden; it is a discipline, instilled and strengthened through one's choices. In the excruciating spot that Hermione found herself in, smarting from Malfoy's earlier insult and confronted by her own prideful treatment of Ron and the barrier it put between them, she had to test her true self against these extremes—and to recognize that the reality of who she is lay somewhere in between. She is neither the lowly outcast Draco marks her as nor the all-important bigshot she has presented herself as in class. She is intelligent and clever, book-smart and logical, yet she needs others to keep her weaknesses in check and to complement her strengths.

Second, humility, compassion, and empathy—to make a positive difference—must be made manifest in one's actions and interactions with others. Doing so, especially when the stakes are high and there's a price to pay, requires courage, a virtue that animates much of the plot of the series. Most of the major characters are afforded an opportunity to demonstrate courage. These opportunities come when something or someone they value is in jeopardy and they must act to protect them. Some characters, like Peter Pettigrew, choose cowardice to preserve themselves rather than defy their fear and risk themselves for something or someone more important. Sirius Black acknowledges that Peter was in a difficult spot—caught between Lord Voldemort and a hard place: betray the Potters or die. But the fear Pettigrew felt was no excuse for his infidelity. To borrow a line from Nelson Mandela, courage is not the absence of fear but the "triumph over it." Sirius puts the lie to Peter's sniveling excuses: "What was there to be gained by fighting the most evil wizard who has ever existed? . . . Only innocent lives, Peter!" Peter stubbornly clings to his fear to vindicate himself: "You don't understand! . . . He would have killed me, Sirius!" Black is having none of it; the right choice in such a situation is as chilling as it is clear: "THEN YOU SHOULD HAVE DIED! . . . DIED RATHER THAN BETRAY YOUR FRIENDS, AS WE WOULD HAVE DONE FOR YOU!"

That sounds incredible for anyone to have done such a thing, to have faced the Dark Lord with the prospect of certain death. But Professor McGonagall does what Pettigrew fails to. She revolts against the Death Eaters who have taken over Hogwarts, with the final straw being Amycus Carrow's willingness to allow children to take the brunt of Voldemort's fury in his invasion of the castle. In a phrase reminiscent of Pettigrew, Carrow asks, "Couple of kids more or less, what's the difference?" McGonagall, like Sirius, realizes what's at stake: "Only the difference between truth and lies, courage and cowardice, . . . a difference, in short, which you and your sister seem unable to appreciate. But let me make one thing very clear. You are not going to pass off your many ineptitudes on the students of Hogwarts. I shall not permit it."

At least one Hogwarts student takes to heart the lesson in courage McGonagall and the other faculty teach: Neville Longbottom. Neville, to put it mildly, is an unlikely foe for Voldemort but one who nonetheless dares to oppose him. Rowling vividly captures Neville's panic as Voldemort uses him as an example—pinning him down with the sorting hat and setting it on fire. Once Harry breaks him free, Neville moves quickly, and in one of the most dramatic scenes of the books, takes out Nagini, the children's greatest enemy:

> The slash of the silver blade could not be heard over the roar of the oncoming crowd, or the sounds of the clashing giants, or of

the stampeding centaurs, and yet it seemed to draw every eye. With a single stroke, Neville sliced off the great snake's head, which spun high into the air, gleaming in the light flooding from the Entrance Hall, and Voldemort's mouth was open in a scream of fury that nobody could hear, and the snake's body thudded to the ground at his feet.

It's a memorable moment, but again, Neville—like Hermione—has been prepared for such a time as this; the courage he displays here has been built through earlier decisions and courageous acts. Even if the stakes were smaller then, they were nonetheless challenges to be overcome. A memorable training ground for Neville's stand against Voldemort, for example, was his earlier stand against his friends, stopping them in *The Sorcerer's Stone* from leaving the common room in order to prevent punishment to the whole house. For this act, he is rewarded with ten points for Gryffindor, as Dumbledore announces, "There are all kinds of courage. . . . It takes a great deal of bravery to stand up to your enemies, but just as much to stand up to your friends." Crucially, Neville challenges his friends out of a pure heart, not for selfish reasons. Courage is not to be confused with rash and dangerous action; it is instead principled action in the face of fear. For this reason, C. S. Lewis elevates courage above other virtues: "Courage is not simply one of the virtues, but the form of every virtue at the testing point."[8] Neville stands up to his friends because he loves them. Love being the motivating virtue for all the others and the most important of all the virtues practiced by the characters and taught by the series.

In fact, what most attracts readers, what accounts for the Harry Potter phenomenon is this simple yet profound truth: that love will, in fact, save the world. But, and here's the kicker, love costs. Love is no insubstantial, sentimental thing; it is tough as nails and powerful. It requires force and a humble, courageous act of will. For, as Plato has argued, the virtues truly are unified—they support and reinforce one another to enable us to become the people we ought to be. The education Harry Potter offers is to recognize the value of humility, courage, and most importantly love and to steel us to embrace the cost and to impress deeply upon us that that cost is worth the reward. This pattern—of a desperate situation, a dramatic self-sacrifice, and a hope affirmed through that sacrifice—runs throughout the series and appears both in the overarching narrative and the smaller stories that make up the whole. Through these depictions, Rowling is training her readers to see beyond the immediate and to recognize the even deeper reality of a world ruled by justice and redeemed by love. Individual enactments of humility, courage, and love are inseparable from justice and love's ultimate triumph. In the soil of Rowling's books, the reader's moral imagination can grow alongside those of the central characters. Not only is love what is being taught to these characters (and readers) as they grow up; it's the catalyst for their learning.

In the popular documentary *Won't You Be My Neighbor?* Fred Rogers reminds us that "love is at the root at everything, all learning, all relationships, love or the lack of it." The arc of Harry's story highlights this deep truth. As powerful as the series' climax is—where Harry surrenders himself to Voldemort to save his beloved friends and professors—it could never have happened if it weren't for his mother's sacrificial act to protect him from Voldemort as a child. And not in the obvious way, that Harry would not have lived were it not for his mother's protection. Rather, as book makes clear, Lily Potter denies herself in favor of her son, finds courage to stand up against an implacable enemy despite the overwhelming odds that he will prevail, and plants deep within her son a knowledge of love's power that cannot be shaken. Harry loves well because his mother first loved him. As Dumbledore explains to Harry: "Your mother died to save you. If there is one thing Voldemort cannot understand, it is love. He didn't realize that love as powerful as your mother's for you leaves its own mark. Not a scar, no visible sign... to have been loved so deeply, even though the person who loved us is gone, will give us some protection forever. It is in your very skin."

Even still, Harry must grow into that love, step by step and choice by choice. He does so with the encouragement of loving mentors and pseudo-parents. Dumbledore, especially. As a precursor to Harry's self-sacrifice in *Deathly Hallows*, Dumbledore allows Snape to kill him. That Dumbledore took this step bolsters the encouragement and support he offers Harry at King's Cross Station. Rowling's online venture *Pottermore* elaborates on this important scene in the following commentary that's helpful for underscoring how Dumbledore's character is simultaneously formed and revealed through his actions:

> [D]espite the faults, despite Dumbledore perhaps not being the perfect wizard Harry thought he was, never before has Dumbledore seemed more heroic. For men and women are not born great. They learn greatness over time—from experience, from mistakes. Dumbledore looked at his deeds, at his flaws, and he had the wisdom to confront and overcome them; he fought the

greatest nemesis there was: himself. . . . Who better to teach the next generation of wizards? Who better to face Lord Voldemort? Who better to send Harry on his way from King's Cross station, with one last piece of wisdom: "Do not pity the dead, Harry. Pity the living, and, above all, those who live without love."

The wisdom Dumbledore offers Harry is wedded to his practice; more importantly, it has grown out of that practice. And Harry has learned well, as he goes out to surrender to Voldemort. It's a beautiful picture of someone who has embraced and embodied the moral education of these many years. It's one that resonates with readers, as sales and the popularity of the books and its ancillary products shows. But what readers do with that story matters just as much as the story itself. Have we embraced our own moral education inspired by these books? William James reminds us that without putting what we learned through literature into practice, the experience is the opposite of educative; it is utterly self-indulgent:

> The weeping of a Russian lady over the fictitious personages in the play, while her coach-man is freezing to death on his seat outside, is the sort of thing that everywhere happens on a less glaring scale. . . . One becomes filled with emotions which habitually pass without prompting to any deed, and so the inertly sentimental condition is kept up. The remedy would be, never to suffer one's self to have an emotion at a concert, without expressing it afterward in some active way. Let the expression be the least thing in the world—speaking genially to one's aunt, or giving up one's seat in a horse-car, if nothing more heroic offers—but let it not fail to take place.[9]

Rightly read, good literature—the enchanted and non-enchanted varieties alike—habituates our hearts and minds outwardly, to practice humility, bolster our courage, and embrace love. We can—and should—lament our current state of affairs, how the worst of times are at present being instantiated: the bitter rivalries, the no-holds barred angry rhetoric, and the general sense of despair. We also can—and indeed we must—fasten our present hopes to the eternal verities that will not disappoint. Good stories can show us the way.

Part II: Hope & Goodness

12

How Do You Like Them Ethics?

As NBC's breakout sitcom *The Good Place* opens, Eleanor Shellstrop finds herself in a dilemma. She has died, and a cosmic mismanagement lands her in the Good Place, a secular version of heaven, completely by mistake. Confessing the error will almost certainly mean her removal to the Bad Place and eternal torture. So what should she do? It is out of this predicament that all the series' hijinks ensue. In considering this tension, we find that two organically connected questions lie behind this delightful show: (1) whether morality requires that we do good for goodness' sake and (2) whether reality itself is committed to morality.

Starring Ted Danson as the demon Michael and Kristen Bell as Eleanor—sweet, teentsy, and no freakin' Gandhi—the show blazes a trail of brilliant fun from Nature's Lasik to Ya Basic! As proof that moral philosophy professors aren't as bad as the show's running gag suggests, consider ethicist Chidi Anagonye's *Hamilton*-style rap musical: "My name is Kierkegaard and my writing is impeccable! / Check out my teleological suspension of the ethical!" Or how one day in class Eleanor dismissively asks, "Who died and left Aristotle in charge of ethics?" to which an exasperated Chidi replies, "Plato!"

Although the show is a comedy, the picture that emerges is one of tragedy, tragicomedy at best. Nobody, it turns out at the close of season 3, has made it into the Good Place for centuries. Not even Doug Forcett is likely to make the cut, even though he's the show's quasi-prophet who accidentally stumbled on the secret of the afterlife and has arguably led a faultless life ever since. The reason for this regrettable situation is life's complexity. Even good-intentioned behavior often results in a number of unintended bad consequences, yielding a net loss of "points" rather than a gain. The relative importance of intentions versus consequences is one of the vital philosophical questions the show raises. After discussing what the show has to say on the matter, we will offer our own view and why, if we're right, the context of *The Good Place*, it turns out, is much more tragic than comic. Then we will consider the evidence of morality itself to see if it might suggest a different outcome. But enough of this bullshirt. It's high time to take a swig from a putrid, disgusting bowl of ethical soup.

What Makes an Action Right?

Before reviewing how philosophers have answered the intentions/consequences question, let's first consider the question itself. Some might say that actions are neither right nor wrong. The whole enterprise of morality, they suggest, is misguided. Perhaps life is meaningless or the category of morality is confused. A committed nihilist might insist there's good reason to think there's ultimately nothing to this morality business at all. There are simply no moral truths to be found.

This isn't quite the position of Mindy St. Claire when she counsels Eleanor and company not to mess with ethics ("Mindy St. Claire"). Instead, she advises them to look out for number one. In principle that leaves open the possibility that she believes in objective morality and that we can know what such morality tells us to do, but that she is simply indifferent to it. Perhaps she sees morality and self-interest as so much at odds that she simply gave up on what morality had to say. As she sees it, the more reliable path to happiness concerns promoting what's best for oneself. Interestingly, the moral theory of ethical egoism says that doing what's in one's own ultimate best interest is our moral obligation. This is one way of maintaining a vital connection between what morality says and what's best for us. There's no particular evidence to suggest that Mindy held such an ethical account. What we know is simply that her life was about "making money and doing cocaine"—finding what happiness and fulfillment she could in her circumstances.

The better representation of a nihilistic approach is what Chidi flirted with after becoming aware of his impending eternal doom in the episode "Jeremy Bearimy." Making his vile Peep-M&M-chili concoction in the middle of class, quoting Nietzsche's immortal lines about the death of God, losing heart about morality and meaning—this is the stuff of nihilism commonly understood. Of course defenders of Nietzsche would quickly suggest it's a bit of a caricature, and they have a point; but we'll leave that interesting discussion to the side for now.

Most people still think it's important to consider what makes actions right or wrong. This is the arena of "normative ethics," which has two main strains in the history of philosophy. Chidi discusses both of them in his lectures. One is the Kantian idea that what makes an action right is that it comes from the right motive. Immanuel Kant, the first philosopher mentioned in the show, serves as both ethical touchstone and punchline, a "lonely, obsessive hermit with zero friends" whose ideas nevertheless challenge the characters to wrestle with fundamental questions of right and wrong. The only truly good thing, he thought, is the "good will," which requires that our moral actions be motivated by respect for the moral law. Consequences, on Kant's understanding, don't capture the heart of an action. It's the motive that counts. We should do the right thing because it's the right thing to do, not for any other reason, at least if our action is to retain its moral worth.[1]

One reason Kant found the emphasis on consequences to be dubious is that we're notoriously bad at predicting them. We might try to do something that will result in a good outcome, but the effort can backfire and we end up doing far more bad than good. So it's not the consequences that matter morally. Obviously ethical egoists would disagree. But a narrow focus on self-interest alone strikes many as myopic. A broader "consequentialism" called utilitarianism says an action is right if it produces the best overall consequences for all who are affected by an action. The philosophical nerd best known for promoting utilitarianism is John Stuart Mill. Whereas Kant put the moral focus on intention, Mill generally put it squarely on consequences. Chidi's lecture on Mill has Eleanor initially enamored of utilitarianism's simplicity, Jason's convoluted but surprisingly apropos example of framing "one innocent gator dealer to save a 60-person dance crew" notwithstanding.

Mill did see the possibility that a good-intentioned action might end up doing more harm than good. He handled that sort of possibility by distinguishing between the worth of the moral action and the intention of the moral agent. A well-intentioned action that surprisingly backfires is, in retrospect, a wrong action, but the doer of the action is not necessarily culpable for it. So in this way Mill carved out some space for intention too.[2]

We might side with Kant, or with Mill, or argue for some sort of combination of the two views. As *The Good Place* goes on, it becomes clear that the world it depicts represents a sort of synthesis of Kant's and Mill's ideas. There's a strong emphasis on doing the right thing for its own sake—which sounds like Kant. There's also an important consideration of consequences, but without Mill's distinction between the status of an action and the quality of the agent who performs it. Unintended consequences, even those that can't be reasonably foreseen, can function over time—and almost inevitably will in this increasingly complicated world—to doom one to the Bad Place. For this reason, Doug buying his grandmother flowers actually costs him points, given that his purchase inadvertently supported labor malpractice, environmental abuse, and sexual harassment. This is why nobody has made it to the Good Place for centuries, leaving Chidi and the gang to work out a better system come the final season.

Should It Bother Us?

Should this seemingly unfair feature of the universe of *The Good Place* bother us? It would seem patently unjust to be held eternally responsible for the unforeseen and unforeseeable consequences of our best-intentioned actions. The surface problem is the complexity that renders moral decision-making so complicated and uncertain. But the deeper problem is that the world of *The Good Place* is apparently governed by incompetent administration and a bad moral theory.

Some commentators have noted how secular *The Good Place* is. There is no positive mention of God, for example. There's the Judge, but she's enthralled by *NCIS* and blindsided by the world's complexity. So she doesn't qualify as God in any traditional sense. She's as much at the mercy of the system as anyone. There are also layers of various bureaucracies, like the superficially benign but actually feckless, benighted, and ineffectual "committee," which is more ready to create subcommittees than to correct injustices in the point system. Though they're impeccable rule-followers, questions of actual justice, fairness, and suffering don't drive them.

It's all portrayed hilariously, of course, but viewers find themselves rooting for Eleanor and Chidi, Jason and Tahani—and even Michael! It does and should bother us that the system is flawed, the presiding administration unjust, the reigning hierarchies uncaring. It also understandably bothers the characters themselves, because they continue to make their case, expose the unfairness, and appeal to some standard of goodness and decency that could give mankind hope for a better fate.

But should the callous administration and flawed system of such a world detract from the characters' commitment to do the right thing, to grow morally, to become better people, to discharge their duties? The show suggests that it shouldn't. Its message is that, even if doing the right thing is inconsistent with happiness, it's still worth doing. Eleanor's an exemplar of this approach, especially in her public confession in season 1 that she does not belong in the Good Place. She has all the reason to suspect this confession will land her in the Bad Place, but she comes clean nonetheless. Morality is worth doing for its own sake. Once the characters' eternal fate in the Bad Place seemed sealed, any effort on their part to do good—by helping those they love escape a similar destiny—must be coming from a pure motive since it would help only others, not themselves. In this seemingly Kantian spirit, the show implicitly extols the heroic virtues of commitment to the moral life irrespective of consequences for oneself.

This approach, though, doesn't really resonate with Kant. Although he downplayed the importance of consequences and counseled commitment to duty for duty's sake, Kant wasn't indifferent to the moral agent's well-being. He thought human beings reside both in the noumenal and phenomenal realms—the world as it is and the world of appearances, respectively. If we were purely noumenal creatures, he argued, then commitment to virtue for its own sake and nothing else would be enough, but because we're also phenomenal creatures, we're hardwired to care about issues like our own happiness. So, it's true that Kant thought that our moral motivations shouldn't include our desire to be happy. But it's also true that Kant thought our desire to be happy is morally legitimate.

The show gestures toward this with Eleanor's conclusions in "Pandemonium," the final episode of season 3. Even though she thinks reality is basically meaningless, she finds she can't let go of the desire to find happiness. "I guess all I can do is embrace the pandemonium, find happiness in the unique insanity of being here, now." Kant might suggest that the heroic depiction of being moral for its own sake irrespective of consequences is both correct and incorrect. It's true that we should be motivated by morality alone, but it's false to think that we can set aside questions of ultimate happiness as if they're unimportant. They remain important—and even more, they remain important to morality. The very institution or enterprise of morality itself, to make full rational sense, to remain rationally stable, requires a greater correspondence between virtue and happiness than The Good Place seems to allow.

The Coincidence Thesis

Although Kant is the philosopher best known for talking about the need for such correspondence between virtue and happiness, several thinkers before him recognized the connection. Questions about morality and the afterlife have a long history in philosophy. In his *Pensées*, French mathematician and philosopher Blaise Pascal asserted that the immortality of the soul is so important that one must have lost all feeling not to care about knowing the facts of the matter.[3]

Continuing on the same general theme, the great English philosopher John Locke is well known for emphasizing the importance of rewards and punishments in moral motivation. The forthrightness with which he occasionally emphasized their centrality, in fact, has elicited from some quarters accusations that he fell prey to the misguided notion that the matter of moral motivation can be reduced to aiming for a beneficial outcome—something more practical or prudential than intrinsically moral.[4] However bluntly or crassly drawn some of these connections may be, Locke was right to insist on an ultimate reckoning and balancing of the scales—something emphasized both by the Hellenistic Socrates in the Apology and the Hebraic St. Paul in Acts 17. *The Good Place*, in its own way, underscores this insistence on justice. Although the characters find themselves in a skewed system, they cannot let go of the conviction that there's a standard above the broken system that ought to hold sway. Unless ultimate reality is itself committed to justice, many of our most cherished hopes for the rectification of wrongs and redemption of sufferings are in vain.

Locke thought that humans can appreciate the intrinsic goodness of virtue, and even its appeal, but this is not nearly enough to motivate virtuous behavior, especially when doing so is costly. To remedy this problem, on Locke's view, clear and explicit sanctions are needed to ensure that the virtuous course of action will always be the more attractive option. What if being or doing good were to produce, rather than good consequences, horrible ones? What Locke seemed to recognize—as did many other major philosophers, from Augustine to Anselm, Bishop Butler to George Berkeley (and that's just the As and Bs)—is that morality and ultimate happiness need to go hand in hand if morality is to be a fully rational enterprise. To retain its authority in our lives, morality requires the stability of cohering with ultimate happiness.

Some philosophers have called this the "Coincidence Thesis," which says that the moral life is, or is at least likely to be, good on the whole for the virtuous agent. The rationality of morality requires it, but certain experiences of evil can shake this conviction. How can we believe in such a thesis? How can Chidi and Eleanor, especially after they find out that nobody's made it to the Good Place for centuries? Scottish philosopher Thomas Reid, for one, saw no way to defend the coincidence of virtue and well-being apart from supposing that the world is under benevolent administration.

Reid offered a few arguments in support of the Coincidence Thesis, according to which well-being and virtue go together. He made it clear that virtue and well-being are distinct, but a benevolent deity secures their coincidence. As Reid put it,

> While the world is under a wise and benevolent administration, it is impossible, that any man should, in the issue, be a loser by doing his duty. Every man, therefore, who believes in God, while he is careful to do his duty, may safely leave the care of his happiness to Him who made him.[5]

As it happens, Reid would agree with the writers of *The Good Place*, convinced that genuine virtue requires being committed to the moral life for its own sake, not for some reward. Importantly, though, he saw no way to make sense of that commitment apart from holding that there is just and benevolent administration of the world, ensuring that an agent's virtue and well-being coincide, if not in this life, then in the next. As Reid put it, "Virtue is his [i.e. God's] care. Its votaries are under his protection & guardianship."[6] Reid thought a commitment to the Coincidence Thesis, though virtuous, natural, and intuitive, goes beyond the evidence in some sense. Another step is needed. For Kant, these considerations provided the material for an argument for God's existence.

Kant held that a rational moral being must necessarily will "the highest good," which consists of a world in which people are both morally good and happy, and in which moral virtue is the condition for happiness. Kant was less concerned with questions of happiness per se than with questions of what makes us worthy of happiness. He held that a person can't rationally will a virtuous life without believing that moral actions can successfully achieve such an end, which requires that the world be ordered in a certain way. This conviction is equivalent to belief in God, a moral being who is ultimately responsible for the character of the natural world. So Kant would reject both the suggestion that happiness is irrelevant to the moral life and the suggestion that the world features a huge disconnect between virtue and happiness. *The Good Place*, potentially anyway, seems to represent a thought experiment in which the Coincidence Thesis is simply false. But Kant would say that rather than such a scenario enabling the purest morality of all, it would render the moral enterprise less than rationally stable. What morality and what rationality would dictate us to do would be at odds. Morality wouldn't really make full rational sense. Thus the tragedy.

Incidentally, Kant was known for a second moral argument for God's existence (or rational belief in God), which we can call his "argument from grace."[7] In light of our corrupt motivations and inward bents, Kant thought we must believe in God to give us the needed resources to be virtuous—to cure us from privileging our desires and inclinations over our moral duties. More could be said about this, but it's only mentioned here to identify another critique he'd offer of *The Good Place* universe. It had become a world in which the moral life was irremediably impossible to achieve with no divine resource to rectify it. Rational commitment to the moral life requires believing it's possible. If it isn't possible, the moral enterprise, once more, is compromised.

Benevolent Administration

Many of us have a nagging conviction that the moral life is worth doing for its own sake. Morality has autonomy or independence; morality is its own thing and reward. If this is correct, what does it reveal about reality?

Earlier we mentioned Reid, who held that the Coincidence Thesis lies deep in the moral life. Reid thought it a virtuous coincidence that the moral life is, or is at least likely to be, good on the whole for the virtuous agent. At the same time, Reid recognized that certain experiences of evil can shake this conviction. Terence Cuneo explains, "Reid sees no way to defend the coincidence of virtue and well-being apart from supposing that the world is under benevolent administration. There is an important sense, then, in which Reid's ethical views are ineliminably theistic."[8]

It might be thought that insisting that virtue and happiness ultimately coincide is self-centered. How is this different from Mindy St. Claire's me-first attitude? But if Kant was right, we as human beings can't help but to care about our eternal destinies and to desire enduring joy. It's not irrational to be concerned with such things, but rather quite natural and altogether human. The idea that happiness and virtue ultimately coincide is not, on this score, myopically selfish. Rather, morality, to be the fully rational thing we suppose it to be, must feature such resonance with happiness. Not all self-interest is selfish. So-called eudaimonists are so convinced of the inherent connection between virtue and happiness they tread the verge of equating them. Kant was not inclined to conflate them, but still he saw them as connected. This is why moral action should be done for its own sake and why the stability of morality requires benevolent administration. Kant happened to think a personal and loving God not only could but absolutely would ensure the airtight correspondence between virtue and happiness.

Some might suggest that there is a good nontheistic way to ensure such ultimate correspondence. Consider the possibility of karma instead of a theistic universe. In the episode titled "You've Changed, Man," something like reincarnation or transmigration of souls is hinted at as a potential solution to the broken system. Couldn't an atheist opt for something like that to make everything bonzer? Yes, but in light of the incalculable complexity of a system of karma featuring its plethora of precise calibrations, such a moral order postulated by nontheistic reincarnation paradoxically provides evidence for the existence of a personal God after all. Who else is crunching the numbers and directing the whole show? So Kant at least would be inclined to think theism—not a mechanistic universe, a rule-obsessed committee, or a free-for-all pandemonium—is the more plausible explanation of the benevolent administration that morality and rationality would be at odds without.

Tragedy, Comedy, or Cincinnati?

Until the final season, the question loomed whether the show's depiction of the afterlife constituted a comedy or a tragedy. Simon Critchley has written that the world is "a tragicomedy defined by war, corruption, vanity, and greed, and entirely without the capacity for redemption. Perhaps this is why it is so hard for us to parse the difference between tragedy and comedy. Who knows, perhaps Socrates was right in the *Symposium* after all: the tragedian should be a comedian and vice versa."[9] With the finale now in the books, *The Good Place*, in its own way, seems to contain elements of both tragedy and comedy.

The show's aforementioned steadfast adherence to secularity makes it stand in contrast to the robustly religious conception of the afterlife held by those earlier thinkers like Pascal or Locke, St. Paul or Kant. And the show's tragic elements are thrown in relief by these points of departure. At the beginning of this chapter, recall that two central questions reside at the heart of the show: (1) whether morality requires that we do good for goodness' sake and (2) whether reality itself is committed to morality. Now we can qualify and clarify that claim. Doing morality for morality's sake echoes a recurring and resounding note in the show. But if benevolent administration is needed to make morality and rationality cohere, the universe of *The Good Place* is not really as committed to morality as it might first appear. The highest authorities are often benighted, callous, ineffectual, and little concerned with justice. In fact, absurdly, voices of good and evil are accorded the same weight in final determinations—as if fairness requires treating them equally and impartially. That Shawn from the Bad Place, for example, might still mount a coup and set up a whole new and deeply unjust system remains a possibility. Whether the reformed system stays in place is a wholly contingent matter. But as we saw earlier, a world ungoverned by a just authority undermines the Kantian notion of the rationality of doing right for the sake of rightness alone.

The show's conclusion enables us to extend this analysis. A feature of secularism is what Charles Taylor calls its "immanent frame," which inclines the modern mind to find fulfillment without recourse to any transcendent source. Rather than the beatific vision as humanity's ultimate end and best destiny, the highest good becomes, at worst, garden-variety amoral trivial pursuits like the perfect video game performance or jamming with a Magic Guitar. But at least at moments the show seems to recognize an even deeper value: that bonding with other people may be a more satisfying endeavor. In this way, the show affirms Ernest Becker's conclusion that the modern relationship is all that many of us have left after the "death of God." We see this in Chidi and Eleanor's relationship. By the final episode, however, we also come to see that even this love ultimately falters.

Perhaps this is because even human loves fall short. They admit of boredom and fail to satisfy. Understandably so since, as Becker puts it, "No human relationship can bear the burden of godhood."[10] But what if that's all there is, as *The Good Place* intimates? What if all we have to look forward to is monotony-induced enervating ennui, relieved only by the dissolution of the self? What else is to be said but that this would be a tragic state of affairs? Such a picture is one in which the highest possible good isn't large or transcendent enough to satisfy forever. It would be profoundly sad if eternal joy were an oxymoron, a contradiction in terms. Only an infinite good could liberate us from such a fate. Who knows what joys of life redeemed may bring, when fecund light and love unending sing?

The Good Place, despite its recognition of the flaws in a broken system, either can't or won't imagine for its characters a source of unending bliss and eternal satisfaction. If the show is right, however much we might wish to follow Schopenhauer in crediting mortality as the source of meaning, life for Chidi and company is tragic indeed. Although *The Good Place* may be second to none as a brilliant sitcom, we have principled reason to hope for an even more divine comedy.

And that, in the words of our paragon of moral wisdom Eleanor Shellstrop, is how you get ethics'd in the face.

13

The Handmaid's Tale Evokes a Longing for Peace and Justice

Margaret Atwood's 1985 novel *The Handmaid's Tale* has plenty of fodder for an engaging drama: a relatable and likable protagonist, a fully imagined world peopled with a diverse cast of characters, exaggerated yet believable hostilities, and a deep commitment to effecting justice. All of that makes for a compelling adaptation to Hulu's visual medium. In this story are dangers viewers will understand and hopes they can root for.

The book's trappings are dystopian, chillingly so, and with a distinctly feminist flair. A rabidly patriarchal, theocratic authoritarian regime has taken control of the United States (now called the Republic of Gilead). Women have lost all freedom and are relegated to a handful of domestic roles marked by strict dress codes. For example, the titular handmaids wear striking red gowns made more shocking by the stark contrast of their white oversized bonnets. Because of their fertility in an era marked by barrenness, handmaids are enslaved to serve as surrogate birth mothers for wealthy families. Rape is not only sanctioned in Gilead; it is institutionalized, with a ceremony involving the so-called commander, his wife, and the handmaid.

Despite the oppressive world depicted in the novel's pages, readers can easily connect with its protagonist, a handmaid named Offred (literally "of Fred," the name of her commander). Her plight epitomizes the human condition as she wrestles with injustice, strives for survival, seeks peace and community in a world fraught with evil, and asserts her unique personality even as societal strictures and structures stifle her freedom. Add Atwood's lush poetic prose to this well-drawn portrait of Offred, and *The Handmaid's Tale* is often poignant and heartbreaking in its beauty. Visually depicting such imagery should prove a worthwhile endeavor for the series' creators.

As we waited for the initial three episodes to air back in 2017, promising promos stoked our excitement for the series. *Mad Men*'s Elisabeth Moss would play Offred, Reed Morano would direct, and publicity photos hit the web. Atwood's story really was taking visual shape, and it was intriguing to watch play out. But the publicity took a bizarre turn in March of that year when Hulu hired actresses to roam ominously around the South by Southwest film festival in full handmaid attire.[1] In a case of life imitating art, another group—unsanctioned by Hulu—turned up to protest an abortion-related vote in the Texas legislature.[2] As the premiere date drew nearer, expectations were running quite high. Although the show was in production well before November of 2016, Donald Trump's election had imbued the atmosphere surrounding *The Handmaid's Tale* with a surprising urgency.

Noting that the series "border[s] on being too relevant," Dominic Patten told his readers that "it is not to be missed."[3] Hank Stuever claimed that Hulu's series is not simply timely but is "essential viewing" for our fractured society.[4] Although the book was written over thirty years ago, many—such as Jen Chaney—underscored resonances between Hulu's depiction of Gilead and our current political moment: "'There would be no mercies for a member of the Resistance,' says Offred. . . . You hear her say this, and you know she's talking about a resistance completely different from the grassroots movement against the Trump administration. You shudder anyway."[5]

In a passionate, especially personal review, Emily Temple expressed the fear she felt before watching the show that it wouldn't be any good. Then she confesses a bigger fear: that it wouldn't be good enough. But good enough for what? The rest of Temple's review offers some insight, pointing to entrenched patriarchal patterns in American culture that need disruption: "We need to start with our children. Or else we'll all be sobbing in our bedrooms, and much harder than I did, and for much longer, and not because of what we're watching on television."[6]

If the series' reviews and promotional material are to be believed, the needed disruption starts by facing who we are in the cultural mirror provided by *The Handmaid's Tale*. So suggested Atwood herself in an op-ed for the *New York Times*: "If this future can be described in detail, maybe it won't happen. But such wishful thinking cannot be depended on either."[7] The hyperbole that ran through Hulu's promotional material bespoke a passionate concern for our country's political, cultural, and spiritual challenges. Those viewing *The Handmaid's Tale* as a contemporary allegory cited various pieces of evidence: Trump's authoritarian tendencies; the growing nationalistic and isolationist impulse he rode to victory; his overt attacks on institutions important to a thriving democracy (e.g., the press and the courts); and the resurgence of the religious right who looked to Trump to promote a conservative cultural agenda, complete with pro-life and religious liberty planks that some consider retrograde and discriminatory.

For many, the world in *The Handmaid's Tale* looks eerily similar to our contemporary moment. And the paranoia that fills the frames of Hulu's series captures that feeling well. Opening with a frantic car chase and the brutal arrest of Offred and her young daughter, the show is unflinching in its depiction of the abuse of power, perversion of religious belief, and disintegration of community. Setting aside its apparent political agenda, the series offers a vivid, memorable glimpse into the depravity of mankind—how cruel, how prideful, how self-serving, and how apathetic we can be and often are. Janine (later Ofwarren) suffers a nervous breakdown after being condemned as responsible for a sexual assault she endured; the rebellious Moira is reduced to a compliant automaton by physical and emotional coercion; and hanging bodies of those executed for resistance line the city walls, warning all against rebellion.

Still, the series—like its textual predecessor—insists on human uniqueness, creativity, and dignity. In Offred's actions, viewers see the human spirit striving against overwhelming odds, as she occasionally breaks protocol with a friendly word or smile. Offred risks friendship with Ofglen when callousness would be the safer course. She even seems tender toward Serena Joy, her commander's wife. This indomitable assertion of the human spirit amid rigid oppression is beautifully reflected by Offred's behavior during Ofwarren's childbirth. The other handmaids chant a prescribed mantra while encircling Ofwarren, but Offred cuts through the crowd and stays at Ofwarren's side. She alone speaks words of comfort, telling her, among other things, that she's "doing great."

In moments like these, it's easy to believe the series might match its boosters' expectations. Perhaps *The Handmaid's Tale* will wake us up to our inhumanity and force us to acknowledge the destructive path we seem to be set on. Perhaps in these scenes we'll recognize the humanity of the other, our contribution to their degradation, and our need to reverse course.

Or perhaps not.

Sweet moments are not the rule for the series. And typically they're initiated by and reserved for handmaids, the victims of the oppressive state, and never for the functionaries of the state itself. Serena Joy and Commander Waterson are somewhat fleshed out, but their attempts at human interaction are awkwardly portrayed (and even rendered grotesque in the ceremony scenes). The series may recognize both mankind's depravity and dignity, but (at least in early seasons) it has yet to show those qualities much mingled in a single character—a feat its source material pulls off masterfully in figures like Offred's mother. Such one-dimensionality might work in the series' imaginary world. However, when read as political allegory, as so many reviewers have insisted, it becomes more problematic, perhaps even a cautionary tale in itself. What Jonathan Swift says of satire seems applicable here: *The Handmaid's Tale* "is a sort of glass wherein beholders do generally discover everybody's face but their own."

For all its promotional moralizing, there is no "us" in Hulu's *The Handmaid's Tale*. Instead, its world is one where enlightened progressives have been beaten down by fundamentalist zealots, idealistic passivity their fatal flaw. Offred's reflection in episode three captures this conviction: "Now I'm awake to the world," she says. "I was asleep before. That's how we let it happen. . . . Nothing changes instantaneously. In a gradually heating bathtub, you'd be boiled to death before you knew it." And, lest there be any doubt, traditionalists are the ones turning up the heat. It's tempting for viewers to fixate on this divide, for liberals to identify with the hapless handmaids and conservatives to resent their representation as heartless oppressors. But we might hope that the threads of compassion woven throughout the currently available episodes will deescalate the political rhetoric swirling around the series. May these grace notes sound again in future episodes and even increase.

But attending to and honoring the humanity of the other, especially while acknowledging one's own weaknesses and guilt—this goes against our inward bent, our self-regard. What we must do, we cannot do on our own. What we long for is unavailable through spectacle or the marketplace. *The Handmaid's Tale* points us toward the need for hope; it tells us such an abusive world absolutely cannot stand. But as Offred's enthusiastic participation in the execution of an accused rapist shows, the demand for justice left untempered by love turns to brutality. An honest look in the proverbial mirror shows that we—all of us, without exception—are both handmaid and commander, victim and perpetrator.

Hope for perfect redemption lies outside the contaminated heart of man. Justice comes only through the slow work of grace; only through daily surrender to Christ will peace abide. Any other promise is Pollyannaish and mere siren song, enticing us with possibility but leading us to destruction. Evil is real, and more hideous than we can put into words; Christianity is rigorously honest about this world's darkness. Such darkness, though, is not confined to those of particular political persuasions or select portions of the ideological spectrum. It's ubiquitous, infiltrating each of our hearts. Christianity offers a far bleaker diagnosis of our fallenness and corruption, and is an equal opportunist in its condemnation. At the same time, however, because of God's amazing grace, it offers a far brighter prognosis if we but acknowledge our radical sin, our bent to self, and through repentance plead for God's mercy—to be forgiven, healed, and transformed.

This is a communal process, something God works into us as the church practices repentance and forgiveness together, as Tish Harrison Warren explains in *Liturgy of the Ordinary*:

> We are quarreling people, but God is reforming us to be people who, through our ordinary moments, establish his kingdom of peace. Believing this is an act of faith. It takes faith to believe that our little frail faithfulness can produce fruit. . . . And it takes faith to believe that God is making us into people—slowly, through repentance—who are capable of saying to the world through our lives, "Peace of Christ to you."

Imperfect human beings can never truly envision or enact the perfect mechanism for redemption; we're too flawed ourselves, too limited in our understanding and our power, too prideful, too self-concerned. Is that not the truth of Gilead? And doesn't that also reveal the beauty of our God? It's the glorious "Peace of Christ" that we need. He acts on our behalf at great cost to himself to effect the only peace available—restoring us to himself and then, and only then, with one another.

14

How to Resist Evil: Nonviolence in *The Passion of the Christ*

The Passion of the Christ has been described as the best movie people don't want to see twice. It gives horror and slasher films a run for their money. Mel Gibson's relentlessly graphic depiction of the death of Christ presents us with gruesome violence that goes well beyond anything described in the Gospels. Jesus is beaten by Jewish guards prior to his trial before the Sanhedrin, he is dropped off a bridge, his arm is dislocated during the crucifixion, and he endures an unusually severe flogging and scourging at the hands of sadistic Roman soldiers. What is the purpose of all this violence? Clearly, it is to amplify emotional impact.

Not often noticed, but equally worthy of attention, however, is Jesus' non-violent response. At no point does he attempt to avoid or resist the violence inflicted on him. In the opening scene he reveals his anguish in a remarkable prayer: "Father, you can do all things. If it be possible, let this chalice pass from me. But let your will be done, not mine." We see a man who seems to know the horrors in store for him, in fulfillment of prophecies he takes as applying to himself. With all his might he wishes he could avoid these horrors, but he senses that such suffering is God's plan, and so he's willing to submit to it. Accepting of his fate, he endures the suffering, refusing to resist, obedient to his calling. Indeed, at times he seems almost to invite it, as when he painfully climbs to his feet after his hideous flogging by Roman guards. Refusing to hit back, refraining from complaint, he remarkably endures the pain and shame.

In these ways, the film's extreme violence subverts itself by showing the ultimate emptiness of violence in the face of all-conquering love. Indeed, in some ways the film's depiction of Jesus' practice of non-violence goes beyond Christ's teachings, a fact that will prove important for us. Such a vision seems plainly to be Gibson's faith-based conviction as a Catholic filmmaker. But can this belief in the futility of violence be justified as a reasoned conclusion from evidence that does not presuppose any theological convictions?

Jesus' Teachings on Nonviolence

Jesus' practice of nonviolence during his Passion remarkably resembles his teaching of nonviolence during his ministry. Several scenes in the film focus specifically on Jesus' teachings on nonviolence. These include the flashback to the Sermon on the Mount, in which Jesus preaches forgiveness and love of enemies, which he then later models on the cross himself. Another flashback features Jesus washing his disciples' feet, while warning them to expect persecution as followers of him, which they must meet meekly and without fear—in contrast to Peter's vehement denial of knowing Christ when persecution for it seemed likely. Also pertinent is the scene in the Garden of Gethsemane, where Christ watches sadly as his disciples fight the Jewish guards and he instructs Peter to put down his sword, quoting the Jewish proverb that "all who live by the sword shall die by the sword." Jesus, far from joining in the fight, instead restores the ear of the guard that Peter had cut off, to the guard's utter astonishment. Peter's greater willingness to brandish a sword to defend Jesus than to be persecuted for Jesus was the exact opposite of the harder path to which Jesus had called him. Christendom's lamentable history of holy wars, inquisitions, and crusades is sad testimony that Peter has too often indeed been its guiding example.

Admonitions to "turn the other cheek" and "go the extra mile" derive from Jesus' instructions (Luke 6:27-28; Matthew 5:39-41), and examples could be multiplied. Included among such teachings are "hard sayings"—like "resist not evil"—that Jesus himself put into practice and also expected his disciples to follow, even unto death (Matthew 10:17-22; 10:38-39). What did Jesus mean by these strongly pacifist-sounding sayings? The earliest Christian communities seem to have taken Jesus' teachings on nonviolence and love of enemies quite seriously, refusing military service, declining resort to secular courts, praying for their persecutors, and submitting unresistingly and even joyously to the lash, sword, or cross.[1] Taken literally, however, these sayings are so demanding that attempts have been made at least since the time of St. Augustine to limit their scope or blunt their force.

Let's look briefly at five leading interpretations, several of which may contain insight into this matter.

The traditional Catholic approach to Jesus' hard sayings is to treat them as "counsels of perfection" addressed only to a select few who choose to pursue a higher calling of moral and spiritual perfection. On this view, Christ laid down two kinds of moral directions: "precepts" and "counsels." Precepts are commandments binding on everyone that cannot be disobeyed without mortal sin. Counsels, by contrast, are recommendations for those who wish to undertake, either for a lifetime or a period of time, a more perfect imitation of Christ's example (by, for instance, taking vows of voluntary poverty or chastity). Protestant Reformers strongly opposed the Catholic doctrine of super-meritorious actions, insisting that Christ called all his followers to be perfect, as their heavenly Father is perfect (Matthew 5:48).

Even if we grant that some of Christ's ethical directives are counsels, it's doubtful that his teachings on nonviolence fall into this category, since they occur in the midst of directives that are clearly commands (don't divorce, don't swear, and the like). Moreover, some of the ethical directives the Catholic tradition treats as commands, such as the commandment to love God with all one's heart and soul, are in fact *more* difficult to fulfill than many of the alleged counsels, such as turning the other cheek or going the extra mile. In this way, the Catholic two-class ethic interpretation is problematic. In fact, as Catholic theologian Hans Küng notes, the counsel-precept distinction has largely dropped out of post-Vatican II Catholic moral teaching.[2]

Another way of understanding Jesus' radical ethical teachings that makes them largely irrelevant to most Christians today is to see them as short-term emergency legislation for the end-time. On this view, first popularized by the German theologian and medical missionary Albert Schweitzer, Jesus fully accepted the "futurist eschatology" endorsed by Jewish apocalyptic sects of his day. Believing that God would intervene immediately and dramatically in human history, Jesus taught a rigorous, perfectionist ethic that makes sense only if one assumes that practical concerns like burying one's dead father (Matthew 8:22) or giving away all one's money or clothes (Luke 6:30, Matthew 5:40) are unimportant given that God's apocalyptic kingdom was immediately at hand. Why worry about hanging on to your coat if there's never going to be another winter?

Although Jesus' ethical teachings may have been colored by his beliefs about the end of the world, it doesn't follow that those teachings were intended only as short-term crisis legislation or lack permanent validity. Jesus' commandments to avoid swearing, anger, divorce, lust in one's heart, showy displays of religiosity, and so forth were clearly intended as intensifications of the Old Law, but there is no reason to believe that Jesus saw these as being applicable only for a few short weeks, months, or years. The same should be said of Jesus' teachings on nonviolence, which are also presented as sharpenings of Old Testament demands.

Many Protestant theologians, following the great Reformation thinker Martin Luther,[3] argue that the real purpose of Jesus' demanding ethical teachings was to bring us to our knees by showing us the impossibility of achieving righteousness through good works. In Luther's view, when Jesus commanded his disciples to "resist not evil" and "turn the other Cheek," he didn't mean to exclude legitimate secular duties such protecting one's family, punishing criminals, and taking up arms to resist foreign invasion or domestic insurrection. Jesus' ethical teachings nevertheless demand absolute, uncompromising obedience to God's holy will, a standard of perfection that all human beings can achieve. Such teachings, heretofore, humble our pride and teach us that salvation comes through truth and grace, not through any righteousness of our own.

Certainly, Jesus lays down a highly demanding ethic and rules out any sort of boasting before God (consider Luke 18:9-14). Recent New Testament scholarship, however, has argued that Jesus' teachings on nonviolence cannot be limited to purely individual, non-civic actions, as Luther claimed, but have social and political implications as well.[4] Further, many of Jesus' ethical teachings, while demanding, are not impossible to fulfill (don't swear, don't pray ostentatiously, and so forth). And as John Howard Yoder points out, if Jesus' purpose were simply to teach the futility of achieving salvation through good works, it's hard to see why he offered such detailed ethical principles or felt it necessary to sharpen Old Testament rules that in many cases were already extremely demanding.[5]

Some have claimed that when Jesus said "resist not evil" he meant exactly what he said: all violence and resistance to evil is wrong, regardless of the reasons, circumstances, or costs. Such absolute pacifism has been defended by Leo Tolstoy, the great Russian novelist, as well as by some of the historic "peace churches" such as the Anabaptists and Mennonites. Tolstoy goes as far as to claim that Christ totally forbids armies, police, and criminal courts, since these all involve the use of force and violence.[6] Absolute pacifism has implications that most people would understandably find very hard to accept because they grate against deep intuitions. An absolute pacifist, for example, would have to condemn any use of force, no matter how moderate and restrained, to protect a helpless child from assault, arrest a serial killer, or prevent a terrorist attack that could kill thousands. Refusing to use even minimal force to protect the innocent seems inconsistent with Christ's teachings to love one's neighbor as oneself (Mark 12:31) and to treat others as we would like them to treat us (Luke 6:31). Consequently, Christians should not conclude that Jesus commanded absolute pacifism unless this is the only plausible interpretation of his teachings.

Fortunately, other interpretations are possible. Jesus himself used force in driving the money-changers out of the Temple with whip of cords (John 2:14-16). At least some of Jesus' disciples carried swords (Luke 22:49), although Christ would not permit their use to prevent his arrest. The Old Testament clearly sanctioned the use of force in a variety of contexts, and although Jesus heightened the demands of certain Old Testament teachings, he rarely if ever explicitly rejected them. Most of Jesus' pacificist sayings are focused on individual, self-regarding conduct (such as "if any one strikes you on the right cheek"), not on conduct involving the welfare or protection of others. And St. Paul, after repeating Jesus' commandments never to avenge wrongs or repay evil for evil (Romans 12:17-19), urges Christians to obey the governing authorities, since these authorities are ordained by God to restrain the wicked and serve the common good (Romans 13:1-5). In light of these facts, it's unlikely Jesus believed in absolute pacifism.

None of the four leading interpretations of Jesus' teachings on nonviolence considered so far seems entirely satisfactory. How, then, should these teachings be interpreted? Perhaps part of the solution lies in two characteristic features of Jesus' teaching: his occasional resort to hyperbole and his opposition to the kind of letter-over-spirit approach to rules adopted in Jesus' day by many Pharisees.

The use of hyperbole (deliberate overstatement or exaggeration) was commonplace in Near-Eastern cultures of Jesus' time, and Jesus himself often used exaggerated language to drive home a point. "If anyone comes to me and does not hate his own father and mother and wife and children and brothers and sisters, yes, and even his own life, he cannot be my disciple" (Luke 14:26). This is just one example of Jesus' sayings that, while clearly extravagant, would not have deceived his listeners. It may well be that there is a similar touch of hyperbole in his pacifist sayings, which Jesus' certainly intended to be taken seriously, even radically, but probably not literally or without qualification.

Jesus' opposition to treating rules as rigid absolutes supports this reading. In his view, even divine commandments like "Remember the Sabbath day, to keep it holy" (Exodus 20:8) must be interpreted flexibly and with an eye to core Biblical values. Contrary to the Pharisees' approach to religious rules, which too often stressed the letter of the law over its spirit, Jesus taught that the Sabbath commandment should not be interpreted as prohibiting hungry people from eating (Mark 2:23-28), sick people from being healed (Luke 6:6-11), or children or animals from being rescued from a well (Luke 14:5). In a powerful scene in Gibson's film, Mary Magdalene is prevented from being stoned according to the prescribed punishment for her transgressions. Rules aren't impersonal, Jesus believed, but come from a personal lawgiver and are often phrased in broad, general language and should not be construed with wooden literalness or rigid legalism in disregard of higher values or the rule-maker's general purposes and intentions.

Jesus' teachings on nonviolence, likewise, lay down a general norm that must be applied intelligently in light of his other teachings. Roughly, Jesus seems to be saying this: Be zealous agents of peace and reconciliation; respond to hatred with love and forgiveness; when abused, be prepared to suffer hardship, loss, or indignity rather than to respond with violence or vengeance; never use force without need and never in ways inconsistent with fundamental Gospel values. This paraphrase brings out clearly how Jesus' sayings on nonviolence were intended as implicitly qualified general norms rather than as absolutes without exception.

Why Did Jesus Believe in Nonviolence?

We have argued that Jesus taught an extremely demanding but not absolute or unqualified ethic of nonviolence and nonresistance. On any plausible interpretation, this ethic is a deeply challenging one, not reasonable by the world's standards. Jesus' explanations for his teachings on nonviolence bring out their radical nature.

First, he says, we should respond to violence and hatred with love and forgiveness because this is what God does, and we should imitate God and seek to fulfill his will in all things, even as he himself did what he saw his Father doing. "Love your enemies, and do good, and lend, expecting nothing in return and your reward will be great, and you will be Sons of the Most High; *for he is kind to the ungrateful and the selfish*. Be merciful even as your Father is merciful" (Luke 6:35-36; emphasis added). Recall the beginning scenes of *The Passion*, where Jesus interferes with the violent resistance put up by his disciples in the Garden of Gethsemane.

Second, Jesus undermines many of the usual justifications for violence by pointing out that, with the dawning of God's kingdom many things that seem to be unmitigated evils are in fact blessings to those who love and serve the Lord. "Blessed are you when men revile you and persecute you and utter all kinds of evil against you falsely on my account. Rejoice and be glad. for your reward is great in heaven" (Matthew 5:11-12). The thought is well dramatized in the scene toward the end of the film in which the "good" thief is promised happiness the very day of the crucifixion. "Blessed are the poor, the hungry, and those who weep, for God has great things in store for them" (Luke 6:20-21). Are you concerned that if you don't respond to violence with violence, evildoers will escape punishment? God will give them the punishment they deserve (Matthew 25:31f). Are you worried that if you don't fight back, you may be robbed, beaten, or killed? "Do not fear those who kill the body but cannot kill the soul" (Matthew 10:28); "whoever loses his life for my sake will find it" (Mathew 16:25).

In short, what Jesus calls for is a radical reversal of worldly values and "common-sense" assumptions, a thoroughgoing conversion (*metanoia*) to a God-centered way of thinking and living. From a worldly point of view, it is an unqualified evil when a good person is robbed or mistreated, and aggressors deserve to be repaid in kind. But from a God-centered point of view, such concerns fade in importance. As Peter asks (sounding here a bit like Socrates and the ancient Stoics), "Who is there to harm you if you are zealous for what is right?" (I Peter 3:13). Nothing that the violent can do to a person, or take from them, can cause them deep or lasting harm if God is on their side. From a personal standpoint, therefore, all that ultimately matters is faithfulness to God—His "kingdom and His righteousness" (Matthew 6:35).

The Ethics of Nonviolence

Willingness to endure the cross seems rooted in a profound moral faith that entrusting ourselves to God's hands and suppressing our violent impulses will be vindicated and can play an important part in ushering in God's kingdom. Is such trust in nonviolence promoting the cause of peace likely to be justified by unassisted reason alone? Suppose that we understand such trust as grounded in the conviction that we ought, morally, to be strongly committed to the cause of peace and nonviolence. This question can then be posed: Can standard secular moral theories undergird a strongly pacifist commitment to live nonviolently in the face of temptations to do otherwise?

Philosophers generally distinguish between two broad types of ethical theories: consequentialist and nonconsequentialist. Consequentialists believe that one should always act for the greater good, whereas nonconsequentialists believe that some acts are wrong even if they do produce the best net outcomes for everyone affected by the action. Caiaphas, the Jewish High Priest in the film, reveals his commitment to consequentialism when he defends Jesus' execution by saying, "It is expedient that one man should die for the people, and that the whole nation should not perish" (John 11:50).

Utilitarianism is the most common version of consequentialism, and comes in a couple of varieties. Act utilitarianism mandates those individual actions that best promote overall utility (for example, the maximizing of pleasure and minimizing of pain for the greatest number). An act utilitarian would probably say, in extreme cases, it's morally permissible, indeed morally obligatory, to torture an innocent child if that's the only way to get a terrorist to reveal where he's hidden a nuclear bomb. Rule utilitarianism, in contrast, dictates that there are certain kinds of actions that should never be done, even if on occasion they promote utility in the short term, because in the long term they are likely to undermine it. So the rule utilitarian would probably insist that torturing an innocent child, for whatever ultimate purpose, is morally ruled out because it's the sort of behavior that, if practiced, will likely detract from long-term utility.

Can Jesus' ethic of nonviolence be defended on consequentialist grounds? It's easy to think of examples in which, say, jailing an innocent person or murdering a political opponent would promote the best consequences for everyone involved, yet Jesus' ethic would plainly condemn such acts. When it comes to act and rule consequentialism, only rule utilitarianism holds any hope of justifying a strongly pacifistic approach to life, and only when based on the highly questionable assumption that no rule permitting forcible resistance to evil could promote long term utility. This however would entail an absolute pacifism that goes beyond Jesus' ethic and that we saw we have good reasons to reject. So whereas act utilitarianism seems to permit actions it morally shouldn't, rule utilitarianism at best justifies an absolute pacifism that seems to yield unpalatable results.

Models of the Passion

If we take the Passion of Christ, those sufferings he surrendered to at his crucifixion, as a faithful application of Jesus' teachings about nonviolence, and interpret his teaching of nonviolence as identifying a moral obligation to renounce violence in most cases and in his own death particularly, then Jesus would have been obligated to do what he did, based on a duty that ruled out any right of his to refuse to do it. And if Jesus in fact was laboring under such an externally imposed moral obligation that precluded any right of his to do otherwise, then he would have been blameworthy for refusing to follow through with his mission. In the movie, when mockingly challenged to come down from the cross by the defiant thief, for instance, Jesus would have been sinful to do so. Given the extraordinarily difficult obligation that was imposed on him, though, he still might be deemed praiseworthy for doing it. We can call this the "duty model of the Passion." A quite different account insists that Jesus was under no obligation at all, but was perfectly free morally to avoid the cross. Jesus' sacrifice was, on this view, an act of pure generosity and grace. Jesus is praiseworthy for having gone to the cross, for he didn't have to in any moral sense, so he wouldn't have been blameworthy for refusing to do so. We can call this the "freedom model of the Passion."

Is there a principled way to split the difference and characterize Jesus' going to the cross both as obedience to God's perfect will and something that Jesus morally had to do, on the one hand, while also something altogether praiseworthy, gracious, and as more than just doing his duty, on the other? Perhaps there is, but we suspect that to find this synthesis we need to introduce aspects of ethics beyond just rights and duties. Surely the Passion isn't properly understood merely as Jesus' discharging a moral duty and thereby avoiding wrongdoing. Rights and duties are not all that ethics is about, and Jesus' Passion just doesn't seem reducible to such categories. There's another way to capture a way Jesus may have "had to" go to the cross, As God the Son, Jesus shared in divinity that, on classical interpretations, is perfectly loving. Jesus, being who he was, couldn't be less than perfectly loving. His obedience was tested somehow in his human vulnerability and in the crucible of pain, but his divine perfection dictated he should do all he could to make the resources of God's grace available. The moral constraints on his behavior, on this view, are internal to his character, rather than externally imposed standards. So it's accurate to say Jesus morally had to do it, given his identity and nature, and it's also appropriate to accord Jesus maximal praise for his willing sacrifice. Knowing that his sacrifice would make God's grace so available, Jesus was morally constrained by his own perfection to express his love sacrificially. We can call this the "character model of the Passion."

Where does pacifism fit in? It depends on which model of the Passion we adopt. The duty model would dictate that nonviolence is a moral obligation imposed by Jesus' teachings and faithfully discharged by Christ himself. Applied to a non-absolutist understanding of pacifism, it would imply that we generally have no right to self-defense, even if we retain rights to defend others. On the freedom model, in contrast, pacifism would be a purely supererogatory act, one that we are praiseworthy for performing but not blameworthy for not performing. We would be not be obligated to follow Jesus' hard sayings on nonviolence, though doing so would be praiseworthy. Opting out of pacifism would not be at all blameworthy. Rights to defend oneself and others would be consistent with this approach. This view conspicuously resembles the two-ethic analysis discussed earlier.

Our favored take on pacifism and nonviolence, however, follows the character model. As all followers of Jesus are called to perfection, all have been called to follow Jesus' example and to become the kind of people for whom violence is less and less an option. To say merely that nonviolence is a moral duty or that self-defense is not our moral right is to conduct the discourse on the wrong level. Perhaps we do retain a right of self-defense. But Jesus would call us, on occasion at least, not to exercise all the rights we may have, even as he didn't exercise all his own prerogatives, like his moral authority to assert his innocence or point out that what was happening was unjust. This is a useful reminder that rights, despite their importance, need not always dominate ethical discussions. The greater the sacrifice, the more likely we may need to forego genuine rights, but Christ's Passion teaches us that nothing we might be called to sacrifice compares with what he sacrificed for us.

Jesus meant to teach either that we don't have a general right of personal self-defense or that even if we do, we're often called to lay it aside, following his example. Recall from the movie that Jesus said nobody took his life from him, but that he laid it down of his own accord to accomplish the work to which God had called him (see John 10:18). Those inclined to affirm such rights are hard-pressed to do so on consequentialist grounds. Nonconsequentialists, though, can correct what they consider to be this deficiency among the utilitarians. Seeing whether Jesus' teachings on nonviolence can be defended on nonconsequentialist grounds is more difficult, because these theories are so varied. Some nonconsequentialists, like Immanuel Kant and certain contemporary situation ethicists, claim that ethics can be reduced to a single fundamental ethical principle (for instance "Always act on principles that you would like to see everybody act upon" or "Always do the loving thing"). Others hold that there are several basic moral principles ("Tell the truth," "Do no harm," "Act justly," and so forth) and then offer ways of prioritizing the principles to reach concrete outcomes.

In general, however, it's hard to see how a nonconsequentialist theory could do the job. All leading nonconsequentialist theories accord primacy to a right of self-defense that conflicts with Jesus' radical ethic of nonresistance. And from the standpoint of natural reason, how can such a right be denied? There are times, as Jan Narveson notes, when it's either him or us. And the pacifist seems to be insisting that it always ought to be so. But why? The other guy is the guilty party, for heaven's sake![6] So the nonconsequentialist is going to have a difficult time making sense of either denials of rights to self-defense or exhortations to lay such rights aside. Historically, of course, most advocates of radical nonviolence have been motivated by religious conviction, including Buddha, Mahatma Gandhi, Martin Luther King. Jr., and Dorothy Day. Secular accounts of ethics seem ill-equipped to imbue us with the sort of confidence in the ultimate workability of such an approach and the power of love to conquer evil. In the end, as Dietrich Bonhoeffer wrote, "The cross is the only justification for the precept of non-violence, for it alone can kindle a faith in the victory over evil which will enable men to obey that precept. Only such obedience is blessed with the promise that we shall be partakers of Christ's victory as well as his suffering."[8]

15

"And Death Shall Be No More": Going beyond Transhumanism for Kids

Death seems an odd topic for a children's book, but author Gennady Stolyarov II explains that he wrote *Death Is Wrong* to share with kids what he wished he would have learned growing up: that dying is not inevitable, that through science, medicine, and technology, human beings can and should pursue ways to eradicate death.[1]

Stolyarov is one of a growing number of transhumanists, a loosely confederated group of academics and lay thinkers who seek to transcend human limitations through technological innovation. For many transhumanists, one of the limitations to be overcome is death; these so-called immortalists point to a number of organisms, including jellyfish, lobsters, and tortoises, as evidence of the possibility of extending all life, including and especially human life. Inspiring children to embrace this possibility and to strive toward its execution is the point of Stolyarov's book. He has even launched an Indiegogo campaign to distribute *Death Is Wrong* to 1,000 children free of charge.

At first blush, Stolyarov's argument is laughable: poor little finite creatures riddled with death and sin and weakness engaging in a benighted and futile effort to transcend such limitations through their own limited and meager resources. The unforeseen consequences of such grand designs are far from frivolous, however; they are fodder for many a science fiction and dystopian story that revels in revealing the perilous folly of man's hubris.

As initially unsettling as some of Stolyarov's ideas may be, of course, they resonate in a real way with core Christian convictions. As Romans 5 explains, death is not an essential feature of life. Sin brought death into this world, and it is sin that gives death sway over individuals and mankind. This entrapment, this state of being beholden to death, is what Stolyarov laments, and rightly so, but his lamentation misses the mark insofar as he aims to quash a biological symptom of evil without recognizing its spiritual source or true remedy. In light of biblical revelation, Stolyarov's dream of extended life is merely a caricature of the eternal life available only through relationship with Christ. Thinking otherwise reveals a misunderstanding of the nature of man and the nature of sin.

The secular humanism from which transhumanism derives affirms human beings are valuable free agents but divorces that truth from its foundation—that we are created and sustained by God and bear His image. God is the Source of our life, our value, and our activity. Sin involves a denial of this divine will, a turn toward our own interests, achieved through our own means, and only Christ's redemptive work through the cross and resurrection atones for sin and allows a rapprochement between sinful humanity and a holy God. This promise, we should remember, is available here and now, not awaiting us only beyond the grave.

John 17:3 tells us that to know God and Christ is eternal life. *Aiōnios*, the Greek word translated eternal here, bespeaks a quality of life, not merely a quantity. Our fulfillment is found in knowing God and Christ, not just knowing truths about God, but knowing God Himself, which can infuse our life even now with the touch of the eternal and the authentic ring of the transcendent rooted in divine reality rather than the wishful and dangerous thinking of extreme self-interest and self-reliance. That wishful and dangerous thinking is writ large in Stolyarov's project—invoking the specter of a modern-day Babel. More importantly, Stolyarov's is a mindset of which we are all guilty in the countless ways we trust ourselves rather than God.

It's a tempting trap, leaning on one's own understanding. God has invested in us the capacity for rationality and creativity, the very qualities Stolyarov turns to in his search for deliverance from death. But as longtime Asbury College president and Old Testament scholar Dennis Kinlaw explains in *The Mind of Christ*, "nothing eternal takes place until God acts," a truth Kinlaw notes that even Abram and Sarai forgot in their machinations to produce the child God promised them: "[Abram and Sarai] interfered with God's will for their lives, because they did not believe God would miraculously accomplish what he had promised them. In their eager desire to find an heir, they engineered their own way to do what God had already assured them he would do." In short, they looked to their own understanding and as a result compounded their troubles.

Only trusting the adequacy of God's provision can instill a hope for salvation—including Death's death—that won't disappoint. Death is wrong, yes. It's hideous and horrific, one of the last enemies to be overcome. Jesus came not only to defeat death, but to offer us eternal life, starting now, and because of his death and resurrection, death has been dealt a death blow. Like Paul, we can even trash talk death, because its sting has been removed. To all appearances it may look like the end, but those appearances are misleading. Death is not the victor; it's a vanquished foe. And that's the good news we can share with our children.

16

Three Billboards Outside Ebbing, Missouri Shows Us a World Full of Meanness

No pleasure but meanness. Such is the ethos of the Misfit, the hardened criminal whose presence looms over Flannery O'Connor's iconic short story "A Good Man Is Hard to Find." Even before he appears in the story's climactic final scenes, the Misfit serves as the story's bogeyman, with the grandmother warning her family away from Florida where this escaped felon and his cronies are headed. At the story's outset, the nature of the Misfit's crimes is only vaguely referenced, as the grandmother encourages her son to read "what [the paper] says he did to these people." But we learn just how ruthless he is when he and his fellow convicts slaughter an innocent family—children and all—in cold blood.

Even worse, the Misfit seems to have convinced himself that he's justified in his actions—he's angry at his imprisonment, in denial over his guilt, and resentful of outside help. He has fully rejected faith in Christ's resurrection and, in turn, has embraced the lifestyle that he says follows such a denial:

> If [Jesus] did what He said, then it's nothing for you to do but throw away everything and follow Him, and if He didn't, then it's nothing for you to do but enjoy the few minutes you got left the best way you can—by killing somebody or burning down his house or doing some other meanness to him.[1]

It's a typical O'Connor story that way, where violence and existential questions meet, where ideologies are tested in the laboratory of real life. Just how poorly the Misfit's philosophy fares in this test is evidenced by his eventual acknowledgement that he finds no real pleasure in life even though he's given full vent to his nihilistic impulses.

Martin McDonagh's *Three Billboards Outside Ebbing, Missouri*, is another such story, overflowing with violence and populated by damaged and damaging characters. In its tone, dialogue, and situation, McDonagh's cinematic world seems directly inspired by O'Connor, a connection encouraged by the appearance of her iconic short story collection as reading material for one of the characters. Other implicit references to O'Connor's style and thematic concerns abound, and they provide a redemptive framework, both for making sense of the graceless economy that governs these characters' lives and for imagining other, life-affirming possibilities.

The story centers on a mother's (Mildred Hayes, played by Frances McDormand) misguided attempt to get justice for her murdered daughter by publicly shaming the town's police chief for failing to discover the perpetrator. In her quest, Mildred rents three adjoining billboards, starkly confronting the community with the brazen red-and-black sequential message: "RAPED WHILE DYING"; "AND STILL NO ARRESTS?"; "HOW COME, CHIEF WILLOUGHBY?"

It's a heartrending scenario: an unspeakable crime never solved, a mother unable to find peace, a horrific injustice left unresolved. But rather than stir up sympathy for its characters, *Three Billboards* instead points to the damage done when an aggrieved person fashions her pain into license for self-indulgence. Mildred has become so consumed by unrequited vengeance that she's unleashed her rage on the police force and, by extension, the town. The film documents a breakdown in fellowship with others that is both responsible for and a result of Mildred's obsession. She's so fixated on how her daughter's murder affected her that she's blind to how it has also affected her son and ex-husband and, especially, to how her own untamed fury damages those around her, often brutally.

Deputy Jason Dixon (Sam Rockwell) is Mildred's foil. Like her, rather than quell his inner demons, he unleashes them on innocent victims. A racist drunk emboldened by the authority of his badge, Dixon is a menace to the town. He is known to abuse his position and is alleged to have beaten a black man in his custody, a charge whose veracity is underscored by his actions in the film. Like O'Connor's Misfit, Dixon rationalizes his behavior, finding solace in his mother's excuses for his actions and comfort in her belief that he's special and entitled.

Both Mildred and Dixon have overcompensated for the wrongs inflicted on them—an abusive marriage, a fatherless childhood—and have stoked resentment indiscriminately at a world that's brought them harm. The two seem intent on testing out the Misfit's hypothesis that a world devoid of Christ's resurrection is lawless and, ultimately, meaningless. In this way, then, *Three Billboards* succeeds in effecting an apologetic-in-negative by putting on full display the poverty of such a life bereft of grace.

The audience recognizes the tragedy of this attitude. It's honestly hard to miss, as Mildred foregoes opportunity after opportunity to relinquish her despair and to choose instead to see others, to look beyond her pain and attend to those for whom she's responsible. She lets no slight—perceived or real—go unreturned, including those levied by children.

In the film's most poignant—and, unexpectedly enough, hopeful—thread, Chief Willoughby (Woody Harrelson) bears the brunt of Mildred's animosity. He does so with a dignity and mercy lacking in the other major characters, a contrast made even more vivid given that he's facing a terminal diagnosis. While certainly flawed, Willoughby offers a Christ-like example of turning the other cheek in the face of Mildred's indecency. He can do so because—unlike Mildred—he finds strength and purpose in something beyond himself: his family's love and a firm commitment to his community. Willoughby, in fact, is the only character to speak of love, and he advocates it through deed and word, leaving a letter for Dixon admonishing him to release the hate that's driven him thus far. Given Dixon's heinous racism, many viewers understandably decry this moment, but it does open him up to the possibility of redemption. Furthermore, grace notes like this—relatively rare, often muddled, and undoubtedly incomplete—encourage viewers to think beyond the given and envision a world unbound by our material realities of death and decay, hostility and corruption. Even Mildred seems to long for such a world, though she only allows herself a moment to revel in the possibilities.

In one of the film's most beautiful scenes, one that seems almost out of place, Mildred is planting flowers at the billboards. It's a rare peaceful reprieve for both her and the audience. She sees a deer and finds it a safe sounding board, musing about what conclusions can be drawn from her daughter's unsolved murder: "Still no arrest, how come I wonder, because there ain't no God and the whole world's empty and it doesn't matter what we do to each other?" Despite Mildred's behavior to this point and her apparent belief that life is meaningless and that she can mistreat people with impunity, she unexpectedly concludes, "I hope not."

This "hope not" might be as far as *Three Billboards Outside Ebbing, Missouri* can go, but its accurately bleak depiction of a world without grace instills a powerful longing in viewers that reality might actually be otherwise. That perhaps, as the Misfit acknowledges, Jesus really did throw everything off balance. His resurrection, if true, might just set us free from the calculating, destructive logic of sin. It might just give us a path to justice unencumbered by our failings.

17

Living in the Not Yet: *Mockingjay – Part 1* as Microcosm of the Fall

M*ockingjay – Part 1*, which swept away its box-office competition when it opened in 2014, has a decidedly different feel from previous *Hunger Games* films. Katniss—the consummate hunter and outdoorswoman—is now squirreled away underground in District 13. Her movements are restricted, and, in attempting to harness her charismatic spirit as propaganda for the rebellion, the district administration squelches it instead. In this latest in the *Hunger Games* franchise, the girl on fire has lost some of her spark.

Manohla Dargis of *The New York Times* reads this shift as a mistake, saying the filmmakers have lost sight of the main character and turned the intriguing female-driven story into a "generic action-flick" blockbuster.[1] The film retains the violent clashes characteristic of author Suzanne Collins' trilogy, yet with very little direct involvement from Katniss. She is, as Dargis notes, somewhat on the periphery here, most especially at the film's peak—a daring raid on the Capitol she can merely watch unfold on monitors in District 13's war room.

Yet, rather than reveal a mistake on the filmmakers' part, such scenes highlight a shift in the story's focus, or rather a sharpening of a theme that's been there all along. Behind the violence and gaudy spectacle of the first two films lies Katniss's longing for community, her strong desire to bond with others, protect her friends and family, and live with those she loves in peace and harmony. Her entrance into the Games themselves was not a political maneuver designed to bring down the tyrannical President Snow, but a spontaneous almost involuntary attempt to protect her sister by sacrificing herself.

In a way *Mockingjay – Part 1* returns Katniss to this (non-Rawlsian) original position, searching for a way to keep her loved ones safe, not knowing whom to trust, what those in power want from her, or how to satisfy them and avoid negative repercussions for the innocent. Except now she's quickly learning the impossibility of accomplishing these goals given her current situation. At the close of *Catching Fire* Katniss learns that District 13 was not destroyed as she once believed. And she learns she has misjudged several key figures: head Gamemaker Plutarch Heavensbee concocted the plot to rescue her from the arena, a plot supported by her presumably apolitical mentor Haymitch Abernathy. So from the outset of this third film, Katniss realizes that she is embroiled within a deceptive system, unable to fully grasp its machinations.

The film's opening scene establishes this conflict that will ultimately drive the entire film, as Katniss crouches hidden in a utility corridor of District 13. She's there to avoid the administration who is pressuring her to become the rebellion's figurehead, yet Katniss questions their motives and their tactics. In filling the role of the Mockingjay, will she simply become a pawn in another level of the Games she thought she'd escaped? And who might become the casualties of her decision?

What we see through Katniss's uneasiness in District 13 is the outworking of the Fall, as Adam and Eve's sin separated them from God but also from each other. Human beings, made for relationship—inhuman almost without them—throw roadblocks in the way of the very relationships they need to thrive. A ruggedly individualistic protagonist, though great fodder for Hollywood drama, fits less well within the biblical paradigm of community. At the consummation of His creation, after declaring all He made good, God indicates that Adam's solitude is, in fact, not good. Man is not meant to be alone. As explained by theologians such as Karl Barth and Emil Brunner, our having been made in the image of God entails this capacity for and necessity of relationships. God creates Eve to provide that needed companionship for Adam, and in turn Adam provides companionship for Eve; the benefits of their relationship (and all relationships) are mutual.

After Adam, no human being has entered this world unattached. And yet, this side of Eden, those relationships are fraught with danger. Turning inward, unregenerate man seeks to satisfy his own needs, often at the expense of others. Scriptures are rife with example after example: Adam blames Eve for his sin. Cain murders Abel out of jealousy. Abram passes Sarai off as his sister to protect himself. David sacrifices Uriah for his obsession with Bathsheba. The pages of history and literature are peppered with many more tragic instances of such treachery. Human beings destroy relationships by quarreling, deceiving, exploiting, manipulating, and abandoning the very ones they are meant to support, serve, love, nurture, encourage, and build up. Katniss experiences the effects of these behaviors—definitively from the Capitol which uses others overtly but perhaps also from District 13 whose admirable motives to overcome the brutal President Snow might mask troubling manipulation.

Such is a common-enough theme in the dystopian genre to which *Hunger Games* belongs. *Fahrenheit 451, Brave New World, We*: the inhabitants of these fictional worlds have no meaningful agency; the government, as in District 13, determines right action without input from the governed, for the good of its citizens. But a paternalistic tyranny is a tyranny nonetheless. In *God in the Dock*, C. S. Lewis insightfully explains the demeaning attitude on which such action is based:

> Of all tyrannies, a tyranny sincerely exercised for the good of its victims may be the most oppressive. It would be better to live under robber barons than under omnipotent moral busybodies. . . . This very kindness stings with intolerable insult. To be "cured" against one's will and cured of states which we may not regard as disease is to be put on a level of those who have not yet reached the age of reason or those who never will; to be classed with infants, imbeciles, and domestic animals.

Healthy relationships and the community dependent on these relationships, rather, embrace the dignity of and insist on respect for all parties involved. True love—the necessary cement for relationships—"does not insist on its own way; it is not irritable or resentful; it does not rejoice at wrongdoing, but rejoices with the truth. Love bears all things, believes all things, hopes all things, endures all things" (I Corinthians 13:5-7).

And indeed Katniss still clings to the hope that the community for which she has sacrificed so much will prevail. She lives now in the not yet, as do we all. Amid the effects of the Fall, at the mercy of others' selfish strivings, and prone to give in to an easy cynicism that believes no good will come, let us rather live the promise of full communion and reconciliation, knowing that this, too, shall pass.

18

Weighing Death in *Buffy the Vampire Slayer*

The opening scene of *Buffy the Vampire Slayer*'s "The Body" episode is as unforgettable as it is heart-wrenching. Bright colors dominate the shot as Buffy, clad in a vivid red sweater, comes home to find inside the door a beautiful flower arrangement that her mother Joyce received from a recent date. "Still a couple of guys getting it right," Buffy quips as she calls out to her mother, offering to pick up her sister from school. But this cheery scene quickly gives way to horror as Buffy finds Joyce's body lifeless on the couch, victim of a fatal aneurysm.

Frantic, Buffy tries everything she knows to rouse Joyce—shaking her, yelling, and eventually performing CPR with the guidance of the 911 operator. All to no avail. Her mother remains limp, agonizingly non-responsive. The surreal scenario described is emotional enough. Add in the stark contrast between Buffy's flurry of activity and Joyce's immobility, and the effect is jarring. Buffy moves from room to room, couch to phone and back again, her arms and legs and whole being intent to set right what has gone dreadfully wrong. All the while, the camera lingers on Joyce's body—her eyes open, her face expressionless, her limbs splayed inelegantly out.

It may go without saying, but "The Body" is not the usual campy fare of Joss Whedon's trailblazing comedy-action series from the late 1990s. Death was nothing new to the show, of course. How could it be with "slayer" right there in the title? In fact, death was arguably the supernatural thriller's stock-in-trade, as Buffy and her "Scooby gang" of loyal friends regularly fought the undead. They risked life and limb nearly daily to save the school and town from the "forces of darkness"—vampires, demons, and even ghosts and ghouls. But "The Body" was the first time death came this close and was made so personal. It was also the first time death became utterly unimaginable and unmanageable.

Over the course of the five seasons that led up to "The Body," viewers had been delighted by Buffy's preternatural physical prowess, Giles' staid demeanor in the face of danger, Willow's winsomely nerdy research and computer skills, and Xander's goofily charming and disarming humor. These characters may have faced countless dire circumstances, but they always knew just how to handle them—and did so joyfully, with plenty of verve and style to boot. Given that their hometown of Sunnydale rests atop a "hellmouth," the friends have had more than their share of challenges—usually on an apocalpytic scale, such as when they stopped the ancient, powerful vampire Master from initiating the catastrophic Harvest; or thwarted the demonic Ascension of Mayor Wilkins; or defeated countless other Big Bads threatening to tear apart the fabric of reality and make high school even more hellish than it already is. Whatever the danger, Buffy and her friends invariably charged in, dealt with the situation, and always—always—overcame. "The Body" is the first time we see their powers rendered impotent to remedy the situation.

Instead, the gang is downright bewildered by Joyce's death, their ability to process and come to terms with it stymied. Death, the ultimate thief, simply does not compute, particularly not the death of one so young. Despite Joyce's recent bout with a brain tumor, for example, Buffy insists to the EMTs that the surgery has taken care of all that. "She's fine now," Buffy repeats, but somehow without conviction. Over the course of the episode, viewers see her replay fantasies of arriving home earlier, rescuing her mother when the emergency hits, and clutching her in the nick of time from the jaws of her ignoble fate. However, even if Buffy had gotten there before the attack, the doctor makes clear that her mother's death was inevitable.

Willow, too, struggles in her own distinctive way. Unable to rectify the situation, she longs to console her friend but knows that there is little comfort she can offer, a sober truth reflected in her earnest attempts to find the perfect outfit to wear to the hospital. It's a sweet but ultimately absurd attempt to mitigate the agony of Joyce's loss. Xander, too, finds his characteristic humor woefully inadequate to the situation, so he seeks someone, anyone, to blame for the death:

perhaps it was Glory (the supernatural villain of season 5), or the doctors who should have anticipated the problem. But when Xander exhausts his list of possible culprits, he is left with only rage, punching the wall and bloodying his fist in the process.

Anya, as a demon-turned-human, is new to the experience of death. She plays the child in response, which further unsettles the friends. She naively asks foolish and taboo questions about whether they would see Joyce's body and whether her body would be cut open. When Willow lashes out, begging her to stop asking such questions, Anya articulates the confusion and dismay felt by the others, including the viewers:

> I don't understand how this all happened. I mean, I knew her, and then she. . . there's just a body, and I don't understand why she just can't get back in it and not be dead anymore. It's stupid. It's mortal and stupid. And Xander's crying and not talking, and I was having fruit punch, and I thought, well Joyce will never have any more fruit punch ever. And she'll never have eggs or yawn or brush her hair, not ever. And no one will explain to me why.

In scenes like these, and many others, "The Body" forces viewers to feel the simple awfulness of death. Such is Whedon's goal, as he explains in the DVD commentary. Having lost his own mother suddenly when he was just 27, Whedon hoped for a more honest portrayal of death than is often shown on TV: "My experience with death is that apart from a lot of people hugging at funerals, it seldom brings people together. It actually tears them apart. And I had always learned from TV that death made everybody stronger and better and learn about themselves. And my experience was that an important piece had been taken out of the puzzle."[1]

By contrast, all throughout "The Body," viewers must sit with the brute and brutal fact of death and let it weigh on us. The episode provides very little relief. "The Body" is devoid of the show's characteristic hip music; instead, painful silence casts a pall over the whole episode. Rather than the signature whimsy between friends, they interact only awkwardly. There are no answers, none offered or even allowed. Instead, the show complexifies the questions and emphasizes their tragic implications and intractable nature. Such as in the final scene, when Buffy's sister Dawn sees her mother's body one last time in the morgue. She experiences the tension of knowing that the body laying on the slab both is and is not her mother. "She is gone," Buffy reassures her; "[i]t's not her." But if that's so, Dawn asks genuinely, then "[w]here'd she go?" It's a question that, fittingly, yields no response as the screen turns black and the credits roll.

Christians especially may find this scenario uncomfortable. Death has been defeated, after all, and we have a great hope—the great hope—in Christ's resurrection. And of course that is so. We can point to scripture after scripture extolling that truth, and they are great comfort when death rears its ugly head and wields its horrific power. Christians surely do not mourn as those without hope (I Thessalonians 4:13). Still, we might ask ourselves if talk of the resurrection is sometimes deployed too quickly or cavalierly, less as comfort in the face of death and more as means to avoid facing the ugliness and brokenness of death. And if so, do we risk minimizing both death's devastating sting and, by extension, the glorious promise of the resurrection?

To Whedon and the cast's credit, they viscerally convey death's atrocity and call us to ponder death's gravity. In this way, "The Body" is a powerful and poignant fictional reminder of just how terrible is this last great enemy of humanity (I Corinthians 15:26). Such a sober-minded view of death—one that truly acknowledges how dreadful it is, how far beyond human capacities to subdue, how irremediably awful it truly is—can reawaken our imaginations to the beautiful mystery of the resurrection's promise to vanquish this final foe, once and for all, and brace our hearts as we await creation's final redemption.

Both John Henry Newman and Søren Kierkegaard warned Christians not to settle for religious jargon but to strive to understand its fundamental theological import. Rather than offering a sanguine retort to Dawn's final question, one that conveys too light a view of death, Christians are not only permitted but are also encouraged to existentially feel the appalling force of death—the utter helplessness of human beings relying on their own resources in the face of it, the appearance it projects of all hope being lost. And through that lens, we may better understand and appreciate the wonder and power of the resurrection and of the God who is making all things new.

19

The Man in the High Castle and the Necessity of Moral Faith

Amazon Studios heavily invested in the success of their original television series *The Man in the High Castle*. Reportedly, the second season cost upwards of $107 million to produce, or about $11 million per episode.[1] And they're not finished yet; at the time of this writing, the third season was set to release in early October of 2018, with a fourth season already in pre-production. It is far from clear whether or not Amazon's gamble will pay off in terms of soliciting new subscribers for their streaming service, but the studio's choice of this program as one to boost makes sense, both because of its rich source material (adapted from a novel of the same name written by legendary science fiction author Philip K. Dick) and because it taps into the anxieties and concerns of our highly charged political moment. Judging from comments Isa Hackett—Dick's daughter and a producer on the show—made at 2018's Comic-Con,[2] later seasons will focus even more intently on the resonances between the characters' situations and what's currently transpiring in American government and culture.

For viewers' sake, however, and for the integrity of the show, it would be regrettable if the series veers too far into political territory at the expense of the philosophical possibilities embedded in the tale itself. To view the story through a staunchly sectarian or provincially partisan lens would, in truth, drain it of its real power to illuminate transcendent truths that undergird and give meaning to the particularities of our present moment. In fact, doing so would be antithetical to the show's central moral concerns, especially how good can flourish in a world overrun by evil. Limiting the source or manifestation of evil merely to one political ideology would undercut the answers the show provides—or at least inchoately intimates.

The Imaginative Possibilities of Alternate History

The Man in the High Castle presents an alternate history, set in 1962, in which the Axis Powers defeated the Allies and won World War II. The United States has been partitioned up, with the Japanese Pacific States taking over the West, the Greater Nazi Reich in the East, and a no-man's land neutral zone separating the two. This intriguing premise makes possible for readers and viewers to experience what Darko Suvin calls "cognitive estrangement," which for him is the defining feature of science fiction texts.[3] By introducing a "novum," or "device or machine that is absolutely new," science fiction opens up fresh ways of imagining our world.[4] For Dick in particular, such cognitive estrangement—the audience's immersion in a highly believable world that differs so dramatically from its own—makes possible penetrating insights into the nature of human existence and the moral challenges we all face. In this way, the story navigates the continuum between the philosophical and the practical, culturally embedding in American guise the central issues at the heart of the human condition.

In the case of *The Man in the High Castle*, the change in global fortunes owes to Nazi technological superiority. It is they who have better weapons; it is they, in fact, who have developed and used the nuclear bomb, which in topsy-turvy fashion dealt the final blow to the Allied forces. Axis technological and military dominance brought their cultural dominance as well, with the Nazi program of ethnic cleansing, totalitarianism, and the cult of Hitler gaining a stranglehold on the East, and Japanese models of ancestor worship, systematized and enforced self-sacrifice, and twisted devotion to the emperor reigning supreme in the West. Such a situation is pregnant with speculative possibility, especially ones centered on moral concerns. American superiority, with its commitments to human dignity and freedom—at least in principle—enshrined in its founding documents, has been dethroned, and an ethos of power, where might makes right, is now the operative law of the land.

This leaves viewers—and characters—with existentially pressing questions: what makes an action right or wrong? What imbues value, what is the measure by which we can judge a person's motivations, what makes it possible to deem a social structure as good or evil? Is there something—or someone—beyond the historical and material conditions in which we find ourselves that underwrites such truths? *The Man in the High Castle*, while not fleshing out a fully formed ethical system, does at least reject any sort of relativism that would tie these transcendent categories to fleeting and fickle human activity.

A Web of Characters

To explore these questions, the show traces the distinct but overlapping stories of five central characters, all implicated within the machinations of Japanese and Nazi rule and faced with hellish situations to navigate with both their lives and souls intact: Juliana Crain, her boyfriend Frank Frink, both of whom are attempting—unsuccessfully—to live quiet lives in San Francisco; Joe Blake, a conflicted undercover Nazi agent; John Smith, an American Army officer–turned–Nazi leader; and Nobusuke Tagomi, Trade Minister of the Pacific States. These characters assume a variety of postures toward the Nazi and Japanese regimes. Some of these responses are more problematic than others, but all are laden and fraught with moral implications. The audience is invited to judge the characters' behavior—sometimes sympathetically (as with Frank Frink who is trapped between saving his sister and saving his girlfriend), other times admirably (such as when Juliana risks her life to save Joe's), and often harshly (which is the case with most of John Smith's actions). The characters do not have the luxury of theorizing about or washing their hands of ethical obligations. They must act, and in so doing, they reveal their core beliefs.

Although the show is sweeping in its scope—portraying large-scale systemic immorality and its destructive consequences—its ultimate focus is individual choice, never absolving altogether any character or excusing his or her corrupt actions due to societal pressure, no matter how crushing that pressure is. The show celebrates the beauty and goodness of those who would endure that pressure and manage to resist the pervasive temptations of fear or power or despair that would break the will of many. Especially through the character of Juliana, *The Man in the High Castle* champions what Robert Adams calls moral faith,[5] the lived-out conviction that human life is worth living, that the moral life is rational and practicable, and that morality is valuable in itself.

In a delightful twist that exemplifies the imaginative power of Dick's work and points with poignancy to the story's themes, there is another layer to this alternate history, an alternate alternate history, if you will. The Resistance, as the underground rebellion is known, smuggles realistic-looking newsreel footage of a reality closer to our own—wherein the Allied Powers prevailed over Germany and Japan.

These films, going by the title *The Grasshopper Lies Heavy* (an allusion to Ecclesiastes 12:5) and produced by the mysterious Man in the High Castle (Hawthorne Abendsen), offer hope that the world need not be what it currently is, that another reality—a better reality—is possible. The television adaptation, contra the novel, hints that these scenes are more than mere possibilities; instead, they offer a glimpse into an alternate universe—something the third season will explore further. But viewers need not subscribe to a multiverse hypothesis to appreciate the role these films play in expanding the characters' moral imaginations and in bolstering their resolve to effect justice, battle evil, retain hope, and enact love where they can.

Juliana as Exemplar of Moral Faith

Seasons 1 and 2 have so far traced the positive effect the films have had on Juliana, who is far from a committed member of the Resistance. However, very early on, when her sister Trudy entrusts the film to her before being killed for possessing it, Juliana is resolved to carry out the charge with which she's been entrusted. For the Resistance, these films may be the way out of oppression, as Trudy calls them, but for Juliana, they provide a way through the challenges she faces, a means—and a justification—to endure, to retain her moral convictions and to live them out against the odds. They provide a touchstone for the moral faith she needs to honor her sister and to jeopardize her own safety to protect others such as John Smith's son Thomas. While we see others fail to practice such moral faith, Juliana seems always able to find, even in the most loathsome characters, what Adams describes as "sufficient value in the lives of such finite, needy, suffering, ignorant, motivationally complex, and even guilty creatures as we are."[6] She never surrenders to the Nazi view that pits strong against weak or embraces the Japanese apotheosis of duty above human dignity.

Such a commitment costs her dearly, but that is precisely what moral faith demands, as Adams explains: "What we must resist most strongly here is an ultracompetitive view of the pursuit of human good as a sort of zero-sum game, in which every good that anyone enjoys must be taken away from someone else."[7] Juliana's commitment to love and justice shines all the brighter in the darkness of this dystopian world. For this reason, she is, as Abendsen tells her in the final episode of season 2, "the only hope any of [them] had." She can offer this hope because of her constancy, appearing again and again in all the films depicting life in the alternate worlds but always behaving the same, always betting "on the best in us." Abendsen says that in these films he witnessed her "bet[ting] on people no matter what the world said about who they were, who they should be." In a line that comes close to Adams's description of moral faith, Abendsen explains that she acted out of a moral conviction: "That woman would do anything to save a sick boy—a Nazi boy, even—because she would believe he deserved the chance, as slim as it might be, to live a valuable life." Importantly, the faithfulness Juliana demonstrates is not dependent on contingent historical realities but on something that goes beyond those particularities.

In an early episode from season 1, a Nazi agent mulls over the question of what's beyond our world; the answer he returns is unsatisfactory, dependent on which governing power has the standing to enforce their view. Juliana's behavior puts the lie to such a system that would bow to political expediency or military might, surrendering one's moral code to the whim of human authority. The films reveal how fleeting and feckless that superficial authority can be, despite transitory appearances. Good and evil, right and wrong, robustly construed and seriously reckoned with, cannot find their origin in flimsy and ephemeral material circumstances or the finite and fallible human beings that inhabit them. *The Man in the High Castle*, although it doesn't offer specifics, provides powerful testimony that there must be something more. And that is certainly a substantive starting point that steadfast believers in a good God can work with.

20

Hold Fast to the Good: *Fahrenheit 451*, the Love of Books, and the Value of People

The 2018 HBO adaptation of Ray Bradbury's *Fahrenheit 451* attempts to update the classic story of censorship and entertainment run amok in light of new technology and our ubiquitous social media culture. It's a laudable effort, and Michael B. Jordan and Michael Shannon put a memorable twist on Guy Montag and Captain John Beatty. A small caveat here at the start: it's easy to be skeptical about the wisdom of adapting this particular book to film, given its overt critiques on the logic and deficiencies of a spectacle-driven society. There's just something odd about using a screen—big or small—to bemoan the decline of the written word's cultural primacy of place. Even still, Bradbury himself approved of François Truffaut's 1966 version, and critics have made a compelling case that the film's visuals pay homage to the role of books in shaping an inviting and hospitable world, one much more attractive and life-giving than the mechanical world of the firemen charged with burning them.

Whatever reservations we have about the film versions notwithstanding, one scene, powerful in the book and brilliantly captured by each adaptation, dramatically and memorably depicts the central conflict of the story. It is a scene that stands out even on one's first encounter with Bradbury's story and that readily comes to mind when we think of what it means to take one's commitments seriously. When one has recognized the value of a thing or person, what obligations does that recognition entail? As Bradbury's story suggests, the greater the value, the higher the price.

Montag's crew raid a house on an anonymous tip. There they find it overflowing with books—illegal all. As they enter the house, they find one lone woman sitting at a desk; in the recent version she reads

John Steinbeck's *The Grapes of Wrath*, unmoved by her unexpected visitors. The firemen search the house, and room after room is overrun with books. They are stacked floor to ceiling in piles that crowd tables, bookshelves, and chairs. This "regular Tower of Babel"—as Beatty calls it—is so jam-packed that the banned materials leave only a small path for the men to walk through.

These books—any books—are an offense to the futuristic America Bradbury has imagined. They require too much time, provoke too much thought, and unsettle easy answers. True-believer Beatty expounds on the dangers inherent in making these writings freely available: "Do you want to know what's inside all these books? Insanity. . . . One expert screaming down another expert's throat. . . . Each one says the opposite, and a man comes away lost, feeling more bestial and lonely than before." This forbidden fruit, Beatty suggests, dazzles with promises to unlock the secrets of the universe but leaves readers more disoriented and confused than before. Happiness, on this worldview, comes from being spoon-fed the knowledge needed to get along: "If you don't want a person unhappy, you don't give them two sides of a question." In fact, you don't give them a question at all.

The stronger Beatty makes his case against books, the more intrigued about them Montag becomes; he snags one and tucks it into his coat before the others are doused with kerosene. As the house is readied to burn, Montag tries to get the occupant to leave. But she remains steadfast, defiant in the face of the firemen's destruction. Montag's conscience has been pricked: "Are we just going to leave her?" he asks as Beatty says to let her be. Coldly, the captain gives her one last chance to avoid the fate destined for her books: "Look, miss, do what you like, but you know as well as I do that these books are gonna burn."

And then comes one of the most memorable scenes of the adaptation: the woman stands atop a pile of kerosene-soaked books, opens her jacket to reveal additional books strapped to her waist, pulls out a single match, which she strikes and drops to the floor. She has done the firemen's job for them, willing to die for the books she cherishes. Bradbury elevates this sacrifice, making it akin to religious devotion, by having her allude to the apocryphal last words of Protestant martyr Hugh Latimer: "Play the man," she says, a line concluded by Latimer with the hope that his present suffering will one day be rewarded: "We shall this day light such a candle, by God's grace, in England, as I trust shall never be put out."

What makes this scene so memorable is the deep conviction readers and viewers sense in the woman's commitment to her books. She values them so highly that, for her, they are worth her very life. Coming after Beatty's denigration of books as societal troublemakers, responsible for all manner of unrest, the woman's sacrifice is all the more poignant. Clearly she thinks otherwise and hopes her immolation will convince viewers of the raid's livestream to challenge the status quo, to give books a chance. And of course if someone is willing to give her life for the cause, anything so intuitively significant and sacrificial certainly merits close attention. Even if her strategy doesn't seal the deal for those watching the fire, it might at least give them pause to reconsider the party line. It does just that for Montag and sets him on a rebellious course.

But as memorable as the scene is, the question of the source of the value of these books remains unanswered—at least in this latest adaptation of *Fahrenheit 451*. It's clear that the filmmakers (and characters like this woman) highly prize the written word, but it's not clear why—what confers on them their worth? Unmoored from any such anchor, the books take on an almost fetishistic role. In a sharp departure from Bradbury's original story, director and writer Ramin Bahrani introduces an electronic component to the preservation of literature. While the original story relies on an exiled community to memorialize the words behind the written texts, the HBO film entrusts it to technology—a database called OMNIS encoded in a DNA strand and stored inside a bird. Presumably, no matter what human beings do to each other, this literature will live on; the final scene of the film suggests as much, with the bird soaring high above the embattled city. These precious books have left humanity behind and are no longer subjected to their depraved machinations.

In Bradbury's novel version, the opposite is true: the written word itself falls away, and is now imprinted in the memories of the "book people" who have each undertaken to memorize whole books in a throwback to the world of oral culture. The books have been more deeply internalized than before, and community is essential to their survival. While Bradbury never explores any locus of value beyond this human community, he seems to recognize what the filmmakers do not: that these texts cannot stand on their own and absorb any significant amount of devotion without something inherently valuable to underwrite them. For Bradbury, books themselves are primarily a vehicle for human creativity and an extension of the mind of the creator him or herself.

To censor or otherwise destroy them means more than physical annihilation of the material text: it's to dishonor and degrade the people behind the writings. It's also to stamp out the good these reflections on the human condition and our world can offer readers now. The figure of Faber, who is notably absent in the newest version, beautifully articulates the connection: "It's not books you need, it's some of the things that once were in books. . . . The magic is only in what books say, how they stitched the patches of the universe together into one garment for us. . . . This book has pores. It has features. This book can go under the microscope. You'd find life under the glass, streaming past in infinite profusion." Admittedly, Bradbury's framework needs expanding a bit, undergirding the temporal human community with an eternal source of ultimate value—something that classical theism readily provides we should note, but he at least gestures in that direction.

21

Once Upon a Time and Philosophy: Rumpel's Redemption

Once Upon a Time is a fun and sometimes fascinating little TV show (running from 2011-2018). Writing for the show can be uneven—from quite good to painfully banal (Prince Charming as David is a reliable source of the latter)—but several characters are compelling and a few plot points are thought provoking in distinctively philosophical ways. Perhaps the biggest recurring philosophical issue that arises in the series is ethics, issues of right and wrong, good and bad, virtue and vice. The show has both its good and bad characters. Snow White and Prince Charming, along with their daughter Emma and her son Henry, are obvious heroes; Regina and Rumpel(stilskin) are villains. But the heroes have their temptations and feet of clay, and the villains their charms and redemptive characteristics.

For those unfamiliar with the basic story line, the evil queen Regina performs a curse, which sends all the storybook characters we know into this world—to Storybrooke, Maine, to be precise. No one from this world can see the town, and all the storybook characters, arguably except Rumpel and (perhaps) Regina, have no recollection of their previous lives. They reside in the town blithely unaware of what has happened, and carrying on in largely the same way, day after day, at least until a certain day. Regina is the mayor of the town, Rumpel runs an antique shop, and Snow White is Henry's elementary school teacher. Henry, through Snow White, comes to possess a book of fairy tales and somewhat mysteriously becomes aware that they're more than stories. He, and he alone, comes to see that they are true, and he sees it as his task to help the inhabitants of the town remember who they are. Having been adopted by Regina from outside the town (Emma gave him up for adoption outside of Storybrooke), Henry, unlike anyone else in the town, is able to travel beyond its borders. He does so when he's ten, in search of Emma, finds her in Boston—a meeting that takes place in the first episode. He persuades Emma to take him home, and she sticks around to make sure he's happy. Her arrival breaks the loop, and, significantly, the town clock starts to run for the first time. She finds his fantastical claims incredible and assumes he's a troubled kid. Eventually, though, she discovers that what he says is true and that she, in fact, is the only person who can break the spell.

The villains are perhaps the most interesting characters in the show, and the two most compelling villains, Regina (the evil queen/mayor) and Rumpelstilskin (Mr. Gold), have done terrible things. Regina is responsible for the curse itself, for killing the sheriff, for framing Snow White for murder, and for a litany of other villainies. Rumpel, too, has done his worst—killing, conniving, and such. But much of what makes the show inherently so interesting is the possibility of redemption in each case. Although both of these characters are clearly morally bad, there's something deeply likeable about them, and, as the story unfolds and the backstory gets filled in, there's something sympathetic about each character as well. They're anything but stock or one-dimensional villains. Each, at one time, was a very good person, but, as their lives unfolded, their choices shaped their characters in dark directions.

In Regina's case, she was the daughter of an ambitious, diabolical woman with great magical powers, who wanted her daughter to be delivered from a life of servanthood. She manipulated events to bring about a proposal for marriage to Regina from the king. At that point in Regina's life, she harbored no desire for power or marriage to the king; her deepest desire instead was to marry the stable boy Thomas. Just as she's on the verge of escaping from her dominating mother and eloping with her true love, her mother shows up, kills Thomas, and ensures that Regina will marry the king instead. To make matters worse, it was a young Snow White's (honest) mistake that divulged to Regina's mother the knowledge of her daughter's plans to defy her. Regina's loss of her loved one made her seethe in resentment toward Snow White, and go down a path of seeking power and revenge and of using magic in harmful ways, as her mother had done. Ironically, she becomes very much like her own mother, whose ways she had despised so much, and even takes to repeating her mother's mantra that "love is weakness."

Rumpel's story is equally intriguing. Rumpel's father had abandoned him—a fascinating story in itself, which we'll come back to in a moment—and Rumpel, in contrast, wants to be there for his own son. But he's afflicted with a huge character flaw: lack of courage. C. S. Lewis once suggested that courage is the virtue that functions at the foundation of every other virtue; if true, without courage it's hard to sustain a life of much moral integrity. Once we see Rumpel's genuine desire to be there for his son, however, and the fact that he's given cause to believe that his participation in a war into which he'd been drafted would result in his death unless he turned back, his decision to feign an injury to be with his family becomes more understandable. It's perceived by everyone else, though, including his wife, as nothing but an act of cowardice. Bullied by the local military leaders, Rumpel understandably wants to protect himself and his child—even, as he puts it, "all the children," a noble sentiment indeed—and, when given the opportunity, he avails himself of the chance to acquire the necessary power to do so. Suddenly, as the "Dark One" invested with such power, his fear dissipates, and he starts to use the power for increasingly ignoble ends. This strains his relationship with his son, who begs him to stop using magic and who wants them to go to a new land for a fresh start. When the time comes, however, Rumpel's cowardice holds sway, and he chooses not to go with his son.

The difficult circumstances in the lives of Regina and Rumpel don't excuse their decisions, but they do make those decisions a bit more understandable. They at least help explain those decisions, and they probably do something else. They make the watchers of the show root for these characters; there's something recognizable about them, something human, something that resonates. Perhaps, we find ourselves thinking that they're not beyond redemption. Maybe their humanity can be salvaged. Indeed, much of the show is geared toward this very question. Henry functions as the conscience for Regina, and Belle, who sees the good that remains in Rumpel, serves in this capacity for him. In each case, they're encouraged to give up magic, to put a stop to evildoing, to change course. In fits and starts, each experiences some success, but almost inevitably they're drawn back into magic, darkness, and vengeance.

Both stories are compelling, but for us the Rumpel story more so—perhaps in part because we find the actor playing Gold/Rumpelstilskin so delightful. Robert Carlyle's little mannerisms, idiosyncrasies, modulations of voice, physical presence, and gratuitous comical flourishes make for a simply wonderful character to watch. Knowing the goodness that once resided in his heart, too, makes the viewer hope he's not too far gone. Rumpel, though, sees himself as a monster, as something no longer human, no longer a man. In the episode "Skin Deep," Belle tells Rumpel it would be understandable if he were lonely. "Any man would be lonely," she says, to which he replies, "I'm not a man." Belle doesn't give up, though, saying, "So you were a man once, an ordinary man?" Rumpel replies with skepticism, wondering if she's just trying to uncover "the monster's weaknesses." "You're not a monster," Belle assures him.

A few lines later, discussing a courageous act that she's performed, Belle says, "I figured, do the brave thing, and bravery would follow." Belle recognizes the causal connection between actions and character, specifically from actions to character, rather than vice versa—at least before one's character gets cemented into place. But if this can work in a positive direction, it can also work in a negative direction. The notion here that evildoing, a heart of darkness, bad choices and their inevitable trajectory, could actually result in a loss of humanness is, at bottom, a profoundly troubling insight. Yet there seems something about it that rings with sober truth. We can't forever divorce our actions from who we are. Our actions put us on moral trajectories; one who lies enough is no longer just one who lies, but a liar. In time a liar can even start to believe her lies.

Aristotle argues that virtues are tied to our humanity, vices to something else, and an organic connection obtains between our actions and our character. What would make for a stock and, frankly, uninteresting bad guy would be a villain who has a bad character and never deviates or departs from it, never shows any signs of ambivalence, remorse, or potential for anything else. What makes for a more nuanced and believable character, one we both love and hate at the same time, one we can root for, is a good person gone bad, step by incremental step. Part of the beauty of Vince Gilligan's *Breaking Bad* series, for example, was watching a good man go down a dark path, each step implicating him further, sucking him in deeper—until eventually we see the nearly complete devolution of the fellow. Rumpel has gone down this path, too, but however much he himself may doubt it, he seems to retain the capacity to turn—or return. Such a turn requires courage and virtuous actions that, over time and painfully, can reshape his character.

Rumpel is a moral work in progress, but at the time of this writing, it's unclear what the final product will be. His character doesn't seem to have been sealed in quite yet; his actions are still shaping his character rather than simply being its inexorable entailments. He's gone quite a way down a dark path, though, which makes a change in character harder to accomplish. Long habit has made extrication from evil all the more difficult. The great philosopher and psychologist William James, in his *Talks to Teachers*, recognizing the power of recurring actions and entrenched habits in shaping our character and destiny, said that a teacher's primary job is to inculcate the right habits in his students—particularly when they're young enough to be more easily malleable. Change later is possible, but increasingly difficult as we get older and more set in our ways. For Rumpel to change, he really needs to find the courage to turn, the strength to resist temptation, the wherewithal to effect change—exactly when, for lack of doing enough of this beforehand, it's the hardest for him to do so. Whether he will or not, which of these warring factions within him will prevail, makes for gripping television. We have reason to hope for Rumpel's redemption because he's not his father's son. His father is despicably evil, willing and happy to relegate his own son to misery for his own purposes. Rumpel, to save Henry from his (Rumpel's) father's clutches, needs to be willing to sacrifice himself. And, importantly, he's indeed willing to do so. Moreover, when Rumpel's father suggests a parity between himself and Rumpel, the disanalogy is immediately clear—and it's pointed out by, of all people, Rumpel's son, who'd harbored years of resentment over his own abandonment.

What was the difference? It was this: Rumpel's father never regretted his wrongdoing. Rumpel did. As soon as he lost his son, he regretted it, and set himself to the seemingly impossible chore of rectifying it. On the surface, their actions may have seemed similar, but digging beneath the surface, we find that the appearance is misleading. One endorsed his own wrongdoing, embraced it, and gladly let it define him. His second order and first order desires perfectly meshed. The other regretted it, fought to fix it, and didn't try to justify it. In one case there was wrongdoing and perfect reconciliation with it. In the other, Rumpel's case, there was wrongdoing and enough unhappiness with it, enough dissonance, enough guilt, enough regret, enough irremediable tension, that it couldn't entirely define him. It left room for repentance, and a chance for change. That Rumpel is not his father's son gives us reason to think he will find redemption. Now, let's hope.

22

Mark Twain's Tightrope Walk: Caught between Despair and Hope

Over a hundred years after his death, Mark Twain remains one of the most colorful and well-beloved American authors. Even infrequent readers know of Tom Sawyer and Huckleberry Finn who have become iconic characters in the American imagination, and Twain's public persona and incisive wit are the stuff of legend. Born Samuel Langhorne Clemens in 1835,[1] Twain was shaped by the western frontier, both in his native Missouri and through his various travels during his adventurous young adulthood. He in turn shaped the public imagination through his numerous tall tales and humorous sketches of a life largely unknown to the genteel Easterners who devoured his stories. By many accounts, Twain was the most recognized person of his time; his speaking tours, advocacy work, and prestigious honors led to his status as "the first modern celebrity."[2] Considering Twain's most consistent and central themes—he repeatedly wrote withering critiques of institutions and individuals alike—this popularity seems surprising; however, his artful humor helps to account for the discrepancy.

Both prolific and profound, Twain managed to expose social ills and elicit a hearty dose of laughter from his readers, who themselves were often the very targets of his critique. Beginning with his first published story, "The Celebrated Jumping Frog of Calaveras County," Twain lampooned human pretensions, moral hypocrisies, political absurdities, and religious spectacle. As his writing matured, he took on racial oppression and imperialism, capitalism and animal cruelty. His imagination was both expansive and ethical, evidenced by his keen insights that the human condition was indeed pitiable. Even still, owing to Twain's pervasive and characteristic humor, Harold Bush identifies him as an ultimately hopeful writer: "The moral aspect of his writings hinges upon both a desire for and an unshakeable faith in the possibility that things might change and that his work might become an agent for such change."[3] Other critics, however, find claims of this sort wishful thinking. Gabriel Brahm and Forrest Robinson notably identify Nietzschean nihilistic strains that run throughout Twain's work.[4]

Twain's Puzzlements

Honestly it's difficult to adjudicate between those elements of Twain that feel very much like hope and love for humanity and those that resemble despair and disgust for his fellow creatures. These determinations require answering difficult questions, such as how much weight Twain's end-of-life, remarkably scathing writings should get. Should his vociferous commentary on the "damned human race"[5] be excused because of his intense grief over the death of his wife and daughter as he faced his own deteriorating health and imminent demise? If Twain's youthful hope had anything to commend it, might not the very challenges he faced as his life came to a close be the optimal time for it to manifest and have purchase, providing counterbalance to those sorrows? That it didn't, that Twain gave full vent to his angst about the intolerable injustices and everyday indignities of this unimaginably dark period of his life, we suggest, makes him all the more relatable. Regardless of his personal religious convictions—which is a matter of critical debate among biographers and Twain scholars[6]—what the writings of Twain, from the beginning of his career to its end, vividly display is the all-too-human temptation to despair pitted against the all-too-human impulse to hope.

Truth be told, Twain was always a complicated figure. Paradoxical, or at least seemingly contradictory, positions abound in his work. Berkove and Csicsila identify at least eight areas—including democracy and medical fads—where he offered diametrically opposed views.[7] Even after satirizing moneymaking schemes in his cowritten novel *The Gilded Age*, Twain sank $300,000 into an ill-fated typesetter enterprise.[8] He critiqued romanticized visions of the South, most overtly in *Life on the Mississippi*, yet arguably dabbled in his own sentimentalizing of the frontier and unbounded human freedom in *Adventures of Huckleberry Finn*. His most complicated attitudes, however, were reserved for organized religion, especially Christianity, and his relationship with God. What Nathaniel Hawthorne said of Herman Melville seems equally applicable to Twain: "He can neither believe, nor be comfortable in his unbelief."[9] In many ways, Twain's feelings toward Christianity matched those he evinced toward hope; he seemed to feel equally compelled and repulsed by it, desirous of faith but disdainful of its failures. As Reesman puts it, "He was clearly in a constant conflict about God and faith, and never could just leave it alone and move on. He wanted God, but he wanted a better God."[10]

Wrestling with God

Twain's relationship with church and religion began early. His mother was a devout Christian, and he spent much of his childhood singing hymns and attending services. He was familiar with Scripture, and its language, imagery, and themes fill the pages of his writing. Time and again, Twain used religious figures to epitomize boorishness (*The Innocents Abroad*),[11] vapidity ("Little Bessie," collected in *Tales, Speeches, Essays, and Sketches*),[12] and hypocrisy (the Grangerfords and Shepherdsons in *Huckleberry Finn*).[13] In his personal notebooks, he says, with biting flair, that "if Christ were here there is one thing he would not be—a Christian."[14] Satan even serves as the hero of several of his late pieces — most notably in the posthumously published *The Mysterious Stranger*.[15]

And yet Twain persisted with religion. He surrounded himself with Christians; his closest friends and family affirmed a robust faith. From his wife to Congregationalist minister Joseph Twichell to fellow writer William Dean Howells,[16] they all strongly influenced him, even if he felt less comfortable with God than they did. During his years in Hartford, Connecticut, Twain attended Twichell's church regularly and generously supported the ministry with charitable giving.[17] He even took to referring to himself as something of a lay preacher who used humor as his sermons.[18] If humor defined his sermons, the historical record of injustice was his pericope. And no one was immune from his altar calls, including God Himself whom he put in the dock, faulting Him for allowing His creatures to suffer.[19] But herein lies the dilemma that defined Twain's religious struggles: hope for rectifying clear injustice required something uncorrupted by those wrongs. Twain seemed able neither to relinquish his hope for a better world nor to embrace a God of perfect goodness who alone is capable of accomplishing that redemption.

Hoping against Hope

Twain's lesser-known *Pudd'nhead Wilson* showcases these central tensions that define his entire body of work. Here Twain used the story of children switched in infancy to depict the human toll of slavery and its long-lasting, seemingly intractable consequences persisting well past its eradication. The children themselves are innocent, of course, and the slave child's mother Roxy knows intimately the degradation of slavery and desires a better life for her son Chambers, making her choice to switch him with her master's child Tom eminently understandable. And yet her action dooms another to that same misery she wanted her son to avoid. The remainder of the novel's plot reveals both the need for rectification and the impossibility of the characters to effect it, at least not fully. There's always a gap between what needs to be done and what temporal beings alone can do. For example, Tom is ultimately restored to his "rightful" place, but the reader acutely feels the inadequacy of that restoration. In this way, Twain highlights the tenacious human desire for happiness and unwittingly gestures beyond this world for any actual hope of its fulfillment.

But is it wise to hope in a world filled with woe? While Twain was likely unsettled on that question, there is much to commend hope, as painful as it might be to live in the not-yet of its consummation. Without hope what can be said of those who suffer gratuitous evils? Perhaps, as Richard Creel has argued,[20] we are obligated to hope that there is a God who can redeem such suffering. Abandoning hope is tantamount to memorializing those victims as little more than emblems of life's tragic meaninglessness.[21] Perhaps on the other hand, the question is not about wisdom but practicality: can human beings even live without hope, if only a modified hope that life has some semblance of meaning and purpose? What else could enable creativity, motivate and sustain relationships, justify social advocacy? True enough, the pragmatic function of hope isn't necessarily evidence of its trustworthiness. Darwinianism, for example, offers an account of the persistent nature of hope as a necessity for the species' survival. Additionally, Sherwood Cummings offers a compelling case that Twain was, at the least, influenced by Darwin's theories.[22] But even a modicum of reflection on such an evolutionary mechanism reveals that a Darwinian explanation, conjoined with naturalism, erodes the very foundation it purports to offer, explaining hope away. On Christianity, we may well have a moral obligation to hope; on atheism, it is difficult to see how we even have permission. And yet, for Twain, hope for change, for justice, and for good to prevail remained.

However indulgent a cynical Twain may at times have been, however rife and riddled with darkness were some of his words uttered or written at his lowest moments, his better lights that resisted despair and found expression in his persistent satirical commentary on America and the world—acute reflections about its potential and pitfalls, triumphs and temptations—revealed a soaring hope at once audacious and obstinate. It found dogged expression and towering erudition in what Bush calls Twain's apocalyptic voice, which has resonated with readers ever since who likewise want desperately for all to be well.[23]

Is such hope mere wishful thinking signifying nothing, worthy of suppression, and bound to disappoint? Is a poignant recognition of human hearts and a world gone awry cause for unyielding despair, for the sober conviction that ultimately all is lost, pointless, or futile? Or, rather, is it a prelude and necessary prolegomenon to a message of good news and a hope that won't disappoint, of a God who is good—better than even Twain's capacious heart and fertile mind could imagine—a good God who loves us despite all of our unloveliness? Might hope, allied with faith and love, in fact be a particularly vivid example of what C. S. Lewis described as "a desire which no experience in this world can satisfy"—an inconsolable longing as engrained as it is beyond our autonomous grasp for a world redeemed, a divine prescription for an otherwise dismal diagnosis of a lethal malady?[24] If to despair is human, might it be that to hope is divine?

Part III: Love & Beauty

23

Love Potion No. 9 ¾

In the Muggle world people spend vast sums of money on perfumes, body sprays, cosmetics, jewelry, pheromones, body sculpting, skimpy clothing, gym memberships, tanning salons, diet programs, and other means of increasing physical attractiveness and stirring romantic interest. In the wizarding world of Harry Potter there are far more powerful and reliable attractants: magical love potions. Yet there are obvious ethical issues regarding the use of such potions, particularly the nonconsensual use, as occurs in two key episodes in Rowling's stories. So, what do magical love potions have to teach us about love, infatuation, and the ethical treatment of others? In particular, what can we learn from Merope Gaunt's use of a love potion to ensnare Tom Riddle Sr. (Voldemort's father), and her eventual decision to stop using the potion, at great cost to herself and her unborn son?

Violently Pink Products

Love potions not only make for fascinating thought experiments. They're also an important part of the Harry Potter plot. In *Chamber of Secrets*, Professor Lockhart at one point jokingly encourages the students at Hogwarts to ask Professor Snape how to whip up a love potion, and in *Prisoner of Azkaban*, Mrs. Weasley tells her daughter, Ginny, and Hermione Granger about a love potion she made as a young girl.

But in *Half-Blood Prince*, we find several significant references to love potions. The first happens in Diagon Alley, at Weasleys' Wizard Wheezes, Fred and George's magic shop:

> Near the window was an array of violently pink products around which a cluster of excited girls was giggling enthusiastically. Hermione and Ginny both hung back, looking wary.

There you go," said Fred proudly. "Best range of love potions you'll find anywhere."

Ginny raised an eyebrow skeptically. "Do they work?" she asked.

"Certainly they work, for up to twenty-four hours at a time depending on the weight of the boy in question. . ."

". . . and the attractiveness of the girl," said George, reappearing suddenly at their side.[1]

So, in Harry's world, love potions are legal, apparently work only on males (although this isn't explicitly stated), vary in potency depending on the weight of the boy and the attractiveness of the girl, and work for only a limited time without a fresh dose.

The next appearance of love potions comes at Hogwarts, in the newly installed Professor Slughorn's Potions classroom, where Hermione's showing her stuff:

"Now, this one here . . . yes, my dear?" said Slughorn, now looking slightly bemused, as Hermione's hand punched the air again.

"It's Amortentia!"

"It is indeed. It seems almost foolish to ask." said Slughorn, who was looking mightily impressed, "but l assume you know what it does?

"It's the most powerful love potion in the world," said Hermione.

"Quite right! You recognized it, I suppose, by its distinctive mother-of-pearl sheen?"

"And the steam rising in characteristic spirals," said Hermione enthusiastically, "and it's supposed to smell differently to each of us, according to what attracts us, and I can smell freshly mown grass and new parchment and—"

But she turned slightly pink and did not complete the sentence.[2]

On the next page, Slughorn reveals more about this love potion:

"Amortentia doesn't really create *love*, of course. It is impossible to manufacture or imitate love. No, this will simply cause a powerful infatuation or obsession. It is probably the most dangerous and powerful potion in this room—oh yes," he said, nodding gravely at Malfoy and Nott, both of whom were smirking skeptically. "When you have seen as much of life as I have, you will not underestimate the power of obsessive love."[3]

Later in *Half-Blood Prince*, we learn just how dangerous and powerful a love potion can be, when Ron unwittingly eats a box of Chocolate Cauldrons spiked with love potion and becomes madly infatuated with Romilda Vane. From that episode, we discover that love potions act almost instantaneously; that they cause obsessive thoughts, intense excitement, and violent emotions; that they can strengthen over time; and that they can be cured by means of a simple, antidote.

So, what kind of person would actually use a love potion? In our final snippet from *Half-Blood Prince*, we are introduced to one: Voldemort's mother.

Little Hangleton

Merope Gaunt, the local tramp's daughter, harbors a secret, burning passion for Tom Riddle, the wealthy squire's son. An unlikely pair, but Merope is a witch whose powers give her a chance to plot her escape from the desperate life she has led for eighteen years under the subjugation of her father and brother. "Can you not think of any measure Merope could have taken to make Tom Riddle forget his Muggle companion, and fall in love with her instead?"[4] Albus Dumbledore asks Harry. To which Harry offers two guesses: the Imperius Curse and a love potion.

The Imperius Curse, of course, is one of the three "unforgivable curses" in the magical world; it robs victims of their will and is, as a result, a prime example of how magic in Harry's world *can* but *must not* be used to manipulate and exploit others, especially the most vulnerable. Love potions, we've seen, aren't illegal in Harry's world. Perhaps they're not considered as dangerous as the Imperius Curse, because they don't last as long, produce only romantic feelings (as opposed to, say, homicidal intentions), and don't result in total control of the affected person. But it's instructive that Harry sees a particular effect and correctly narrows down the likely causes to either the Imperius Curse or a love potion, reminding us of Slughorn's sober warnings of the love potion's dangers.

After Harry's two guesses, Dumbledore continues,

> Very good. Personally, I am inclined to think that she used a love potion. I am sure it would have seemed more romantic to her, and I do not think it would have been very difficult, some hot day,

when Riddle was riding alone, to persuade him to take a drink of water. In any case, within a few months the village of Little Hangleton enjoyed a tremendous scandal. You can imagine the gossip it caused when the squire's son ran off with the tramp's daughter, Merope.[5]

Dumbledore continues by engaging in some guesswork:

You see, within a few months of their runaway marriage, Tom Riddle reappeared at the manor house in Little Hangleton without his wife. The rumor flew around the neighborhood that he was talking of being "hoodwinked" and "taken in." What he meant, I am sure, is that he had been under an enchantment that had now lifted, though I daresay he did not dare use those precise words for fear of being thought insane.[6]

After Harry asks why the love potion stopped working. Dumbledore adds,

Again, this is guesswork . . . but I believe that Merope, who was deeply in love with her husband, could not bear to continue enslaving him by magical means. I believe that she made the choice to stop giving him the potion. Perhaps, besotted as she was, she had convinced herself that he would by now have fallen in love with her in return. Perhaps she thought he would stay for the baby's sake. If so, she was wrong on both counts. He left her, never saw her again, and never troubled to discover what became of his son.[7]

Harry then asks again whether it's important to know all of this about Voldemort's past, to which Dumbledore replies, "Very important, I think," and "It has everything to do with the prophecy." What does this love potion narrative add to the story, and what might it have to do with the prophecy about Harry's defeat of Voldemort?[8]

Real Love or Mere Infatuation?

So, here's a question: Did Merope Gaunt, Voldemort's mother, love Tom Riddle Sr.? She was certainly infatuated with him, attracted to him, willing to go to extraordinary lengths to have him. But did she love him?

Dumbledore says she did, but another possible answer is no, and here's the case for it: She didn't love him, or at least she didn't love him very deeply, exactly because she was willing to use a love potion on him. Presumably, a love potion, after all, robs a person of his free will. This is what makes love pills or potions an ideal thought experiment to elicit the recognition that real freedom requires more than doing what we want to do. Doing what we want to do may be necessary for freedom, but it's not sufficient. We must also have the freedom to do otherwise. Tom lacked such "libertarian" freedom.

Some philosophers, including Harry Frankfurt, deny that the ability to do otherwise is necessary for genuine freedom. This view especially appeals to those who think that everything we do is strictly determined by the laws of the physical universe or by the sovereign plan of God. They typically accept compatibilism: the idea that free will is consistent with strict determination of all of our actions and choices. Yet even compatibilists will likely deny that Tom Riddle Sr. freely loved Merope. Why? Because even if Tom were doing what he wanted by loving her, he wouldn't have wanted to love her as a result of a magical inducement.

How much could Merope have loved Tom if giving him the potion deprived him of his freedom? It wasn't that she loved him too much; she didn't love him enough, if at all. It was selfish of her. She wanted what was in her interests, not his. She may have felt amorous affection or entertained an unhealthy obsession for him, but clearly she did not feel the deep love that respects the true interests and considered preferences of the beloved.

Not only did she take away Riddle's freedom, enslaving him by the potion, she robbed him of the chance to the "relationship," and we use that term loosely, for although love can be one-way, relationships by their nature are not. Merope didn't create a relationship that provided a context for Riddle to remain committed despite fluctuating feelings to grow more in love as time goes on, to attain love's deeper reaches after the physical attraction and the initial excitement fade, or to become a better person as the rough edges of his personality get smoothed out in the mutual self-giving of a real and reciprocal loving relationship. No, she subjected him to magic that coerced his will into becoming obsessed with her. She could have treated him like dirt after that, and still he'd go on stupidly relishing and accepting whatever she dealt him, for that's the nature of the potion. This is surely a situation that invites abuse, hardly a paradigm of love.

Incidentally, this shows us what's wrong with using a love potion even on oneself to develop feelings for another, a person we perhaps deem worthy of loving. We're inclined to think it at least not as bad to use a potion on oneself as it is to administer it to another person, because the issue of free will doesn't arise in the same way. By choosing to take the potion, our free will is intact. This isn't obviously correct, but suppose we grant it. Still, there's the other issue of becoming a certain kind of person. Think how easy it would be to take the potion—rather than working hard in the relationship to remain committed despite challenges and to grow as a person through relational hardships. With all of the challenges removed, we would lose terrific opportunities to become better persons through the relationship.[9]

Not His Mother's Son

We could imagine that sort of story for Merope, and it's the direction we originally anticipated this chapter to go. It's no shock that a character so thoroughly evil and despicable as Voldemort would hail from such troubled beginnings. It's not a stretch that a man who never loved would have come from a loveless union generated and sustained by magic alone. Nor would it be surprising that a character who from his earliest years harbored such fondness for cruelty and domination would have a mother willing to coerce the will of her mate and a father who would so callously neglect his child after the enchantment lifted.

This view of Merope and Voldemort seems to make a good deal of sense. Its only drawback, so far as we can see, is that it's wrong. Especially where Merope is concerned, the contrast between her and Voldemort is far more important than the comparison. Voldemort's problem is not that he's his mother's son, which in many ways he isn't. No, the problem is that Voldemort is more like his grandfather Marvolo Gaunt and his ancestor Salazar Slytherin. The point in excluding Merope from the list is that she illustrates how, in Harry's world, choices—not innate talent or biological ancestry or magical pedigree—most shape characters and destinies.

Merope is a character who ought to elicit from us compassion and no small amount of respect. What she did to win Riddle was wrong, and radically so, but good people sometimes do bad things. It's not the occasional misdeed that defines us but the habitual practice, the settled character, the persistent pattern of choices that put us on our life's trajectory. We are what we consistently do, as Aristotle put it. Her action was wrong, yes, but we're not convinced she was very bad at all. To the contrary, she shows a remarkable character, all the more so in the face of all the obstacles she had to overcome and the temptations she had to resist. What matters is not merely where she ended up, but also the distance she had to travel to get there.

What matters is the ultimate trajectory her life took and not merely the projected track of her worst decisions. Unfortunately, Voldemort, if anything, ended up following in the footsteps of where his mother was headed until she came to her senses. Whereas she eventually stopped going in the direction of the dark side, he embraced it wholeheartedly. The blood of Slytherin coursed through each of them, but their lives went in diametrically opposite directions. If nothing else, this illustrates, once more, the primacy of choice in Harry's world.

Critics have sometimes complained about the shortage of redeemed characters in the *Potter* books, but Merope is a prime example of one: a character whose background was as tragic as anyone's, whose capacity for misusing magic was as great as anyone's, whose temptations to engage in the Dark Arts were as strong as anyone's, yet whose life showed that not even a person like that is destined for darkness. And if even she wasn't, then Voldemort wasn't, for his upbringing was no more tragic than hers. If his destiny ended up beyond redemption, it was because his own choices, over time, forged a mutilated character from which there was no escape. Character may be destiny, but this makes more sense and is more just if character is the culmination of a truly free set of choices, rather than the inevitable outcome of "blood" or fate. This possibility of true freedom, of goods potentially but needlessly lost, imbues the *Potter* books with an element of tragedy that's often a feature of great literature.

Consider again Merope's tragic home life: physical, verbal, and emotional abuse; a condition of virtual domestic slavery: an absence of love and affirmation; an abundance of violence and meanness. None of this makes her ensnarement of Riddle right, but—and this is part of Rowling's nuanced moral analysis—it ought to soften our critical judgment of Merope, especially since, of her own volition, she eventually gave up using the potion. At the risk of losing the love of her life, her unborn child's father, and perhaps the first happiness she ever experienced, at the risk of rejection and terrible pain, pain that did in fact practically kill her with a broken heart—she did the right thing, choosing character over power, reality over appearance, forgiveness over resentment. And she chose love over hate, letting Riddle leave because that was his choice, despite her continued love for him, indeed, because of her love for him. And despite Riddle's abandonment of her, she still named her son after him, so gracious was her character, which reminds us of Dumbledore's eventual gracious response to Muggles, despite their cruel and devastating mistreatment of his sister. Voldemort, in contrast, chose to exact revenge for his father's abandonment by killing both his father and his grandparents and by rejecting his Muggle name and heritage.

The contemporary philosopher William Hasker offers an analysis of freedom quite relevant to Merope's predicament:

> All sorts of experiences and relationships acquire a special value because they involve love, trust, and affection that are freely bestowed. The love potions that appear in many fairy stories [and in the *Harry Potter* series] can become a trap; the one who has used the potion finds that he wants to be loved for his own sake and not because of the potion, yet fears the loss of the beloved's affection if the potion is no longer used.[10]

Merope came to a crossroads in her short, tragic life: through magic she could continue to manipulate Riddle, or she could stop, though at great personal cost. Merope did the right thing. She gave up using her magical powers altogether after Riddle left her, refusing to use them even to save her own life. It might have been grief that led to the loss of her powers, but Dumbledore is virtually certain that instead, she no longer wanted to be a witch. Perhaps she saw its potential for abuse, especially within herself, and she refused to indulge it anymore. She may have recognized within herself the call to the dark side, as it were, and realized that the best way to avoid it was by renouncing magic altogether, never again subjecting another to the sort of tyranny that she herself had been subjected to by her family. She had experienced firsthand what that led to and no longer wanted any part of it.

Certain behavior can skip a generation. The child of an alcoholic not uncommonly sees the ugliness of the addiction and reacts against it, perhaps by becoming a rigid teetotaler, and then his children react against that, and the pattern recurs. Merope so reacted against magic and its abuses and retained such potential for love that she was willing to suffer and be vulnerable. Exhibiting what Voldemort could only think of as weakness, she was willing to fall prey to what he considered the worst thing of all: death. Merope chose the death of her body, rather than the death of her character and her own pain before the domination of another. Her love for Riddle had made her vulnerable to hurt and rejection, as all love does, and her aversion to hurting others the way she herself had been hurt contributed to her premature death. Not surprisingly, given her horrible upbringing, she lacked some of the good qualities that Harry's mother had. But nonetheless, Merope did all that she could to battle the forces of unforgiving fate to break free from the pattern of magical manipulation and coercion.[11]

In this sense, Voldemort is radically unlike his mother, who, despite her tragic history, still retained tenderness of heart and the capacity for love, whereas Voldemort never loved another, never even had a genuine friend or wanted one. And this wasn't because of his tragic beginnings and certainly not because of his mother's moral failing but, among other reasons, because he rejected the pain, vulnerability, and weakness that caring for another as much as for himself inevitably involves. He wanted to be untouchable, and he got his wish, losing his very humanity in the process.

Remember that Dumbledore said that he wasn't as concerned about the young Voldemort's ability to speak to snakes as he was about his obvious instincts for cruelty, secrecy, and domination. Voldemort's abilities didn't define him; his choices did, and sowing his choices reaped a character and a destiny of darkness.[12] He might have chosen not to love in order to avoid dependency or weakness, but his habitual unwillingness to open his heart to another led to the loss of his capacity to do it altogether.[13] What we see in Voldemort is a picture of where the definitive choice of evil and the rejection of love lead: a character in love only with himself but who ends up harming and fragmenting himself in irremediable ways.

Tragically, Voldemort learned from the worst his mother did, rather than from the best, hating what he should have loved, and imitating with reckless abandon what she herself rejected. All of this, of course, only bolsters the contrast between Voldemort and Harry. So much of what distinguishes Harry from Voldemort is that Harry, despite his troubled past and tragic life, never loses his ability to love. He doesn't harden his heart and start to care only about himself. He doesn't cut himself off from others. Far more than Voldemort, he remains his mother's son—the mother whose courage and sacrificial love keep Harry safe from the worst Voldemort can dish out.[14] Her love unleashes a more ancient and powerful magic than any potion can hope to imitate or Voldemort can hope to defeat or even understand.

24

Intuiting the Beauty of the Infinite: Ramanujan and Hardy's Partnership

The *Man Who Knew Infinity*, a 2016 movie based on a book of the same name by Robert Kanigel, recounts the short but remarkable life story of India's great mathematical prodigy Srivivasa Ramanujan. Although what follows is a response to the film, the book is well-worth reading, filled with luscious prose such as in this sample: "The Cauvery was a familiar, recurrent constant of Ramanujan's life. At some places along its length, palm trees, their trunks heavy with fruit, leaned over the river at rakish angles. At others, leafy trees formed a canopy of green over it, their gnarled, knotted roots snaking along the riverbank."

The movie begins by quoting the notable atheist thinker Bertrand Russell (a character in the movie itself): "Mathematics, rightly viewed, possesses not only truth but supreme beauty." It then shows Ramanujan in India, doing his mathematics (without much formal training) while trying to eke out a living for his family. His passion and talent for math are obvious; trying to describe maths (the preferred British abbreviation) to his wife, he says it's like a painting, but with colors you can't see. There are patterns everywhere in mathematics, he adds, revealed in the most incredible forms. Finding himself in need of someone who could understand and appreciate his ground-breaking work, Ramanujan wrote G. H. Hardy, legendary professor at Cambridge, and eventually Hardy invited Ramanujan to traverse the ocean and come work with him there.

This incredible opportunity required Ramanujan to leave his wife behind and endure the long journey and culture shock of moving to England, which contributes to a compelling narrative, with many twists and turns we're not discussing but that make for a terrific, sometimes heart-wrenching tale. Despite the trials and challenges (including a war), what's amazing was how much work Ramanujan and Hardy were able to do over the next five years—publishing dozens of groundbreaking articles.

The divergent worldviews of the two men make the dynamics of their friendship particularly fascinating to chronicle. Ramanujan was a devout Hindu whereas Hardy was a committed atheist—though the first time Hardy says this to Ramanujan in the movie ("I'm what's called an 'atheist'"), he replies, "You believe in God. You just don't think he likes you." Incidentally, this is a key structuring question in C. S. Lewis's moving novel *Till We Have Faces*: whereas both Psyche and Orual believe in the gods, Psyche believed they were marvelous and loving, but Orual thought they were only dark, unkind, and mysterious. In Rudolph Otto's terminology, Orual was familiar with the *tremendum* aspect of the Numinous, but Psyche with both the *tremendum* (the awe-inspiring mystery) and the *fascinans* aspect of the Numinous. *Fascinans* is the aspect of the Divine involving consuming attraction, rapturous longing—and is often connected to the imagination, beauty, even poetry.[1]

The diametric difference in Ramanujan's and Hardy's ultimate worldviews proves to be related to a central aspect of the plot. Hardy is adamant about the need to show step-by-step proofs of Ramanujan's conclusions, while Ramanujan is depicted as functioning on a much more intuitive level. We're not concerned for now what artistic liberties the moviemakers might have taken in this regard, but it is true that Ramanujan would often write down the conclusions of his work and not all the intervening steps. There may be at least a partial explanation of this which is fairly prosaic: paper tended to be in short supply for Ramanujan in India. But it's at least intriguing to consider the explanation advanced in the movie: Ramanujan possessed incredibly strong intuitive skills. Mystifying Hardy, Ramanujan could just see things that few others could and felt little need to offer the proofs.

Hardy—though incredibly impressed with Ramanujan's abilities, likening him to an artist like Mozart, who could write a whole symphony in his head—repeatedly says that intuition is not enough. Intuition must be "held accountable." Proofs mattered, to avoid projecting the appearance of Ramanujan's mathematical dance or art as on a par with conjuring. It isn't that Ramanujan's intuitions were infallible. His theory of primes, however intuitively obvious, turned out to be wrong. Still, though, many of his intuitions were eventually vindicated and proved right. One among other interesting questions that Ramanujan's reliance on intuitions raises is how much discursive analysis they involve. It's a vexed question among epistemologists whether intuitions are a lightning quick series of inferences, or something more immediately and directly apprehended. The quickness with which they come naturally lends itself to the latter analysis, but perhaps there's something to the former option—particularly if much of the analysis is done beneath the level of conscious awareness. In the Sherlock Holmes stories, for example, Sherlock's inferences would come so quickly that Watson characterized them as resembling intuitions; likewise, realizing it's sometimes easier to know something than to explain the justification for it, Sherlock himself recognized the way knowledge can have features that resemble more immediate apprehendings than just the deliverances of the discursive intellect. A couple of real-life Sherlocks, Al Plantinga and Phil Quinn had a dust up some years back on whether basic beliefs are formed inferentially or not.

The difference in Hardy's and Ramanujan's styles, we come to see, is related to their divergent worldviews. Exasperated at Hardy's recurring disparagement of intuition as lacking in substance, Ramanujan finally blurts out, "You say this word as if it is nothing. Is that all it is to you? All that I am? You've never even seen me. You are a man of no faith. . . . Who are you, Mr. Hardy?" The underlying dynamic that brought this exchange to a head was the way Ramanujan connected his own identity to those intuitions. Hardy had asked Ramanujan before how he got his ideas. Now Ramanujan gives his answer: "By my god. She speaks to me, puts formulas on my tongue when I sleep, sometimes when I pray." Ramanujan asks Hardy if he believes him, and adds, "Because if you are my friend, you will know that I am telling you the truth. If you are truly my friend."

In *Till We Have Faces*, we find a similar scene. Orual can't see the gold-and-amber castle that Psyche tells her of, but Orual also knows that Psyche had never told her a lie. One issue here is testimony, and the conditions that need to be in place to take it as reliable. Of course someone could be telling the truth, the best they understand it, and still be unreliable—for perhaps they've unwittingly made a mistake, or they're delusional or confused.

At any rate, Hardy's reply is transparent: "But I don't believe in God. I don't believe in anything I can't prove." "Then you don't believe in me," Ramanujan responded. "Now do you see? An equation has no meaning to me unless it expresses the thought of God."

Hardy remained skeptical of Ramanujan's theology, but couldn't dispute with the results. He would go to bat for Ramanujan to get him a fellowship at Cambridge, and in his impassioned defense of Ramanujan's accomplishments he extolled his incredible originality, by which Ramanujan could apprehend so much truth otherwise missed. On Hardy's view, the creativity and originality, though they provided Ramanujan a lens through which to see, didn't subjectivize Ramanujan's findings; rather, they were a tool for seeing farther and seeing more.

This contrasts with, say, Simon Critchley's interpretation of the poetry of Wallace Stevens. On Stevens's view according to Critchley, the only reality we experience is mediated through categories furnished by the poetic imagination, rendering our perspectives products of the imagination and, thus, subjective—yet still able to be believed despite their fictive nature. This is what some might call a more "postmodern" perspective than Hardy's more traditional view that there's an objective reality we're able to discern, however imperfectly and through a glass darkly.

In real life, when Hardy died, one mourner captured the mathematician's sensibilities this way:

> [He had a] profound conviction that the truths of mathematics described a bright and clear universe, exquisite and beautiful in its structure, in comparison with which the physical world was turbid and confused. It was this which made his friends . . . think that in his attitude to mathematics there was something which, being essentially spiritual, was near to religion.[2]

Hardy didn't believe in God, but he did believe in Ramanujan and in the objectivity of mathematical truth. He wrote of his Platonism in his *Mathematician's Apology*, and the movie captures this too. In one of his defenses of Ramanujan in the film, he related the story of the way Ramanujan said mathematical truths are thoughts of God—a view parallel to, say, Plantinga's view that modal and necessary moral truths are also thoughts in the mind of God. Then Hardy added:

> Despite everything in my being set to the contrary, perhaps he's right. For isn't this exactly our justification for pure mathematics? We are merely the explorers of infinity in the pursuit of absolute perfection. We do not invent these formulae—they already exist and lie in wait for only the brightest minds to divine and prove. In the end, who are we to question Ramanujan—let alone God?

Though math, on Hardy's view, is discovered, not invented, it may take those with prodigious talents to uncover its deepest truths. Speaking of which, near the start of the film Hardy had said, "I didn't invent Ramanujan. I discovered him." Even more than the math, this is a movie about men and their remarkable friendship and fertile partnership across radically divergent and conflicting paradigms. The humanity of the film is its best feature of all.

After five years of collaboration between these unlikely friends, Ramanujan returned to India, having contracted a fatal disease—likely tuberculosis. Within a year he died, at the age of just 32. Hardy was crestfallen when he heard the news, and grieved the loss deeply. Near the end of the movie, he reflected on his collaboration with both Ramanujan and another colleague, Littlewood, saying he'd done something special indeed: "I have collaborated with both Littlewood and Ramanujan on something like equal terms."

Paraphrasing Hardy, he once commented that out of 100 points, he would give himself 30 as a mathematician, 45 to Littlewood, 70 to Hilbert. And 100 to Ramanujan. In the year Ramanujan spent in India before his death, he poured his brilliant findings into another notebook. It was lost for a while, but when found, the importance of its discovery was likened to that of Beethoven's "10th Symphony." A century later, these formulas are being used to understand the behavior of black holes.

25

J. K. Rowling: In Praise of Imagination

Scribblers in the 2014 blogosphere were abuzz with talk of *Harry Potter* author J. K. Rowling's most recent revelation. Hold on to your broomsticks: in what she admits likely qualifies as apostasy and a clear departure from the canon, she laments pairing Ron Weasley and Hermione Granger! The polyjuice-potioned *Daily Prophet* (devilishly resembling the internet) leaked portions of a new interview with the popular author,[1] setting in motion all manner of bubbling-cauldron heads, whose collective commentary rivaled the blast of a Howler.

Faster than a Knight Bus, more efficient than the Sorting Hat, Rowling's heretical disclosure transformed garden-variety Muggles into rabid partisans: "Ron's a dork!" "Ron's loyal, funny, and a good friend!" "Harry's perfect for Hermione!" "Harry's a brat!" "Did Dumbledore really wear so suspiciously floral a bonnet?" (Oh wait, that was a different debate.[2])

Before this animated dialogue took on Twilight-esque proportions, release of the full interview provided context. Charming and disarming, Rowling's interview with Emma Watson (who plays Hermione in the films) taps into all there is to love about the literary phenomenon of the Potter series: the realistic, likeable characters, the fully-developed fantastical world, the author's almost maternal concern for her characters and fans, the portrayal of friendship and love and courage and sacrifice, and the universal relevance of the central coming-of-age story.

The interview served as a time turner, taking us back and reminding us of how special the *Potter* series was, how exciting it was for this generation to watch it all unfold. It wasn't anything like the best literature ever, but so what? And it was certainly better than plenty. The series was able to cast its spell by drawing us in and engaging our imagination on a scale much broader than the question of who got the girl. The books have their share of romances, awkward first dates, and even misguided, manipulative flirtations with love potions, but these are seamlessly woven into the much broader mosaic of an unforgettable world carefully and exquisitely wrought by Rowling. Trips to Hogsmeade, a revolving cast of Defense against the Dark Arts teachers, the whomping willow, Quidditch, Ollivanders, the Forbidden Forest, flying cars, Platform 9¾, Gringotts Wizarding Bank, butter beer, house elves, chocolate frogs, invisibility cloaks: all of these and more create a rich world emanating from Rowling's lush imagination—a world many of us loved to visit, and may again, and should do so without guilt.

Christians are called to serious business, it's true, but God wants human beings to delight in him and his world. In "Words of Delight" (an essay collected in *The Christian Imagination*) Leland Ryken builds a case for the pure enjoyment of literature for its own sake. Drawing on Ecclesiastes 12:9-10 that declares the Preacher's desire to use "words of delight" in communicating truth, Ryken argues that "[l]iterary style and technique call attention to themselves and are experienced as something gratuitous, going beyond the functional needs of communication, possessing a refreshment or entertaining value that is self-rewarding." Sometimes things aren't just delightful because they delight, but delight us because they're delightful.

Such is the case with Rowling's series, and through delightful engagement with it, readers are pointed to the ultimate reality, as C. S. Lewis explains in Chapter 13 of *The Screwtape Letters*. Through the voice of Screwtape, Lewis argues that simple pleasure in reading can draw people to God because "[t]he deepest likings and impulses of any man are the raw material, the starting-point" that gets people in touch with reality and directs them toward a homecoming, toward self-recovery—because, as Screwtape acknowledges, that pleasure is "unmistakably real."

Pleasure and truth, enjoyment and substance, work and play, need not be at odds. If the good, the true, and the beautiful ultimately cohere and form an integrated whole—and they do if the Christian story is true—then that which charms and enchants us, mesmerizes our attention, enthralls and delights us, may well do so because contained within it are seeds of truth. The big narrative of which we're a part as Christians is that we serve a God at work redeeming the entirety of the created order—not just atomized selves. So whenever anything captures the imagination of a generation on so grand a scale as *Harry Potter* did, Christians have an opportunity. They can lament and cast aspersions, dismiss as frivolous, or they can be intentional to look for signals of transcendence and intimations of truth. Rowling's work contains plenty. We live in a world infused with hints of the redemptive all around us, and we shouldn't miss the opportunity to point them out. This includes valuing stories like Rowling's that, however imperfectly, point us to The Story.

26

Rats in God's Laboratory: *Shadowlands* and the Problem of Evil

Love is something more than an accident that bubbled to the surface of the human condition, a fortuitous experience or fuzzy feeling deriving from a particular collocation of atoms. It's the wild truth, the essence of what is ultimately real and what we as human beings were designed for. Love is the end towards which we rightly strive. Without love, life is an emaciated caricature of its true potential. Love on such a view goes all the way down to the core of reality. It's truly what life's meaning is all about.

Loving relationships—both earthly and divine—do however require a willingness to suffer. Grasping this truth may help us to cope with various aspects of suffering caused by these relationships. Richard Attenborough's beautiful 1994 film *Shadowlands* (based on a stage play written by William Nicholson) powerfully depicts such a hard lesson, learned in the context of an unlikely and moving love story between an Oxford don, C. S. (Jack) Lewis (played by acclaimed actor Anthony Hopkins, who won a British academy award for his performance), and an American poet, Joy Gresham (played by Debra Winger).

Jack at Oxford

The opening scenes of *Shadowlands* showcase the complexity of C. S. Lewis. His colleague and fellow Inkling J. R. R. Tolkien once said of Lewis that we'll never get to the bottom of him. In the classrooms of the hauntingly beautiful Magdalen College at Oxford, Lewis exemplifies the erudite professor of English literature. In an early scene from the movie, we see Professor Lewis closing the window to his classroom and reading to his students about a garden and a fountain. In the midst of this garden grows one perfect rosebud, which he says is an image. But an image of what? The ensuing discussion makes clear that the rosebud is an image of courtly love, which prompts Lewis to ask his students, "What is love's one essential quality?" One student tentatively begins, "Un. . ." The professor interrupts his student, "Unattainability. The most intense joy lies not in the having, but in the desiring. The light that never fades the bliss that is eternal, is only yours when what you most desire is just out of reach."

In the classroom, Lewis projects a persona that is polished, aloof, and dispassionate. At high table with his colleagues, or in the local pub, he can be found discussing his popular children's novels, which show him to be an expert storyteller with a rich and deep imagination. Beyond a teacher, scholar, and author of beloved children's novels, Lewis is also a popular religious speaker and writer. *Shadowlands* includes excerpts from some of his more famous talks given to Christian laypeople, most of which are addressed to what philosophers call the Problem of Evil. Perhaps the most succinct articulation of the Problem of Evil is to be found in the writings of the Scottish philosopher and skeptic, David Hume: "Is he [God] willing to prevent evil, but not able? Then is he impotent. Is he able, but not willing? Then is he malevolent. Is he both able and willing? Whence then is evil?"

Lewis himself had suffered in his own life. As a young boy, he lost his mother to cancer. Despite his prayers for her healing, she died. This unanswered prayer was likely one of the contributors to his atheism, which persisted for several years before he eventually reclaimed his faith later in his life. Attenborough takes some liberties to characterize Lewis's aloofness as a result of this early traumatic loss. Having gone through the painful childhood ordeal of losing his mother, the film suggests, he constructed a wall around his heart to prevent further hurt. Whether or not this is true of the real-life Lewis, such barriers likely serve to block intimacy and rob us of the best that life has to offer. For the meaning of life is bound up in loving relationships, which require an accessible heart and a willingness to be vulnerable, and this inevitably will involve pain and suffering.

A Megaphone to Rouse a Deaf World

The Problem of Evil is very hard to resolve. For believers, or theists, it presents what is probably the biggest obstacle in the way of religious faith. A scene from *Shadowlands* includes the following snippet from Lewis's popular talks on religious questions, in which we can catch a glimpse of the sort of answer he provides. Referring to a tragic loss of life that had taken place not long before the talk was delivered, Lewis asks where God was on the night that it happened? "Why didn't he stop it? Doesn't he love us?" He continues, "I'm not particularly sure God wants us to be happy. He wants us to be able to love and be loved. He wants us to grow up. It's because God loves us that he makes us the gift of suffering. To put it another way, pain is God's megaphone to rouse a deaf world."

Lewis then likens us to blocks of stone, and God to the sculptor who carves the forms of men: "The blows of his chisel which hurt us so much are what make us perfect." In a later talk containing similar reflections, he continues, "We think our childish toys bring us all the happiness there is, and our nursery is the whole wide world." Then, unwittingly anticipating events to come, he adds, "But something must drive us out of the nursery into the world of others. And that something is suffering." A moment's reflection on Lewis's words reveals that such sentiments do little to really solve the Problem of Evil. In fairness to Lewis, this smattering of insights does little to exhaust his writings and reflections on this philosophical topic. In real life, Lewis wrote an entire book devoted to this topic, *The Problem of Pain*. Such memorable phrases as "megaphone to rouse a deaf world," and images of pain planting "the flag of truth within a rebel fortress" come from this famous book. Here, Lewis avails himself of perhaps the two most important resources that are at the theist's disposal in contending with the Problem of Evil. The first is human freedom, which accounts for those evils that are inflicted at the hands of other persons (what philosophers call "moral evil"). The second resource has to do with what philosophers call "natural evil": in an imperfect world—one that is littered with cancer, earthquakes, and heartache—pain seems required for us to develop both morally and spiritually.

Shadowlands highlights just one aspect of Lewis's thoughts on these matters: Why bother to love at all when losing loved ones hurts so much? Instead of providing a comprehensive catalogue of Lewis's insights, the movie highlights the difference between Lewis's theoretical reflections on the Problem of Evil, or what we might think of as "book knowledge" on the one hand, and his personal contentions with it, or "experiential knowledge, on the other hand. Philosophers sometimes make a similar sort of distinction between knowledge about something or someone on the one hand, versus actually knowing that thing or person on the other. Someone may know all about you—

your gender, profession, marital status, hobbies, and interests—without knowing you. Likewise, thinking about pain and suffering is not the same as experiencing it in one's own life.

Shadowlands depicts Lewis, having lost his mother, as carefully guarding his heart to prevent further hurt, while at the same time engaging in academic reflections about pain and suffering. In Lewis's preface to *The Problem of Pain*, he admits that his treatment of the subject matter is more about the intellectual, or theoretical, aspect of the Problem of Evil than it is about the personal or experiential variant. Philosophers carefully distinguish between the theoretical, and personal (or pastoral), Problem of Evil. Most philosophers confine their attention primarily to the former. But the difficulty with this sort of approach towards this particular problem is that it threatens to ignore the fact that evil is typically felt in sometimes brutal experiences of an intensely personal nature. Merely reflecting on the fact that thousands of children die each year of cancer will typically not tug at our heart strings, but watching our own child die of the same disease is unbearable. Joy Gresham will provide that personal struggle with suffering that would bring Lewis out of his self-imposed shell and invest his life with new meaning.

Joy

Shadowlands portrays Lewis's tranquil and settled life interrupted by the outspoken, and occasionally brusque, Gresham. When we meet Joy, she has just come out of a marriage, and has been corresponding with Lewis after having read several of his books. In real life, Joy had two sons, but the movie casts her as having only one son who is around the age of Lewis when he had lost his own mother. After cultivating a friendship with her, Lewis agrees to marry Joy in order to extend his British citizenship to her so she can remain in England. The marriage is strictly a formal affair, and both go on living separate lives just as they had before they ever met.

Lewis's willingness to marry Joy covertly, concealing it from even his best friends, suggests some sense in which Lewis is emotionally inaccessible. But Joy had already begun chipping away at Lewis's heart, preparing him to see an element of authenticity in her emotional life that was lacking in his. Joy touches an emotional and experiential chord in Lewis that had been silent for too long.

Early in their relationship, Joy claims that personal experience is everything. Lewis replies by asking if reading is thus a waste of time.

"No, it's not a waste of time," she answers, "but it's safe, isn't it? Books aren't about to hurt you." To this, Lewis responds that just because something hurts doesn't make it truer or more significant. This interesting exchange between Jack and Joy demonstrates something important about the nature of their relationship. Although she is attracted to Jack's intellect, Joy is equally captivated by his emotional struggles. This brief dialogue also shows that Lewis has retreated into the world of books and ideas, closing himself off to emotions and personal experience. In a pivotal scene that shortly follows this exchange, Joy sees this troubling aspect of the life that Lewis had arranged for himself. She accuses him of surrounding himself with those who are weaker, younger, or under his control. Neither the brother with whom he lives, nor his gang of friends with whom he associates, challenge him. They point him in the direction of doubt and fear, not hope or love. Nobody can touch him. Nobody can penetrate the walls he had constructed around his heart, not even Joy. Her willingness to confront him on this issue does eventually have some impact, and offers a refreshing challenge to his settled and studious life.

Rats in God's Laboratory

What happens next is summed up by Lewis in another of his religious talks.

> Yesterday, a friend of mine—a very brave, good woman—collapsed in terrible pain. One minute she was fit and well, the next minute she was in agony. She's now in the hospital and this morning I was told she's suffering from cancer. Why? See, if you love don't want them to suffer. You can't bear it. You want to take their suffering onto yourself. If even *I* feel like that, why doesn't *God*?

The Problem of Evil comes home once again to Jack, now an adult, in an intensely personal way. Joy's prognosis looks bleak. At the very same time, Lewis is developing feelings for his wife. In a truly touching scene, Lewis apprehends the extent of his affections, "How could Joy be my wife? I would have to love her more than anyone else in this world. I would have to be suffering the torments of the damned at the prospect of losing her." As tears roll down his cheeks, Lewis finally recognizes the depth of his love for Joy, and the height of the barriers that he had erected around his heart. Lewis decides to marry Joy, but this time before God and the world. As a boy he had reacted to pain by guarding himself from further hurt. As a man, he opens his heart to Joy and allows himself to become vulnerable.

Treatments follow. Prayers are offered. And signs of hope appear. Joy's cancer goes into remission, and she's allowed to return home, where she and Jack enjoy a season of blissful married life. But in time the cancer returns, and the end draws near. At her deathbed Lewis movingly confides to his wife that she is the truest person he has ever known, and that he never knew he could be so happy as she had made him.

When Joy dies, Lewis plunges into despair, and his faith in God is shaken to its very foundations. Realizing that he may never see her again, unable to remember her face, terrified suffering is just suffering after all, Lewis seethes in angry resentment. Finding the consolations of faith empty, he becomes convinced that it is all a bloody awful mess, nothing more. "I've just come up against a bit of experience, Warnie," he confides to his brother (played by Edward Hard). "Experience is a brutal teacher. But you learn. My God, you learn!" A friend tries to comfort Lewis by reminding him that we see so little here, and only God knows why these things happen. Lewis replies, "God knows, but does God care? . . . No, we're the creatures, aren't we? We're the rats in the cosmic laboratory. I have no doubt that the experiment is for our own good, but it still makes God the vivisectionist, doesn't it?

Notice that Lewis does not lose his faith. Instead, he offers a poignant example of a person of faith who is wrestling with the anguish of unanswered prayer. And when we think about it, we realize that it is only the religious believers who really *have* to struggle with this problem. Atheists can and do struggle with pain and suffering, but to whom can they complain? For why should it be any different? The believer, though, faces the full brunt of the challenge. The believer can either renounce her faith altogether, or try to come to terms with the existential struggle and inevitable cognitive dissonance that comes from trying to make sense of such seemingly needless suffering in a world that was created by a loving God. For her the question of why God allows such evil to persist is almost insuperable. The possibility that there is an ultimate answer to the Problem of Evil of which we are currently ignorant makes it all the harder to swallow.

For Lewis, rejecting belief in God is simply not an option. Both his intellect and his imagination point to theism. Another option would be to reject the traditional understanding of God's nature. If God is not wholly powerful (omnipotent) or wholly good (omni-benevolent), then there is no Problem of Evil, for he just might not have the power or will to do other than create an imperfect world with imperfect creatures. Harold Kushner, in his book *Why Bad Things Happen to Good People*, questions God's omnipotence, claiming that there are simply some things that God can't do, like heal certain diseases. Kushner claims that he'd rather believe in a less-than-all-powerful God than one who is so cruel as to allow children to suffer and die for some exalted purpose. Although Lewis doesn't go that route, he is tempted by the possibility that God is not, after all, good, or if God is good, his goodness is so beyond our comprehension as humans that we do not even recognize it as such. Lewis becomes haunted by images of God as divine vivisectionist or cosmic sadist.

Suffering Over Safety

In one of the last scenes of *Shadowlands*, Lewis finds Douglas, Joy's son (played by Joseph Mazzello), and talks with him about his mother's recent death. Not knowing what to say to the young boy, Lewis had avoided saying anything. "Jack," Douglas eventually asks, "Do you believe in heaven?" After only a moment's pause, Lewis answers, "Yes, I do."

> "I don't believe in heaven," Douglas replies.
> "That's okay." Jack assures him.
> "I sure would like to see her again," Douglas utters.

Then, as he begins to weep, Jack answers brokenly, "Me too," and envelops the boy with his arms. This event is pivotal, for in the next scene Lewis seems more at peace. We find Lewis meeting with a student. In contrast to the earlier scene, Lewis now opens his window. Instead of offering clean pre-packaged answers to his own questions, he now listens to the student. The movie ends with Jack contrasting his response to pain as a boy to that of a man. Now he chooses suffering over safety in order to love. Of course, neither this scene nor the movie addresses the entire Problem of Evil, but they do offer some insights into one important aspect of it.

So, why should we love when losing hurts so much? Because to miss out on the love of friends and family is to miss out on much of what makes life meaningful. On our deathbeds, we won't be embracing our checkbooks or stock portfolios, for this is not what makes life worth living. Love does involve pain, for no relationship between imperfect persons can be pain-free. And death will invariably bring all earthly relationships to an end. We can try to avoid the pain altogether, but at the cost of those very relationships that invest our lives with so much of its meaning as well as its pleasure. Of course, it's a mistake to encourage people to remain in (verbally or physically) abusive relationships in the name of love, or submission to God's will. Mutually self-giving relationships are wonderful, but relationships in which one person is doing most or all of the giving are a recipe for disaster. Love does not entail a forfeiture of self-respect, but it does require—this side of heaven—willingness to sacrifice and suffer.

A Grief Observed

After losing Joy, Lewis began to keep a very personal about his grief over losing his wife. Published later as *A Grief Observed*, this book has been considered by some to be Lewis's most spiritual, honest, and forthright work. In this book Leis faced head-on his fear that God is a cosmic sadist, and that we're mere rats in his laboratory. Lewis eventually rejected the vivisectionist hypothesis, if for no other reason than that it's too anthropomorphic—depicting God as too much in our image. The sort of moral obtuseness on which such a theology is based seems inconsistent with the sort of Creator responsible for love or laughter or a frosty sunset.

As an oversimplification for the sake of projecting a particular artistic vision, it's fine for *Shadowlands* to characterize Lewis as saying he didn't know if God wanted us to be happy. But the real-life Lewis never said such a thing. What he said instead is that God is interested in more than merely making us happy. Unlike a kindly old grandfather willing to indulge his grandchildren's every whim, God has other intentions. God's love for us as fallen creatures, just as our love for others, introduces the necessity of pain. God is more like the divine surgeon who will not stop cutting until he has thoroughly removed the malignancy of sin. He is less interested in satiating our palate than in making us healthy, and sometimes the cure can be painful. Ultimately, on his view, our true happiness is attainable all right, and not out of reach after all, but to be found in fellowship with God. Since God is perfectly holy, such fellowship requires a profound moral transformation. Heaven may make the sufferings of this world pale by comparison, but it demands that we first be completely transformed by God's grace, and perhaps perfected through our own suffering As Lewis himself put it in *A Grief Observed*, there are not only tears to be dried, but stains to be scoured.

Choosing Love and Choosing Pain

Shadowlands reminds us: To choose love is to choose pain. And this point can be applied to both the earthly realm and to our relationships with the divine. The Christian tradition has almost without exception heralded the truth that genuine saving faith is to be made fit for heaven, we must be changed, which requires more than mere intellectual assent to certain propositions. To be made fit for heaven, we must be changed and made holy. Sin is no option. After we are graciously forgiven, salvation requires transformation of character. But this process of liberation from sin is not easy. Biblically, it's often depicted in terms of being refined by fire as our whole inward orientation has to change from being, in Lewis's terms, "mercenary and self-seeking through and through." But this process of the self becoming dethroned in favor of our heart's rightful inhabitant can be a painful one. Lewis believed our egotistic selves constantly attempt to regain the throne. Only by relinquishing control, and by submitting ourselves to God's plan, he thought, can full fellowship with the ultimate source and paradigm of love be enjoyed, and the deepest self-giving fellowship with others be made possible.

The central malady afflicting us is our self-consumed tendency to put our own desires and agendas above all else. Lewis came to see how egoistic and selfish he himself had been, both in his love for Joy and, even more so, in his devotion to God, especially after his faith proved so precarious when he did not get his way. Lewis thought this required a divine iconoclast. Experience needed to shatter the house of cards that was Lewis's false image of God, so that a stronger faith and a clearer image could emerge. That Lewis may have thought God used Joy's death in his life does not mean that God orchestrated it; however, even if Lewis was right, God's redeeming a situation is not the same as his authoring it. Nor is God's bringing good out of a tragedy a denial of its badness.

As the scene with Joy's son Douglas illustrates, although Lewis never stopped believing in God or heaven, he did become less confident that he knew all the answers to the most difficult of questions. His faith convinced him that there are answers, but not necessarily that he had been made privy to them. He came to understand that sometimes grief simply has to be endured. His own sufferings sensitized him to, and made him more sympathetic with, the sufferings of others. When Douglas claimed not to believe in heaven, Lewis did not correct him, but held him in his arms and cried. More than philosophical or theological admonition, sometimes such open-hearted participation in grief is the best and most spiritual response to pain. We can wait for greater clarity once our eyes are not blurred with tears.

Although a certain element of mystery remains in any discussion of the Problem of Evil, maybe the best we can do is echo contemporary Christian philosopher Nicholas Wolterstorff's insight (after his own tragic loss of a loved one):

> God is love. That is why he suffers. To love our suffering sinful world is to suffer. God so suffered for the world that he gave up his only Son to suffering. The one who does not see God's suffering does not see his love. God is suffering love.
>
> So suffering is down at the center of things, deep down where the meaning is. Suffering is the meaning of our world. For Love is the meaning. And Love suffers. The tears of God are the meaning of history.[1]

Suffering love is, for a believer like Lewis, both the abstract meaning of history, and the very personal meaning of life.[2]

27

About Time: A Romantic Comedy That's Actually about Love

The critical consensus on *About Time* labels it sentimental. Not a few reviews compare it to *Groundhog Day,* and the harshest ones call it insufferable with idiotic plot points. We get it, at least somewhat. Richard Curtis's 2013 film is adorable, and adorable often seems trite. Additionally, the characters' adventures with time travel repeatedly violate the film's own metaphysical strictures. However, underneath the adorableness and in spite of the confused timelines, *About Time* reminds viewers of an important truth: Life is sacred—all life, all the time. The film's power lies not in the abstraction of this truth but in its specificity. It works by drawing viewers in, calling them to really notice the profundity of what is often mistaken as merely mundane.

About Time disarms viewers from the start by opening with quirky character descriptions and the charming antics of the family on which the plot centers. At the outset, protagonist Tim (played by Domhnall Gleeson) introduces viewers to his "sturdy" mother, his laid-back father, his dapper yet distracted uncle, and his offbeat, free-spirited sister. The individuals are odd, yet oddly well suited to the whole. They express their love for each other through routine and repetition— what Tim calls "the repeated rhythms and patterns" of their lives— and thrive on the expected. With whimsical constancy, the family takes tea on the beach daily, no matter the weather; they play weekly outdoor movies, defying the rain that would otherwise thwart their plans; and they hold a yearly New Year's Eve party that walks the line between hokey and hip.

Amid this delightful atmosphere, the equally delightful father-son relationship comes into focus. Tim's dad (played by the perfectly cast Bill Nighy) is undemonstrative in his fatherly role, yet this understated devotion—characterized by frequent table-tennis matches and intimate chats—grounds the movie. The viewer learns, along with Tim, the virtue and value of these seemingly insignificant daily acts of love. While Tim recognizes his father's availability to him, it takes him the entire course of the film (assisted by the fantastical time-travel element) to fully grasp its significance. So, too, for the viewer: All that is present at the start of the film accumulates ever-increasing importance as the film fosters our awareness of the value of these people, places, and experiences. It does, in fact, what Christians are called to do—not confer, but rather, honor the sacredness of the other.

Three relationships are at the heart of Tim's lesson about the value of life and the nature of love: a romantic relationship with Mary (played by Rachel McAdams), a sibling relationship with his sister Kit Kat (played by Lydia Wilson), and the aforementioned father-son relationship. These relationships are introduced with simplicity, little preparing viewers for the depth they will develop and sustain over the course of the film. Tim's attraction to Mary, for example, seems no more than a boyhood crush, especially coming as it does soon after his being rejected by his first "love" (which, truth be told, is merely a summer infatuation). At the start Tim may simply be interested in what he might gain from pursuing a relationship with Mary. From the moment he learns about his time-travel ability, Tim directs this newfound skill to seeking out love, as he tells the viewer that "it was always going to be all about love." And the father's advice to use time travel to make his life what he wants it to be translates for Tim to "find a girlfriend."

But in ways this film is a coming-of-age story, and over time Tim discovers the vacuity of his vague desire. Through his involvement with Mary, Tim learns that love has value only when it is directed specifically. A tense scene marks this epiphany for Tim, as awareness dawns that he doesn't want "a girlfriend"; he wants Mary. His entanglement in real life, and real love, has drained his abstracted romantic wish of all its appeal. No longer can "a girlfriend" enchant him—only what Miroslav Volf, in a beautiful passage about his children from *Free of Charge*, calls the "unsubstitutable particularity" of the specific object of his love. At this point, the film breaks out of its romantic comedy template by expanding its investigation of love beyond the erotic. Now Tim's relationship with his sister becomes the new vehicle for the film's lessons about life and love, and it is with her that Tim learns the risks and limits of love. While his father warns him about misunderstanding and thus misusing time travel, Tim's lessons always come through experience. His love for his sister puts him at her mercy, as does love for anyone. Her personal failures become his problems, and he can be—and is—hurt by her actions.

C. S. Lewis is instructive here: "To love at all is to be vulnerable," he explains in *The Four Loves*, "Love anything and your heart will be wrung and possibly broken." Whether through loss or disloyalty or foolishness or accident, others make way for pain. Of course they also make way for joy, but not without risk. Tempting as it might be to exert control of others, to prevent them from intentionally or accidentally causing you—or even themselves—pain, dictating the behavior of others does not demonstrate true love, as Tim learns through trial and error with Kit Kat. Love respects the other's autonomy. In *A Grief Observed*, Lewis explains love as "the constant impact of something very close and intimate, yet all the time unmistakably other, resistant—in a word, real."

Tim's embrace of Mary and Kit Kat in their specificity and otherness reveals how love enlarges our being, forcing our attention outside ourselves. Nowhere in the film is Tim's need to do this presented as clearly as in his relationship with his father. This relationship seems the most prosaic at the film's outset, but by film's end it has become the centerpiece. Of the members of his family, Tim's father is the one Tim may have taken most for granted. But when faced with the possibility of losing him, Tim realizes both the depth of his father's devotion to him and the way in which this devotion is embedded in the quotidian. In a series of increasingly poignant scenes, Richard Curtis (the film's screenwriter and director) reveals how the father relishes his life and his family—and Curtis summons his viewers to similarly relish theirs. The father's true legacy resonates with what Christian should easily see: that every day, every moment, every person is sacred.

What Tim takes the course of the film and a series of time travel adventures to learn, Mary seems to know intuitively: She savors a less than picture-perfect wedding day and looks forward to "lots and lots of types of days," which are the stuff of our lives. By failing to relish the everyday and the thousand small blessings of our lives, or to cherish those with whom we share our journey, or to smile amidst and even laugh at life's travails in our earthly pilgrimage, we relegate ourselves to perpetual discontent, because life is meted out to us in no other way. The trick is to apprehend and truly appreciate how extraordinary the ordinary is.

28
Friendship, Rivalry, and Excellence

Friendship today is a concept that has undergone a fair bit of degradation. It used to be a highly exalted notion. It was thought by many ancients to represent the highest form of love. It was touted as a school of virtue, and as something relatively rare. More recently, casual acquaintances are liable to call each other friends, or even online acquaintances in the form of a plethora of Facebook "friends" and the like. So friendship is well worth exploring, and doing so in the context of discussing tennis affords the extra advantage of identifying some of the challenges posed to friendship at the highest levels of competitive sport.

In tennis, what intensifies the competition is that the game is played directly between the participants. I hit my backhand to your forehand, and your drop shot requires me to run. And at each step along the way, we find a zero-sum game; your earned point means my lost point, and my winning game means a lost game for you. This adversarial structure may not always conduce to friendship. The problem, in a sense, is exacerbated in the case of the Williams sisters. Just imagine facing your own sister (repeatedly!) in the finals of Grand Slams and the sort of cognitive dissonance such an encounter is likely to induce. Winning the trophy means depriving your sister of it: little wonder this is one of the reasons this legendary rivalry ranks near the top of the all-time most dramatic to watch unfold, and every such matchup is bittersweet for the ambivalent participants, by their own admission.[1]

Even though tennis is a sport, many of us on occasion have taken it too far, happy to win by nearly any means available, growing disgusted at ourselves for a missed opportunity or bad execution. Sometimes we even allow a tension to develop with the player on the other side of the court whom we, in our worst moments, think of not merely as a fellow player or perhaps even friend, but the enemy, the obstinate opposition. It's easy to fall into the trap of thinking of the conflict as more than it is We can lose perspective, and rather than just a snapshot of who happens to win on a particular day, a tennis match or other competition is reconceived as practically a death match, a struggle for domination, a chance not just to win a set or match but to vanquish a foe. We see this in rabid political partisanship, conflicts between avid proponents of divergent worldviews, as well as on the tennis court. This means that there's an important issue here indeed. How can rivals (or, for that matter, disputants, interlocutors, dialogue partners, and the like), either on the tennis court or off, be friends?[2]

Friendships of Pleasure

The history of thought has featured several important philosophers and writers probing the question of what friendship is all about—ranging from Plato to Augustine, Aristotle to Cicero, Montaigne to Emerson. What makes someone more than an acquaintance; what makes for a genuine friend? Must a friendship have for one of its basic ingredients warm feelings, or will grudging respect do? Are friendships vital for human flourishing? Are there different sorts of friendships? To get a handle on some of these questions, let's begin with what Aristotle, Plato's most famous student, and one of the most important analysts of friendship, thought was an important sort of friendship, namely, one of pleasure or enjoyment.[3]

Suppose you and a hypothetical tennis partner just have a really good time playing tennis with each other. Foremost in your mind, imagine, isn't the improvement of your game or the moral fiber of your opponent but rather simply the enjoyment and pleasure you derive from playing tennis with this person. Knowing that she seems to be enjoying it as well may even enhance your own pleasure. What really drives such a friendship, more than anything, is this shared enjoyment from time spent together playing tennis. Aristotle would say of such a friendship—and he wouldn't deny that it is a kind of friendship—that what each person most cares about in the friendship is something other than the other person; rather, the pleasure that time spent with that person produces is the driving concern. If a different person could equally well provide the same quantity or quality of enjoyment, the partner in question could be easily replaced; moreover, a friendship of pleasure functions irrespective of the caliber of the other person's character. Perhaps the person is one of integrity and great character, perhaps not; but a friendship of pleasure doesn't require it. Such an issue isn't relevant. Nor are the friendship and its benefits at root due to this integrity, real or imagined, and nothing in the friendship intentionally aims at producing such character. This makes such a friendship a (mere) friendship of pleasure.

Pleasure is not intrinsically bad; in fact, it's probably inherently good. This is not to say, however, that every enjoyment or search for pleasure is morally respectable. So, too, deriving pleasure from a friendship is not necessarily bad. As friendships go, however, such a model does leave something to be desired. In terms of a real-life example from the world of tennis, it would be altogether presumptuous to reduce any friendship on the tour merely to the level of a pleasure friendship. So let's be circumspect here and engage in a thought experiment involving two of our childhood favorites, known for having a great friendship. Björn Borg and Vitas Gerulaitis were dear friends. They spent a great deal of time together, enjoying one another's company immensely, playing tennis regularly, despite their rather different personality types. Before his premature and tragic death, Gerulaitis, in addition to being one of the best tennis players in the world (reputed to hardly ever miss a shot in practice), was notorious for his ebullience and ability to have fun. Whether their friendship was actually a mere friendship of pleasure is beside the point. We're entitled to harbor huge doubts that it was, and so let's not say otherwise. But just suppose that the basis of the friendship were merely the enjoyment they derived from one another's company. Again, this supposition may well be entirely contrary to fact, but if it were true, then such a friendship would have been a mere friendship of pleasure by Aristotle's account. It was a fact that these two were something of rivals, playing some classic matches (that Borg won); so, perhaps counterfactually speaking, if they were friends in the sense of a friendship of pleasure, they were obviously able to function as such friends despite their rivalry and its attendant challenges.

Friendships of Usefulness

A friendship of usefulness or utility is the second form Aristotle explores. Suppose two tennis players develop a friendship because each derives a benefit from practicing with the other. Their games are sufficiently suited to one another's, and the quality of their play is adequately complementary, that they serve as ideal practice partners for each other. Their friendship never goes much beyond the mutual benefit they derive from their shared interest in improving their games, but they get along well and come to regard each other as friends. Aristotle would characterize this as a friendship, to be sure, but a friendship at the level of utility or usefulness. Each is in it for the usefulness the friendship serves. Such a friendship of utility isn't a bad thing, but note that each person is primarily in it not exactly because of the other person considered in her entirety but because of a specific thing that happens to be true about her, namely, that her tennis game conduces to an effective playing and practice partner. In the absence of such a trait, presumably, the relationship probably would not endure.[4]

Friendships of usefulness introduce an interesting twist when one considers rivalries. For friendship and rivalry may be thought mutually exclusive at the highest levels of competitive tennis for the following reason: in a game sometimes decided by millimeters and milliseconds, the slightest psychological advantage can make the difference between winning and losing. If a friendship makes one more susceptible to letting up, feeling bad for winning, sacrificing an advantage, forfeiting a killer instinct, that might make all the difference. Winning at the highest levels requires a kind of ruthlessness, a single-minded focus, a nearly unquenchable thirst for domination, not exactly the stuff of warm fuzzy feelings. When there are two opponents and only one prize, the one who blinks will probably lose. This is perhaps why the friendship between Pete Sampras and Jim Courier cooled as they approached the top of their games and why regarding the 2001 French Open semifinal between Justine Henin and Kim Clijsters, Henin's biographer says, "There was no space for friendship any more, there was too much at stake."[5] Sampras admits to benefiting from the persona that grew up around him on the tour as someone a bit untouchable and unapproachable, which he didn't mind reinforcing.

In philosophy, say, one doesn't rightly construe a friend's publishing a paper as an occasion for feeling diminished, because his or her publishing a paper isn't inconsistent with anyone else publishing their own. We should be happy for our friend; indeed, we can choose to perceive her achievement in a way that enhances us both. It can be something of a source of pride that a friend is faring so well professionally. This is an altogether appropriate occasion to rejoice with those who rejoice. But in tennis there's an added challenge. For rivals are going for the very same goal. One's winning means another's losing. The analogy with academics, to be consistent, would be that two friends are each going for the same dream job, and only one can get it. An academic may be happy for their friend if she gets it, but her getting it precludes anyone else from doing so. Imagine now that such a dynamic were operative not just on some such rare occasion, but all the time. This is the situation in tennis between two top rivals. When one thinks of the magnitude of winning a major, the way it forever changes one's life, one really sees the height of the stakes.

At the same time, there's something paradoxical about rivalries that perhaps carves out an important space for a friendship of usefulness. This is the interesting twist we promised. A great player benefits from other great players. Such rivalries provide a chance to display true excellence, a quality of play that may not otherwise find expression. Nadal pushes Federer to play better on clay than Federer would otherwise have to (for three years in a row, only Nadal was able to beat Federer at Roland Garros). Agassi pushed Sampras to add new elements to his game to meet the former's challenge. Perhaps the most notorious example of all here is the way that Steffi Graf's legacy itself was hurt, obviously through no fault of her own, by her crazed fan's attack on her main rival, Monica Seles. As Mark Foreman has noted, this tragedy hurt not only the game, tennis fans, and most obviously Seles herself, but Graf's own legacy.[6] Rivalries thus understood aren't just consistent with friendships of usefulness; the great rivalries provide the truest test of tennis greatness.

For now, though, let's shift gears and find in tennis history an altogether different example of a friendship of usefulness, not between two rivals per se, but between two legends whose paths overlapped in a fascinating way. Let's consider the complex relationship between Arthur Ashe and John McEnroe. Ashe served as captain of the Davis Cup team through many of the years McEnroe played. As McEnroe's coach, Ashe shouldered the job of reining in Mac, which made for some awfully tense moments. By nature Ashe was a study in equanimity, whereas McEnroe is notoriously irascible. Their diametrically opposed reactions to volatile situations vividly manifested themselves on numerous occasions, one of which we will recount: In a Davis Cup doubles match against Clerc and Vilas, various displays of gamesmanship, delaying tactics, and needling remarks were getting to McEnroe. The Argentinians were rattling him, and the obscenities and verbal jabs between Clerc and McEnroe between points were escalating. After Ashe tried settling Mac down, reminding him that he was representing the United States, Mac seemed temporarily better, until Clerc "looked at him sweetly and lisped, provocatively, You're so nice!" To which McEnroe retorted, "Go f--- yourself!" Ashe was incensed; here's his account of what happened next: "I was stunned. I stormed onto the court, and John and I exchanged some bitter words for a few seconds. This time I thought I might punch John. I have never punched anyone in my life, but I was truly on the brink of hitting him. I had never been so angry in my life. I couldn't trust myself not to strangle him. Of course, if I had, any jury would have acquitted me."[7]

Ashe admitted that as captain and player they were like total strangers. "I wasn't happy about the situation, but I had no stomach for fake camaraderie or ersatz shows of friendship."[8] So far, it sound as if they weren't friends at all, especially when we remember Mac's aversion to authority, which Ashe had come to represent as a coach willing on occasion to stand up to him. But that wouldn't begin to capture the complexity of their relationship, for a genuine friendship did in reality emerge between these two men. McEnroe didn't want Ashe to remain entirely quiet on the sidelines during a match, and Ashe greatly appreciated the talent, loyalty, and excitement Mac brought to Davis Cup. In various ways they did find each other useful, and this was the basis of some semblance of friendship. The friendship was less rooted in pleasure than usefulness, though Ashe did delight in watching Mac's on-court brilliance.

Even that analysis, though, doesn't do justice to their complicated friendship. McEnroe came to grow fond of and deeply respect Ashe, and Ashe, surprisingly, came to respect Mac as well, even if he didn't respect some of his antics and explosions. Regarding Mac's rage, Ashe offered a nuanced analysis that many readers may find surprising. It's tempting for us to think that Mac was the vicious one and Ashe the virtuous one. Mac never held his anger in check; Ashe always did. But appearances can be deceiving. Ashe explained that Neil Amdur's analysis of him may have been right: that Ashe held his emotions so tightly in check due to a certain amount of repression. "Neil traced my repression back to the death of my grandfather and mother in the span of one year during my childhood, and especially my father's grief when my mother died when I was seven." Seeing adult family members openly sobbing and mourning frightened the young Ashe, and to protect himself, he may well have built an "emotional wall." "Each time McEnroe loses control on the court in a Davis Cup match," Amdur writes, "it forces Ashe to deal with the most delicate frames in his psyche."[9]

Ashe came to think that this may have been right, which tempered his judgment of McEnroe. He elaborated:

> I suspect now that McEnroe and I were not so far apart, after all. Far from seeing John as an alien, I think I may have known him, probably without being fully aware of my feelings, as a reflection of an intimate part of myself. This sense of McEnroe as embodying feelings I could only repress, or as a kind of darker angel to my own tightly restrained spirit, may explain why I always hesitated to interfere with his rages even when he was excessive, although I sometimes had to do so. Now I wonder whether I had not always been aware, at some level, that John was expressing my own rage, my own anger, for me, as I never could express it; and I perhaps was even grateful to him for doing so, although his behavior was, on another level, totally unacceptable.

Theirs was a complex relationship, not easily reducible to a preset category. If it's at least best characterized as a friendship of utility, it certainly glimmered with aspects of more. "I developed a deep affection for McEnroe, and also a genuine respect for his character and integrity that defused my outrage at behavior often so different from my own," Ashe wrote. He added, "What bound me to McEnroe was not simply his rage but also his selflessness in making sacrifices to play for our country, and his artistry on the tennis court. I couldn't resist that combination. I began to see him as a brother. He was, in some ways, an incorrigible brother; but our fights were indeed, in my mind, 'intrafamilial.'"[10]

Ashe's depiction of the relationship as practically familial is telling. A relative is someone we're stuck with, someone we're more unconditionally committed to than a friend whose company we might prefer and whose reciprocity is required. A bond formed between these two tennis greats, one that was deep and complex, welding together two men who were in many ways complete opposites, yet at a deeper level kindred spirits. Ashe recognized the virtue in Mac, despite his very public failures, and he saw that virtue can sometimes be less about behavior than the struggle required to behave rightly, a bigger challenge for some than for others. In the Tennis Hall of Fame in Newport, Rhode Island, is a watercolor of Arthur Ashe. John McEnroe donated it to the museum. Ashe's concern about Mac's behavior and his recognition of virtuous aspects of Mac's character reveal that their friendship to some degree and in certain ways shaded into Aristotle's third and highest form of friendship.

Friendships of Virtue

For Aristotle, friendships of both pleasure and usefulness pale in comparison with the highest form of friendship, friendship in the fullest sense. Such friendships exist between friends who are more than just useful to or pleasurable for one another—these are for people of virtue. Virtues for Aristotle are stable character traits achieved by hitting the right mark between the lines, as it were, avoiding both the excesses and deficiencies that make for vice. Through the right achievement of moderation, one achieves the virtue of courage, for example, rather than fall to either cowardice (which is the deficiency) or rashness (the excess). In friendships grounded in virtue, the friend's character and integrity enhance the pleasure and usefulness of the friendship. The friends care about each other's character and enjoy each other for each's own sake and in virtue of each's own goodness, rather than just some benefit the friendship accords. And friends of the highest type genuinely wish good things for each other as well.[11]

A friendship in this sense in the context of tennis might obtain between individuals who, say, grow to respect one another for their sportsmanship and excellence of play. The enjoyment and usefulness derived from playing one another are a direct function of recognizing such underlying character that manifests in tennis. The opponents mutually recognize in each other the way they consistently hit the right note, balancing competitive fire with a respect for the opposition, a desire to win with respect for the game, a desire for excellence with an appreciation of an opponent's superior play. A friendship rooted in virtue like this will be largely free from jealousy; in contrast, a virtuous friend will root for another, not merely and certainly not primarily to win, but to win virtuously. A virtue-friend's winning a tournament, even if it's at her virtuous friend's expense, won't be perceived by the friend as detracting from her; the victory can be a victory for both parties in the deepest sense. Rather than diminishing the losing friend, it enhances both friends, for mutual growth in virtue is possible even if only one can win the tournament. All of this sounds perhaps a bit overly ideal in the crucible of a real-world, world-class rivalry, but supposing it is, it still can constitute something of an ideal of which to be aware, even if one never fully actualized.

So can two tennis rivals remain friends? According to Aristotle, they surely can. What's most clearly at stake is not just a victory but the sort of people the friends are. Win or lose, the friends can share in growth of character and virtue, for such things aren't a scarce resource available for only one. Such rivals can still care passionately about winning and can try their best to beat each other, but they can come to recognize, perhaps in fits and starts, that winning, though important, is not the only or most important thing there is.

For one salient example of a virtuous friendship between two great tennis rivals, let's turn our attention to Martina Navratilova and Chris Evert, whose rivalry and friendship inspired a whole book, entitled *The Rivals*. Ashe presciently anticipated the possibility of such a book when he wrote that "someone could write a book about, for instance, the rivalry between Chris Evert and Martina Navratilova, which was not only glorious and protracted—both were superb players—but also fraught with so many rich overtones deriving from their very different personalities and histories."[12] Navratilova and Evert, by their own admission, are flawed people, like everyone else, and Evert in particular has taken pains to emphasize that she was never quite the innocent princess many early on presumed her to be. We use their example of a virtuous friendship not unrealistically but rather as a recognition of how, in the crucible of real life, a career-long struggle for tennis dominance, altogether contrasting styles of play and public personas, along with an unusual range of life's normal vicissitudes, these two extraordinary women came to care deeply for one another and each other's well-being. And in the process they formed an authentic and lasting friendship that, in many ways, serves as a model worthy of emulation. In the penultimate paragraph of her book about their great rivalry and friendship, Johnette Howard writes, "They are proof that conviction counts, and that by telling the truth, you carve out room for more truth around you. Evert and Navratilova's shared odyssey underscored that if you live honorably, time can leaven the ups and downs, the heartbreaks and the thrills."[13]

What makes the virtuous friendship between Navratilova and Evert all the more impressive are some of the reasons friendship among the top tier of professional female tennis players was especially difficult in their era. Citing an interview of Steffi Graf, Arthur Ashe elaborated on this dynamic, while pointing out that on one level women were more sociable than men on the tour, in terms of union and associational activity and while qualifying his point that the dynamic of which Graf speaks didn't hold so true at the amateur level: "Aggressively seeking dominance and almost careless about the possible consequences, men tend to challenge one another with macho posturing. Women, on the other hand [at the amateur level], seem to take exquisite care not to offend one another and jeopardize their friendships. Frequently, they may even play beneath their top level of skill in order to preserve peace. Not so on the women's tour, according to Graf and several other commentators."[14]

What Graf pointed to in her interview with *Tennis* magazine was an almost poisoned atmosphere among the women players, resulting in her best friends on the tour being men. "The rivalry among women tennis players is overwhelming," she said.[15] In considering why this dynamic of antisocial competition prevailed among the top women players, Ashe found Laura Tracy's analysis insightful in her book *The Secret between Us: Competition among Women*. Tracy refers to the "secret" as this: while women have been socialized by the ideal of femininity to deny that they are competitive and to resist being openly competitive, they have no choice but to be competitive for jobs, possessions, and the like. But the denial of the reality of competition can force women to act subversively and destructively, especially against other women, as they make their way through life. Competition, Ashe summarizes, becomes a clandestine and often self-destructive activity, one that preys on and exacerbates the elements of vulnerability in a woman.

Tracy writes—remember this was several decades ago—that women have been taught that competition is immoral, that they've been socialized against full participation in our economy and our history. They have been taught to be secret competitors, and their secret has kept them subordinated members of our society. Most of them recognize competition only when it's practiced by another woman. Even worse, many of them often don't realize they are in a competition until they have lost it. Unlike men, then, women don't have the masculine ideal of win-at-any-cost guiding them; rather, they can't make competition impersonal the way men can, and thus they tend to be haunted by fears not simply that they will *seem* selfish or greedy but that they actually will *be* that way.

In the realm of professional tennis, competition is the very essence of the activity, and especially with all that's at stake, the context generated is quite different from the rest of the world (well, there's always politics). Where the killer instinct, fierce independence, will to win, willingness to stand alone, and tenacious belief in oneself, not to mention assertiveness and aggressiveness, are what's needed for the highest levels of success, women conditioned by the ideals of femininity (as construed classically) understandably feel huge tensions. Ashe concluded that women were faced by "many more subtle and complex obstacles than have faced their male counterparts on the professional tour," obstacles forged by cultural dynamics owing to understandings of gender and a presumed tension between fierce competition and the ideals of femininity. If some of Tracy's analysis today seems a bit dated, we can hope that's a mark of some societal improvement in this area of gender relations. In Graf's interview, despite the paucity of friendships among the professional women on the tour (at that time), she cited, as Ashe put it, "both Martina and Chris as shining examples of friendship, courtesy, and respect extended to her in the otherwise rather bleak social world of women's tennis, as Graf experienced it."[16]

C. S. Lewis on Friendship

As a scholar trained in both literature and philosophy, C. S. Lewis hoped for a resurgence of the ancient view of friendship as the most fully human of all love and the crown of life. He recognized that friendship is now often thought of as eliminable, an optional diversion. It's true, he thought, that friendship, like art, philosophy, or tennis, is something we can do without, but it's one of the things that can help make life worth living too.

One of friendship's most important distinguishing features, Lewis argued, is that, whereas lovers are face to face, absorbed in each other, friends are absorbed in some common interest.[17] He thought that some shared activity is a prerequisite for friendship, whether it be a common profession, common studies, perhaps even a shared recreation—like tennis. Friends are side by side, focused on a shared passion. This means, among other things, merely seeking friends tends to be futile, for friendships are about something. Friendship is a journey that requires a destination: "If, at the outset, we had attended more to (our friend) and less to the thing our Friendship is 'about,' we should not have come to know or love him so well. You will not find the warrior, the poet, the philosopher, or the Christian by staring in his eyes as if he were your mistress: better fight beside him, read with him, argue with him, pray with him."[18]

Friendship in this sense of a shared venture and perspective certainly seems consistent with a great rivalry. Indeed, considering the likelihood that the challenge of staying the world's #1 player or sustaining a winning streak at Wimbledon is something that can only be understood by those few others with similar experience, rivals in this sense would seem able to share in experiences of which nearly everyone else can't help but remain irremediably ignorant. After Sampras's last major final, he and Agassi agreed to stay in contact. "We agreed," Sampras writes, "that it would be a shame, after all we'd been through together, to lose touch. Besides, we had a lot of things in common, including two kids each. We'd been players since the age of seven. We had a lot of history, a lot of life—a certain kind of life—in common."[19]

René Stauffer's biography of Federer also details in a chapter on Tiger Woods and Pete Sampras how Federer has more recently formed a friendship with them both.[20] Of course what all three hold in common is complete domination of play against the competition in their respective spheres and eras. This makes for the possibility of a unique bond. Since Federer's and Sampras's careers just barely overlapped, and Federer and Tiger aren't in the same sport, there are few of the tensions that can accompany a shared dominance in a field.

Lewis also recognized that, though friendship can be a school of virtue, it can also be one of vice. "It makes good men better and bad men worse," and in a variety of ways. For example, friendships require a certain deafness to those outside the circle, but the partial deafness that's noble and necessary encourages the wholesale deafness which is arrogant and inhuman. The initial humility felt at being part of a group of friends can easily transition into corporate pride and sense of superiority, "a little self-elected (and therefore absurd) aristocracy, basking in the moonshine of our collective self-approval."[21] This brings us to our last account of friendship, provided by a philosopher who wished to turn on its head the notion that the purpose of friendship at its best or in its highest form was to inculcate virtue, construed classically. What Lewis would vociferously reject, this thinker enthusiastically embraced.

The Overman

Rife with aphorism and subject to varying interpretation, Friedrich Nietzsche's writings can be hard to decipher. Like many prodigies in tennis, Nietzsche too was a prodigy, though of the mind, becoming a chaired professor by the tender age of twenty-four. Not easily domesticated or romanticized, his writings are challenging and iconoclastic, typically an effort to turn on their heads a number of Christian teachings and morals. His goal was to effect a grand reversal of ethics, a "transvaluation of values," according to which many traditional Judeo-Christian virtues (such as humility and, importantly, pity) would be seen as vices, while restoring value to such ancient virtues as pride. Among the virtues he wished to extol were strength, courage, and conquest. What were discussed earlier as the "feminine" virtues would have revolted him, insofar as they were seen as enervating. Most charitably construed, his antipathy was a result of his aversion to the way women are typically socialized and conditioned, requiring them to renounce conquest and achievement or, at most, to pursue such goals subversively.

In *The Geneology of Morality* and elsewhere, Nietzsche suggests that in the "master morality" heroic figures or natural nobles actively rather than passively define themselves by, as it were, looking in the mirror and approving of what they see—strength, martial prowess, intelligence, and the like. This leads them to distinguish the good (themselves) from the bad or plain, those lesser persons who fail to exhibit the attributes the masters observe primarily in themselves. But there is something more to the story, for the natural nobles can also recognize one another and regard each other with, if not warmth, a suitable respect.

Perhaps it's not too big a stretch to argue that Nietzsche, to whom art mattered a great deal (and tennis certainly has its aesthetic elements), would have seen the tennis greats as a cut above, potential "overmen," heroic figures, rare individuals of tremendous achievement and prowess. Great tennis rivals of such caliber, he would think, could come to regard each other, after many epic athletic battles, as comrades to a greater or lesser degree. These men and women to some extent look at their rivals and see something worthy of approval, just as they approve of themselves. This, it could be thought, is a valuable aspect of individual competition. Sometimes these rivalries turn into warm friendships; other times, as in the case of McEnroe and Lendl, all that emerges from the rivalry is a sort of grudging respect, coupled with straightforward dislike. Friendship for Nietzsche was less about warm feelings and more about relationships that spurred individuals on to yet greater forms of excellence, achievement, and creativity. The best friend is also the best enemy, inspiring one's best. Friends, he was wont to say, show their mutual devotion by clashing head-on. Life in the modern state withers the will of great souls, so there aren't many such heroic figures anymore; finding one is rare. The possibility of a friendship between two of them is rarer still.

Perhaps the greatest irony of all in Nietzsche's analysis is that such "star friendships" between overmen are best illustrated by pointing not to a pair of friends but a single individual.[22] For unlike Aristotle's goal of an activity of reason that is able to be shared between virtuous friends, Nietzsche would say that the overman ultimately must strive for complete self-definition and independence. The star player might need the other star in order to play his very best, but his goal is ultimately to stand alone, at the top of the heap. He strives to be the winner who has vanquished every other foe—the lone ranger willing to renounce even those friendships with the other heroic figures in order to emerge victorious and achieve the highest level of creativity and make the biggest impact. Who might our example be?

To our thinking, there's one player who best of all in the realm of tennis represents the paradigm of a Nietzschean overman: Jimmy Connors. By his own admission, Connors was not a team player, in part accounting for his aversion to the Davis Cup. When he did get involved, he resented the greater attention paid to his teammate McEnroe. He refused to ever admit that Mac was better, even after his infamous drubbing at Mac's hands in 1984 at Wimbledon. Connors was renowned for keeping his game face on before, during, and after matches, even in the locker room. For him his opponents weren't collaborators but competitors who threatened his bread and butter. Of Connors, Borg wrote in his autobiography that they were not really friends, Connors was the consummate showman, did nothing to forfeit a psychological advantage, fought for every point, saw tennis as an absolutely zero-sum game.

Arthur Ashe had this to say of Connors, indicative of the effect the man produced:

> Connors' effervescence, the stellar quality of his magnetism and drive, lifted everyone. . . . Connors wore an air of such arrogance that he regularly intimidated his opponents even before he had hit a ball. Then he proceeded to smack the ball with a force that bordered on vindictiveness. His twohanded backhand shot was among the most damaging strokes ever seen in tennis. . . . Jimmy's return of serve was unbridled aggression. . . . His heart was always in it, and his readiness to fight never left him. . . . Looking back from the early 1990s, with Connors still playing well, I see that he

was the greatest male tennis player, bar none, in the two and a half decades since the Open era began in 1968. No top player lasted longer as a major attraction or so thoroughly captured the admiration and sympathy of the public for the same length of time. Only Billie Jean King, with her mixture of dedicated feminism, general gifts of leadership, and athletic brilliance, has been more important among all tennis players since World War II.[23]

Some readers may find dubious our application of the Nietzschean overman to Connors. But we'd be hard-pressed to find a more suitable candidate, a player whose fight not just to get to the top but to stay there nearly defies description where the inner impulse to dominate is concerned. If the title does properly apply, in some measure or sense Connors was the best sort of friend to his rivals by Nietzschean standards: not a warm and fuzzy fellow, but one who always pushed them to their limits, never gave up, made them play their best to beat him. He offered them too a chance for greatness. As Nietzsche wrote, perhaps aptly with respect to Connors and his rivals especially, "Let us then believe in our star friendship even if we should be compelled to be earth enemies."[24] In *Thus Spake Zarathustra*, Nietzsche actually offers the paradoxical argument that the best friend may also be an enemy.[25] Looked at from a certain respectable perspective, perhaps Connors would sense and begin to appreciate this sort of tribute paid on his behalf to his (few!) rivals.

Tensions and Other Unresolved Problems

Rather than ending this chapter by telling you whom we think was right and wrong, we will leave it to readers to come to their own conclusions. We have seen a variety of perspectives on the nature of friendship, and a number of ways to construe the connection between friendship and rivals. What remains unclear is how best to understand the tension that emerges within the context of a friendship between rivals when they're competing for the same prize. Whether the tension takes a back seat to the superior goal of a higher shared purpose or can be eliminated by compartmentalizing the competition and the friendship or by women eschewing ideals of femininity or men adopting them is an important question. Along these lines, one might ask whether the tension is an ineliminable aspect of friendship and rightly celebrated or is lamented but thought inevitable and something that must be simply lived with. In any case, it's clear that the tension's existence can serve to make us think about what a true friendship is really all about. It's mildly amusing that an essay on tennis ends with a reflection on the importance of tension!

29

Jerry before Seinfeld: Delightfully Distinct

For nearly thirty years, Jerry Seinfeld has been a fixture of the American cultural landscape. His signature sitcom, the so-called "show about nothing," dominated television during the 1990s, and the comedian himself became a household name. Close to twenty years after its finale, *Seinfeld* remains in syndication, and its namesake has a net worth of $860 million. Seinfeld still commands sell-out crowds on comedy tours and has recently signed with Netflix to distribute new standup specials and host new episodes of his low-key *Comedians in Cars Getting Coffee*.

Bottom line: Jerry Seinfeld is just about as big as it gets in today's America. And yet, ironically enough, he has achieved this iconic status by dealing in minutia. The quintessential observational comic, Seinfeld draws the attention of his audience to the often-overlooked mundane realities that comprise our lives—breakfast cereal, wallpaper, construction tools, laundry, childhood toys, shopping, furniture. And through his comic vision, Seinfeld culls insights on our shared hopes and dreams, our fears and failings, our charms and virtues, our pride and pretensions—insights as brilliant as they seem, after the fact, obvious.

A recent documentary on Joan Didion said that her writing revealed a recurring and remarkable knack for showing the centrality of the peripheral and the universality of the particular. Much the same can be said of Seinfeld's penchant for accentuating the extraordinary of the ordinary. Both artists remind us all of the magic of the everyday and the beauty of the quotidian. Despite this similarity, they manifest this shared trait in remarkably distinct ways. No one would confuse Jerry with Joan. And in these very differences is revealed the allure of diversity's charm.

Seinfeld's delightful pairing of the big and the small, the distinctive and the seemingly insignificant is at the heart of *Jerry before Seinfeld*, the special that kicks off his deal with Netflix. In this combination documentary/standup routine, the comedian returns, literally and figuratively, to his professional roots. Seinfeld once again takes the stage at the Comic Strip, the New York comedy club that gave him his start. Interspersing bits from his show with an assortment of memories tracing his career back to its beginnings, *Jerry before Seinfeld* offers a needful cultural corrective—emphasizing that the comedian's value lies not in his celebrity status but in his unique calling and craft.

It turns out that the Jerry who became Seinfeld was remarkably unremarkable. He grew up in the suburbs of New York, second child of a middle-class Jewish family, with an upbringing marked by no major traumas or spectacular good fortunes. He was simply an ordinary kid. But that ordinary kid had an extraordinary bent toward humor. He couldn't get enough—poring over *MAD* magazines, collecting every comedy album he could get his hands on, and stopping everything if a comedian came on TV. Great performers like Jean Shepherd, George Carlin, and Abbot and Costello transported him from his "boring, regular life" to a realm of wonder and creativity. What captured his imagination, he says, is that these comics held nothing sacred; they just didn't respect anything. It blew his mind to think that he didn't have to simply accept what was handed to him.

Such a lesson might be poison to some kids; to Seinfeld it was liberation. It freed him to discover his unique angle on the world, to believe that his perspective mattered, too. It also enabled him, at twenty-one, to walk away from a full-time construction gig and throw himself completely into comedy, earning nothing but free meals and t-shirts and dealing with hecklers and gigs that bombed. Even still he testifies, "None of this bothered me. I was in comedy, and it just felt like heaven." Thus inspired, it took real work to cultivate his act, develop material, and find his voice. One of the great services Seinfeld has offered us is the inside scoop of what it takes to become a premier comedian, to achieve excellence in one's field. Though a prodigious talent, he was willing to put in the time and effort to maximize his innate skills.[1]

What's true for Seinfeld is true for us all: each of us has a unique voice to share, something we're a genius at doing, which we can do unlike anyone and everyone else. Christians most often say that human value resides most significantly in the fact that we were, all of us, made in God's image, his *imago Dei*. What we all share in this respect is something unspeakably remarkable indeed.

But John Hare points out that there's another vital ingredient to our value as human persons: our distinctiveness. It's not just what we share in common that matters; our differences, too, are a crucial part of who we are and of why we're valuable. No two of us is exactly alike; each of us is designed to reflect a different aspect of our Creator. A prodigious talent and distinctive voice like Seinfeld's is a reminder that each of us is unique, that each of us has a contribution to make that's a reflection of how God made us and what he intended us to do.

Hare writes as follows:

> ... [T]here is a call by God to each one of us, a call to love God in a particular and unique way. Revelation 2:17, in the instructions to the church in Pergamos, refers to a name about which God says, "and [I] will give him a white stone, and in the stone a new name written, which no one knows except the one that receives it." If we think of this name, like "Peter" meaning "rock" (the name Jesus gives to Simon), as giving us the nature into which we are being called, and if we think of this nature, as Scotus does, as a way of loving God, then we can think of the value of each of us as residing in us, in our particular relation to God.[2]

A theistic and Christian picture of the human condition provides a compelling account of human dignity, of incommensurable worth, and of ordained work, not just for humanity as a whole but for each and every individual. This is an account strong enough to sustain our deepest intuitions about the inestimable value of every human person—a profound truth hinted at even in a guy whose concerns canvass nothing. The story of Seinfeld shows that there's something sacred after all.

30

Refusing Counterfeits: *Rear Window* and Our Struggle as Spectators

One of the main themes of Alfred Hitchcock's classic film *Rear Window* is spectatorship. It's a movie heavily about our relationship with art. Among the neighbors that Jefferies (Jimmy Stewart) watches so closely is a dancer, a sculptor, and a musician. More specifically the movie is about cinema, movies, as Jefferies looks out his window across the courtyard into the lives of his various and sundry neighbors. The movie begins with his window blinds going up—the way the curtain used to rise on a movie screen; and his girlfriend later refers to the show being over for now to divert his attention from the stories unfolding before him. She even sports her titillating negligee as a "preview of coming attractions."

Cooped up in his apartment because of an injury, Jefferies falls into the voyeuristic trap of watching the lives of others rather than living his own. As a professional photographer, indulging in voyeurism became his occupational hazard, and the occasion of being home-bound and confined to a chair only intensified the temptation.

But yielding to the temptation carries risks. In light of the cinema analogy, we see that the trap into which Jefferies falls is one to which we are all susceptible. For every book the average college student reads, popular wisdom tells us, he sees something on the order of fifty movies. Movie-makers are the new myth-makers, powerful shapers of the prevailing plausibility structures and thought patterns of our culture, wielding an influence far greater than many realize, and perhaps far more than they ought. Movies can be a wonderful source of entertainment and reprieve from the world. Hitchcock himself loved movies. They can serve eminently worthwhile ends—they can be inspirational, they can be challenging, thought-provoking, even profound. They can also, however, be vacuous, insipid, and mindless.

There is a conspicuous parity between the fluctuating pictures on a movie screen and the flickering images on the wall of Plato's famous cave. Plato asks us to imagine men chained their whole lives inside a cave, able only to watch shadows on its wall. The shadows are but a dim reflection of the outside world—the real world, as it were—and, as a result, such men unwittingly lack knowledge. Their perspectives are shaped by mere appearances, not reality. For Plato, the cave represents the world in which we live, a world of mere appearances. Only through reason can we be put in touch with the real world and actual knowledge rather than opinions based on appearances. His skepticism about playwrights (the movie-makers of his day) came from their implicit crafting of representations of representations, doubly removed from the real thing.

Plato's point is well taken. We need to be careful to distinguish appearances from reality, and opinions from knowledge, and we should be cautioned against a preoccupation with movies and television. When someone suggests that the best news available is from the satirical entertainment-driven *Daily Show*, for example, there's a problem. When we confuse wants with needs, when we confuse pundits for statesmen, or when we settle for personality over character and celebrity over substance, we fall into the same recurring trap of being enticed by dazzling veneers disguising vacuity.

Rear Window has as one of its main insights this particular danger of spectatorship: failure to engage life directly, content with passive viewership without commitment, which results in a life of inauthenticity. One of the recurring motifs we find in the corpus of Hitchcock's work is the importance of personal engagement and commitment. Holding others at arm's length, refusing to commit, and staying at a safe distance is the recipe for inauthenticity.

In one sense the character of Jefferies, committed to finding out whether the neighbor across the way killed his wife, is a seeker of knowledge. But what led to his suspicions wasn't a quest for justice or the natural human desire to solve a mystery or a laudable goal to protect another person, but simply rabid, morbid curiosity, indulgence in voyeurism. Though watching lives from a safe distance can lead to some propositional knowledge, it can also lead to faulty inferences (as it does in Jefferies' case, as he's wrong about nearly everything and everyone), and it can also lead to a failure to achieve knowledge in the arguably far deeper sense than the merely propositional.

Perhaps we underestimate the way instant communication and access to the world's events nowadays condition us to get caught up in the novel and exciting news, catching the waves and getting swept up in the latest break, however banal and ultimately inconsequential. Or we swing the pendulum the other way: we read and hear of tragedies as if they were meant for our entertainment, almost as if they're fictional tales weaved for our amusement, when real lives are at stake and genuine pain experienced. Real people become two-dimensional caricatures, almost fictionalized into something less than human, easily laughed at, mocked, gawked at, trivialized.

Remember for a moment the biblical characterization of knowledge. Adam knew Eve. We're called to know God. This isn't merely propositional knowledge. It's deep personal acquaintance, intimate knowledge of another. It's more than knowing about others; it's knowing them. Substituting propositional knowledge for deep personal knowledge and intimate spiritual and emotional acquaintance lends itself to superficiality and lack or loss of real engagement.

When Jefferies sees his neighbor—Miss Lonelyhearts—nearly driven to suicide by her loneliness, he fears for her life and considers action. But what had stopped him from intervening sooner to provide help in a more practical way—inviting her to dinner, introducing her to a friend? *Rear Window*, perhaps most of all, is about what it means to be a neighbor.

To move beyond spectatorship to real involvement, from a gawker to a real neighbor, requires that we heed the advice of the wise William James, the American pragmatist philosopher and psychologist. In his magnum opus *Principles of Psychology*, James writes about those people who obsessively read novels with such sympathy for the fictional characters they encounter there, but whose emotions, thus aroused, have no bearing on how they treat people in the real world around them. He worries about the person who experiences excellence in a play or concert performance, and leaves that experience at a level of the purely passively aesthetic, not goaded to go and do something excellent himself. James elaborates on this danger (in a passage referenced in our previous chapter on Harry Potter and education):

> The habit of excessive novel-reading and theatre-going will produce true monsters in this line. The weeping of a Russian lady over the fictitious personages in the play, while her coach-man is freezing to death on his seat outside, is the sort of thing that everywhere happens on a less glaring scale. . . . One becomes

filled with emotions which habitually pass without prompting to any deed, and so the inertly sentimental condition is kept up. The remedy would be, never to suffer one's self to have an emotion at a concert, without expressing it afterward in some active way. Let the expression be the least thing in the world—speaking genially to one's aunt, or giving up one's seat in a horse-car, if nothing more heroic offers—but let it not fail to take place.

Reading a book, watching a movie, seeing a concert—all can be great and inspiring activities. Sometimes of course the sheer fun and delight are enough, and nothing further is required. If indulgence alone becomes the habitual pattern, however, and the inspiration and insight such events imbue don't manifest in concrete actions of one sort or another, there's not only a missed opportunity, but a real danger that looms—the risk of inauthenticity and disengagement, of self-consumption rather than neighborly love, of superficiality rather than depth—and such is no wise course.

Having grown up outside Detroit, I (David) attended seminary in the idyllic Wilmore, Kentucky, spending three delightful years there. Occasionally I would watch the local news, charmed by the gravity given to local drama—with occasional exceptions, stories tended to be anecdotal and heart-warming. One Christmas I went home to visit my family and sat down to watch a local Detroit newscast. Although it was the same thing I had watched hundreds of times growing up, on this occasion the unrelenting stories of tragedy and heartbreak gripped my imagination. I had grown far more desensitized to human tragedy than I ever realized. Suddenly, listening to one heart-wrenching story after the next burdened my soul, nearly making me physically ill. I'd grown accustomed for so long to ingesting vast quantities of human tragedies without bothering to digest much of any of it.

Our call is to reflect the light of God's kingdom into the darkest corners of the earth, not to gawk blithely at our disparate and desperate neighbors. Like Jefferies, we must not allow distractions to blind us to the dramatic Story unfolding before us of which we're a part. God has called us to step out of the house and show love to our neighbors, even when it makes us uncomfortable or vulnerable. This is God's kingdom manifesting itself in this world–the ultimate preview of coming attractions.

31

Interstellar and Partiality

Christopher Nolan's 2014 film *Interstellar* tells a sweeping story, speculating on potential widespread destruction and human potential in the face of such prospects. Despite its scope, the film also zeroes in on individual concerns, using the protagonist and his family as the vehicle for considering important ethical questions. One such question centers on the tension between particular and more general moral judgments.

In an early critical scene, Cooper, the main character played by Matthew McConaughey, must decide whether or not to embark on an incredibly ambitious space mission. This mission requires leaving his children behind and risking never seeing them again. But his success in this endeavor could allow for survival of the entire human race, which has few options. A scientist involved in the mission encourages his participation, appealing to Cooper's obligations to mankind: "You can't just think about your family," Doyle says. "You have to think bigger than that." Cooper's response suggests that he recognizes his responsibility involves both the particular and the universal simultaneously: "I'm thinking about my family and millions of other families."

One could not blame Cooper had he participated in the mission solely out of a desire to ensure his own family's survival. But as the above quote suggests, he is also motivated by broader concerns. It seems rather unlikely, in light of Cooper's character, that he would have refrained from the world-saving mission if he did not have his own family to save. Nevertheless, the fact remains that there is something unmistakably particular and concrete about his driving motivation.

And this particularity is emphasized through the touchingly depicted relationship Cooper has with his daughter Murphy. Despite his visceral aversion to leaving her behind, and his arduous effort to part on good terms, he feels compelled and likely obligated to leave. This tension—between duties to his daughter and his duties to the rest of humanity—raises an interesting question: is Cooper morally obligated to complete this mission, a mission for which he is the best qualified? Even if the mission is a success and he returns, it's likely that his children will be considerably older. Does he have a duty to leave them behind? In light of all that's at stake, perhaps he does, but if this is so, it shows something interesting. Parental obligations have their limits. Partiality is permissible, but not sacrosanct.

In the ethics of Immanuel Kant, a person is to follow the categorical imperative, which tells us to act only on those principles we can will to become universal laws. And the principles, or maxims, on which we are to act are to be expressible in universal terms, singular references (like to family) having been expunged. Kant, however, departed on this score from a number of other important ethical thinkers, like Aristotle, who thought that moral judgments are always made in the context of family or polis. Kant's insistence that such particular terms be replaced with universal ones is an interesting claim, but one that leaves many dubious.

Various feminist thinkers, for example, have emphasized that morality is to be understood in more particular terms than Kant would allow. On their view, moral determinations are to be made in the arena of our relationships, as we take into account all the various concrete details and particular specifics of the richly contextualized circumstances in which we find ourselves. We shouldn't be guided by universal and abstract moral principles bereft of reference to those we know, those with whom we have cultivated lasting relationships.

They have a point, of course, which makes understandable the protagonist in *Interstellar* being motivated most of all by a desire to save his own family. But he's also confronted with a truly universal challenge: the planet is slowly dying, and time for rescue is short. The survival of humanity depends on a successful mission. And this crisis, it seems to us, renders unworkable a desire to care only about his own family. Although most of us won't find ourselves in so dire a situation, we live in a much smaller world than we used to. We're aware of human needs that go beyond those of our immediate family, close friends, and nearby neighbors. Because of technological advances, we know about innumerable global needs. If there's a tsunami in Japan, we can watch it in real time. If there are refugees in the Middle East, we can read tweets about them instantaneously. This makes it less permissible to be indifferent to the needs of strangers. Of course, we care most about our close family members and friends, but this doesn't license indifference to others beyond those confines. In fact, we can become so fixated on privileging and prioritizing our loved ones that that very partiality can become perverse.

Recently, we read an article about how so many college-aged kids of today's generation are experiencing a hard time growing up and assuming responsibility. One of the reasons for the phenomenon, it was suggested, is overly protective parenting. Parents are supposed to make their children feel loved and special, no doubt, but parents also have to teach their children that disappointments are inevitable; that, though undeniably valuable, they are not more objectively valuable than others; that achievement requires work; and that failure requires ownership of responsibility. In his examination of Kantian ethics, *The Moral Gap*, John Hare explains the psychological challenges children face upon realizing they are not the guide of their parents' moral compass: "It can be a startling lesson for a child who has been the apple of his mother's eye to discover that his mother is not willing to put pressure on his teacher to get him into a team, or even to make a scene in the shop to get him the last remaining construction set of the kind he wants for Christmas." Yet as most parents know, protecting fragile psyches from such hard truths to avoid their kids from experiencing pain is to confer them permission to remain children, if not infantile.

Neglecting the responsibility to impart these truths, however sober, to their children is a recipe for disaster and perpetual adolescence. Rather than an expression of love, it's to privilege the particular to the neglect of broader truths applicable to everyone. One is implicated in an objectionable form of extreme partiality when her judgments fail to be qualified and regulated by universal truths. C. S. Lewis depicts this insight in a brilliant scene from *The Great Divorce*, where a mother has so fixated on her son that her "love" becomes idolatrous, blinding her to the fullness of reality in which he exists. Sadly, her extreme particularism costs her paradise and is tantamount to choosing darkness over light.

So the feminists have their points to make, but it's a mistake to swing the pendulum toward partiality to the exclusion of what remains true for the whole of humankind. Close personal relationships are particularly vulnerable to corruption, or even abuse, when they're not guided by sound moral principles that apply universally. Every evil in this world is the distortion of something primordially good—wives whose selfless service gets cruelly taken for granted, a healthy sense of self that transforms into pride. Partiality is permissible, but not sacrosanct. Particular obligations obtain, but they don't vitiate more general ones.

32

The Faithful Witness of Fred Rogers

There's a lot that viewers will find unsurprising in *Won't You Be My Neighbor?*, Morgan Neville's 2018 documentary about longtime children's show host Fred Rogers. Most Americans who came of age at the end of the twentieth century are familiar with *Mister Rogers' Neighborhood*, given that the show was on for over thirty years, and the documentary is loaded with iconic images and scenes from the set that are perfect nostalgia fodder. It's all there: the trolley and memorable music, King Friday the 13th and Daniel the Striped Tiger, Lady Aberlin and Mr. McFeely, Mr. Rogers' signature cardigans and his regular, recurring visitors. It's a feel good, emotionally evocative movie if ever there was one, and that good feeling matches the mood of Rogers' show itself, which intentionally offered children familiar feelings of warmth and reassurance. Over the course of its time on the air, the show remained remarkably consistent; its host, thoughtful and kind, and Neville's film nicely captures these dynamics so permanently etched into our memories and vividly returns them to us unchanged.

What has changed, however, is the framing of these familiar features, and therein lies the surprise of the film. Behind the simple sets and low production values of *Mister Rogers' Neighborhood*, underneath the quaint songs and the unhurried storylines lay a profound conviction—children are inherently valuable and deserve the love and respect of those charged with their care. It's a commonplace belief, one that most would readily assent to. And yet, given the contentiousness of our day, we might wonder how genuine such a belief is, how fully committed we are to it. Presented as an homage to Fred Rogers, *Won't You Be My Neighbor?* poses a stiff challenge to viewers: is the world we are making hospitable to the most vulnerable among us? If not, what are we doing to make it so? It's a challenge that Mr. Rogers took to heart and fully lived out. If you want to know what moral apologetics for children looks like, watch a rerun of his show. To him love demanded more than lip service; it informed his approach to all he did.

Mr. Rogers was for just this reason deeply countercultural, even radical. Disrupting the system, turning programming for children on its head, was precisely his intention, as he aimed to use the television medium to work against its most destructive tendencies. An ordained Presbyterian minister, Fred Rogers believed children deserved more from TV than the silliness and violence on offer, the pies in the face, the slapstick comedy reliant on gags and props, vacuous frivolity at best, abject dehumanization at worst. In the 1950s, as television was emerging as a cultural force, Rogers saw the potential for it to be used to connect us, to build real community out of the entire country. And he took on that challenge with all the resources at his disposal—his faith, his musical training, his artistic creativity, his education in early childhood development, his listening skills, his talented and dedicated staff, and his obvious love for children—inviting his young viewers into the safety and security of being his neighbor, to become part of a family who would love, guide, and protect them.

But this neighborhood was no Pollyannaish utopia; in fact, conflict was essential to the stories Fred told—conflict that would be honestly presented and dealt with, not papered over, trivialized, or ignored. Despite its *Leave It to Beaver* feel, the show began in the late 1960s—1968 in fact, perhaps the most heartrending and harrowing year of that most tumultuous of decades. It was a time of unprecedented political and social turmoil, violence, and dissension in the United States, and Mr. Rogers understood it as his job to help children process all of the tragedy and upheaval they were certainly aware of—war, assassinations, racial discrimination—but were often left to their own devices to figure out. Drawing from a concept in music, Rogers explained that he aimed to help children through the difficult modulations of life, some of which are much harder than others to achieve on their own.

His approach was a far cry from seeing these children as consumers merely to be sold a product. As one friend explained, each episode was a sermon, a spiritual message that communicated directly to their hearts. Fred himself said that he saw the space between the TV and the viewer as holy ground, a sentiment verified by the seriousness with which he took his ministry. He crafted every script with care, concerned that the actors follow the lines closely in order to teach the children and help them better understand the world around them. He wrote the songs, voiced the puppets, and produced the shows. And he did so day in and day out, knowing full well that many would miss his point, that he would be mocked with parody, and that he would have to continuously counter the folly of mainstream entertainment.

And that's perhaps another surprising feature of *Won't You Be My Neighbor?* The courage and resolve of Fred Rogers, character traits that enabled his long career but that, regrettably, aren't often associated with the cultural persona of the man himself. We suspect, though, that this is our failure of imagination—to think that kindness, gentleness, and respect are somehow weak or passive. Or perhaps it's a reflection of the nihilism creep in our culture. The life of Mr. Rogers shows that to be truly kind, to be gentle, to demonstrate empathy, and to respect others takes great will. Mockery and cynicism is far easier. But mockery takes a toll; it erodes confidence and trust and wears away the social fabric, a lesson Fred himself learned as a bullied child who had a hard time making friends. He hoped to protect his viewers against such destructive behavior—either enacting it or receiving it. To this end he sought instead to make goodness attractive, "to help children become more aware that what is essential in life is invisible to the eye."

Fred's Christian faith is not the primary focus of the documentary, but it was implicit in everything he did; an attentive viewer will recognize that without it, there would be no *Mister Rogers' Neighborhood*. Junlei Li, director of the Fred Rogers Center, reminds us that Rogers' insistence that all people are inherently valuable, all are deserving of love and capable of giving it, is a fundamental tenet of Christianity. Mr. Rogers taught his viewers to see with spiritual eyes, to look at all people they encounter as image-bearers of God. No one is ordinary, and everyone is unique. His relationship with François Clemmons who played Officer Clemmons on the show testifies to the power of acting on that truth. Fred's simple message, "I love you just the way you are," was meant not only for the children watching but for Clemmons, too. It was a life-changing moment when he finally realized that, Clemmons tearfully recounts: "No man had ever told me that he loved me like that. I needed to hear it all my life. My dad never told me, my stepfather never told me. So from then on he became my surrogate father."

While detractors may balk, and cynics sneer, Rogers' generous acceptance of people is nothing like entitlement; it doesn't enable narcissism. Rather, it's centered on a notion of interdependence—we are responsible for others. We can encourage them toward good or evil. In a PSA recorded after the 9/11 terrorist attacks, Rogers calls us to be Tikkun Olam, a concept from Judaism that means "repairers of creation." "Love is at the root of everything—all learning, all parenting, all relationships. Love or the lack of it." Far from an empty cliché or feckless sentiment, it's the simple truth that it's love that changes the world—sharing that love, teaching others to love, promoting love. Fred embodied what love of God and neighbor—the divine commands in some sense constitutive of all the law and prophets—looks like. Rogers did it in his inimitable and singular way, defying odds, bursting categories, shattering expectations, and debunking stereotypes along the way, but as the film reminds us as it closes, this is an ongoing task and persistent charge for us all. As Rogers shared in his last commencement speech, others have smiled us into smiling, talked us into talking, sang us into singing, loved us into loving. Remember them and do likewise. Mr. Rogers ran his race well, and he has handed the baton off to us. We would be wise to honor his memory, celebrate his life, and emulate his faithfulness.

NOTES

Introduction
1. Charles Taylor, *A Secular Age* (Cambridge, MA: Belknap, 2018).

Chapter 1
1. Kurt Vonnegut, "Make your soul grow." *Letters of Note*, 28 October 2013, https://lettersofnote.com/2013/10/28/make-your-soul-grow/.
2. ---, *Slaughterhouse-Five* (New York: Dell, 19769), 21-22.
3. Ibid., 196.

Chapter 2

Thanks to Greg Bassham, Mark Foreman, and Maria Owen for helpful comments on an earlier draft. Any remaining difficulties in this chapter owe entirely to their patent irresponsibility.

1. Thanks to Christopher and Barbara Roden for the inspiration for such a description, which we paraphrased. All Holmes references in this chapter come from their edited volume of Sir Arthur Conan Doyle, *The Complete Sherlock Holmes* (New York Barnes & Noble, 2009).
2. "Wisteria Lodge," 838.
3. "Veiled Lodger," 1056.
4. "Retired Colourman," 1068.
5. "Naval Treaty," 425-426.
6. *Sign of the Four*, 449.
7. Conan Doyle does characterize Moriarty as a philosopher: "He is the Napoleon of crime, Watson. He is the organizer of half that is evil and of nearly all that is undetected in this great city. He is a genius, a philosopher, an abstract thinker. He has a brain of the first order" ("Final Problem," 440). Other Conan Doyle references to philosophy are less explicable, from "philosophical instruments" in the scientific laboratory to the "brow of a philosopher above and the jaw of a sensualist below" in describing Colonel Sebastian Moran in "The Empty House" (461). Holmes would also assume a half comic and "wholly philosophical" view when his affairs were going awry ("Missing Three-Quarter," 597).
8. "Case of Identity," 47.
9. *Sign of the Four*, 76.
10. *Valley of Fear*, 741.
11. *Study in Scarlet*, 11.
12. "Red-Headed League," 160.
13. Fyodor Dostoevsky, *The Brothers Karamazov* (1880; New York: Bantam Books, 1981), 33.
14. "Blue Carbuncle," 227.
15. "Copper Beeches," 295.
16. "Greek Interpreter," 406.

17. Helen Longino's "Feminist Epistemology as a Local Epistemology" is a powerful example of this in literature. It can be found here: *Aristotelian Society Supplementary Volume* 71, no. 1 (1997): 19-36.
18. "Sussex Vampire," 997.
19. *Sign of the Four*, 76.
20. Ibid., 82.
21. Ibid.
22. Ibid., 140. Interestingly enough, he was more concerned about the deleterious effects of love on his analytical abilities than drugs.
23. "Lion's Mane," 1044.
24. "Six Napoleons," 563.
25. We resonate with Susan Haack on this score; see her "Knowledge and Propaganda: Reflections of an Old Feminist," *Partisan Review* 60 (1993): 556-65.
26. Linda Patrik, the sister-in-law of Theodore Kaczynski, the Unabomber, was once asked what she had learned as a philosopher from the experience, to which she responded, "Based on this whole experience, I have lost respect for tremendous intellect. I have discovered that genius needs to be coupled with heart and loving relationships with people to have a positive impact on society. I now know that intellectual brilliance alone has great dangers" (http://www.union.edu/N/DS/s.php?s=1622).

Chapter 3

1. David French, "How a Fictional Soccer Coach Showed What the World Should Be." *The French Press, The Dispatch.* January 3, 2021. https://frenchpress.thedispatch.com/p/how-a-fictional-soccer-coach-showed.
2. Michaela Flack, "Ted Lasso Is Rooting for You." *Christ and Pop Culture.* November 5, 2020. https://christandpopculture.com/ted-lasso-is-rooting-for-you/.
3. Kevin Baxter, "'Ted Lasso' was icing on a $250 million deal. Now he has his own TV show." *Los Angeles Times.* 14 August 2020, https://www.latimes.com/entertainment-arts/tv/story/2020-08-14/jason-sudeikis-ted-lasso-english-premier-league-apple-tv.
4. Jonny Walls, *Couch Survivor*, Cineline Productions, 2015, DVD.

Chapter 4

1. Those who don't have such a take on New Age and Wiccan theology should insist that an argument be provided here. Though they are right to insist on such an argument, giving that argument would take us too far afield for present purposes. Such a critique, were it to be provided, might focus on such theology's instances of unprincipled syncretism, the way it attempts to put together pieces of theological systems that are composed of mutually exclusive truth claims.
2. Richard Abanes, *Harry Potter and the Bible: The Menace Behind the Magick* (Camp Hill: Horizon, 2001), 96. Abanes uses this spelling to distinguish occult magick from sleight-of-hand magic.
3. Rowling, J. K., *Harry Potter and the Sorcerer's Stone* (New York: Scholastic, 1997), 237.
4. Ibid., 230-233.

5. Epistemology is the branch of philosophy that studies the nature of knowledge, traditionally defined as true, justified beliefs, although the right account of knowledge is a difficult question. Shawn Klein's chapter in *Harry Potter and Philosophy* (Open Court, 2004) elaborates on the challenge of securing knowledge in a world of appearances.
6. Rowling, *Stone*, 177-178.
7. ---, *Harry Potter and the Goblet of Fire* (New York: Scholastic, 2000), 722.
8. ---, *Harry Potter and the Order of the Phoenix* (New York: Scholastic, 2003), 618.
9. ---, *Stone*, 242.
10. ---, *Harry Potter and the Chamber of Secrets* (New York: Scholastic, 1998), 159.
11. ---, *Stone*, 148-152.
12. Abanes, 136.
13. Ibid., 88.
14. Ibid., 244.
15. Alexander I. Solzhenitsyn, *The Gulag Archipelago 1918-1956* (New York: Harper and Row, 1975), 612.
16. Rowling, *Chamber*, 530-531.
17. ---, *Stone*, 5.
18. Martha Nussbaum, *The Fragility of Goodness: Luck and Ethics in Greek Tragedy and Philosophy* (Cambridge: Cambridge University Press, 1986).
19. Tom Morris, *If Aristotle Ran General Motors* (New York: Holt, 1997), 148.
20. C. S. Lewis makes such a case in *Abolition of Man* (New York: HarperOne, 2015).
21. See "The Will to Believe" in William James, *The Will to Believe and Other Essays in Popular Philosophy* (Cambridge, MA: Harvard University Press, 1979). For an insightful analysis of Jamesian "liveness" and religious belief, see Hunter Brown, *William James on Radical Empiricism and Religion* (Toronto: University of Toronto Press, 2000).
22. Originally published in *Harry Potter and Philosophy*, edited by David Baggett and Shawn Klein (Chicago: Open Court, 2004).

Chapter 5

Thanks to Dean Kowalski, Mark Foreman, and Stephanie Deacon for helpful comments on an earlier draft of this essay, and special thanks to Mark for introducing me (David) to Firefly *and to Stephanie for the* Firefly *and* Dr. Horrible *marathons.*

1. As Evelyn Vaughn notes: "Remember how often the show is called a space Western? What some people prefer not to recognize about the Western genre, whether in episodes of *Gunsmoke* or *The Lone Ranger*, is that the majority of its archetypes hail from the Old South, the losing side of the Civil War, as surely as do Mal and Zoe." (see Vaughn, "The Bonnie Brown Flag" in *Serenity Found: More Unauthorized Essays on Joss Whedon's Firefly Universe*, ed. Jane Espenson, with Leah Wilson [Dallas: BenBella Books, 2007], 190-91). Whedon makes clear his negative attitude toward slavery in "Our Mrs. Reynolds" and even more explicitly in "Shindig."

2. Fans of Whedon know that he relishes mixing genres noir and detective stories horror and teenage-girl-coming-of-age stories, and now this. At one point when he wanted to mix noir elements with Westerns in *Serenity*, he found precedent for such a blend in *Pursued*, *The Furies*, and *Johnny Guitar*.
3. See P. Gardner Goldsmith, "Freedom in an Unfree World" in *Serenity Found*, 55-65.
4. Jean-Paul Sartre, *Nausea* (New York: New Directions, 2007), 9.
5. Rhonda V. Wilcox, "I Do Not Hold to That: Joss Whedon and Original Sin," in *Investigating Firefly and Serenity: Science Fiction on the Frontier*, ed. Rhonda V. Wilcox and Tanya R. Cochran (New York Tauris, 2008), 158.
6. Jubal Early, in fact, was a Confederate soldier who also happens to be an ancestor of Nathan Fillion.
7. Lyle Zynda, "We're All Just Floating in Space," in *Finding Serenity: Antiheroes, Lost Shepherds, and Space Hookers in Joss Whedon's* Firefly, ed. Jane Espenson (Dallas: BenBella, 2004), 91.
8. An older but useful book about existentialism and religion is David E. Roberts' *Existentialism and Religious Belief* (New York: Oxford University Press, 1959).
9. William Irwin and Jorge E. Gracia, *Philosophy and the Interpretation of Pop Culture* (New York: Rowman and Littlefield, 2007). 56.
10. Recall again the series theme song. Mal can't do much about powerful entities "burning the land" or "boiling the sea," but what he chooses to do about them and his powerlessness regarding them is not beyond him; in this respect, he is still free.
11. Relevant episodes demonstrating such traits of Mal's include "Heart of Gold," "Shindig," "Our Mrs. Reynolds," and "The Train Job."
12. As Eric Greene writes: "It is more accurate to say [Mal] believed in nothing that was abstract, only in what was immediate. Like many a pragmatic hero in the American Western, Mal is compelled almost exclusively by practical considerations, immediate survival needs, and personal loyalties. Mal is primarily instinctual rather than ideological (Greene, "The Good Book" in *Serenity Found*, 83).
13. Agnes B. Curry, "Is Joss Becoming a Thomist?" *Slayage*, Vol. 4, no. 4, March 2005, https://www.whedonstudies.tv/uploads/2/6/2/8/26288593/curry_slayage_4.4.pdf.
14. Even Sartre himself arguably couldn't be a fully consistent existentialist because his view seemingly entails that it is bad or wrong to live in bad faith.
15. Although this is an interesting and provocative idea, reminiscent in certain respects of Trenton Merricks' intriguing denial of the existence of things like chairs (see his *Objects and Persons* [New York Oxford University Press, 2003]), existentialists may be committing a modal mistake here, spuriously inferring from the contingency of objects their lack of essential properties.
16. An interesting side note: In much of the current philosophical literature on free will, the biggest challenge is scientific materialism. Existentialists are often the ones most vocal in assigning greater primacy to the subjective sense of freedom than to what seems a deliverance of a naturalistic worldview according to which we're complicated organic machines invariably determined to do all we do. In "Free Will in a Deterministic Whedonverse," Thomas Flanson embraces the view that the dominant metaphysical view in

Whedon's fictional worlds is a deterministic one. In support of this, he adduces psychological evidence for determinism, the viability of prophecies in Whedon's fictional worlds (like *Buffy* and *Angel*), and effective predictions (in *Firefly*, such as when Mal predicts Saffron's betrayal and the like). One could respond by pointing to the enduring metaphysical challenges in answering philosophical questions about free will that science alone seems ill-equipped to answer; to the potential consistency of prophecies and libertarian free will (for an informed and accessible recent analysis of this, see Dean Kowalski's "'Minority Report,' Molinism, and the Viability of Precrime," in his edited volume *Steven Spielberg and Philosophy: We're Gonna Need a Bigger Book* [Lexington: University Press of Kentucky, 2008], 227-47); and to the fact that the truth of the proposition "if we are determined, then predictions of human behavior are viable" doesn't entail that "if predictions of human behavior are viable, then we are determined" (see Flanson's essay in *The Psychology of Whedon: An Unauthorized Exploration of* Buffy, Angel, *and* Firefly, ed. Joy Davidson (Dallas BenBella, 2007), 35-49). Whether Joss must be interpreted as a determinist remains to be seen, however, and probably requires a separate essay.

17. A real-life, particularly apt illustration of a governmentally imposed effort aimed at making people better through morally dubious, even hideous, technology is the eugenics movement of the nineteenth and twentieth centuries. Sir Francis Galton coined the term "eugenics" in 1883, but intellectual precursors of the movement go back further—even Plato thought that reproduction should be monitored and controlled by the state. In the name of enhancing the procreation of the genetically advantaged, compulsory sterilization of those deemed inferior was thought justified. In the United States, Woodrow Wilson supported eugenics and, in 1907, helped to make Indiana the first of more than thirty states to adopt legislation aimed at compulsory sterilization of certain individuals. Hitler's infamous efforts to maintain a "pure" German race, killing tens of thousands of the institutionalized disabled while rewarding Aryan women who had large numbers of children, and engaging in mass genocidal practices toward the Jews—whom he considered inferior morally, spiritually, artistically, and physically—are perhaps the best-known atrocities arising from this perverse mentality.

18. In the *Dollhouse* series, in the episode "Omega" Joss rejects a Nietzschean type of nihilism by having Echo refuse to "transcend" with Alpha. This only furthers the argument that Joss is not a nihilist about ethics and value. There are objective standards insofar as slavery or preying on the innocent is wrong.

19. For a much more thorough treatment of the Euthyphro Dilemma, see Jerry Walls and David Baggett's *Good God: The Theistic Foundations of Morality* (New York Oxford University Press, 2011), esp. chap. 2.

Chapter 6

1. W. H. Auden, "September 1, 1939."

Chapter 7

1. Marilyn Adams, *Horrendous Evils and the Goodness of God.* Ithaca, NY: Cornell UP, 2000.

Chapter 8

1. Mark McEvoy, "Interview with John Green. *Sydney Morning Herald*, January 21, 2012.
2. Albert Camus, "The Myth of Sisyphus." *Existentialism from Dostoevsky to Sartre*, edited by Walter Kaufman (New York: Penguin, 1975), 375-378.
3. McEvoy.

Chapter 9

1. Justin Lee, "The Elitism of Fantasy vs The Egalitarianism of Science Fiction: On Ted Chiang's Impersonal Universe," *ArcDigital*, October 14, 2018, http//tinyurl.com/yaxjz7h4.
2. Darko Suvin, *Metamorphoses of Science Fiction* (New Haven, CT: Yale University Press, 1979), 2n.
3. Ibid., 27.
4. Sherryl Vint, *A Guide for the Perplexed: Science Fiction* (London: Bloomsbury Academic, 2014), 135-158, http//dx.doi.org.
5. John Wlson, and Ray Mescallado, "Philip K. Dick," *Magill's Survey of American Literature*, revised edition, September 2006, 1-10.
6. Ibid.
7. Darko Suvin, "P. K. Dick's Opus: Artifice as Refuge and World View," *Science Fiction Studies* 2, 1 (1975): 8-22.
8. *The Man in the High Castle* describes an alternate history wherein the Axis Powers defeated the Allieds in WWII.
9. *The Three Stigmata of Palmer Eldritch* is a dystopian novel of space colonization, blending cyborg technology with religious iconography.
10. *Dr. Bloodmoney* tells a postapocalyptical tale of nuclear holocaust survivors rebuilding society in the aftermath of the fallout.
11. Christian Metz, "Alienation." *The Encyclopedia of Literary and Cultural Theory* (Malden, MA: Wiley Blackwell, 2011). On Marxist terms, alienation refers both to the way human labor is converted into objects that belong to the owners of the means of production and to the experience of living under capitalism, which relies on such a process.
12. ---, "Reification," *The Encyclopedia of Literary and Cultural Theory*. With the term reification, Marxist critics point to the capitalistic process of quantifying human labor as a means to study and manipulate it.
13. Suvin, "P. K. Dick's Opus," 21.
14. Sherryl Vint, *A Guide for the Perplexed: Science Fiction* (London: Bloomsbury Academic, 2014), 135, http://dx.doi.org.
15. Suvin, "P. K. Dick's Opus," 10.
16. Ibid., 11.
17. Ibid., 14.
18. Ibid., 14.
19. In 1974, Dick experienced what he interpreted as a mystical epiphany, which influenced much of his later work.
20. Darko Suvin, "Goodbye and Hello: Differentiating within the Later P. K. Dick," *Extrapolation* 43.4 (2002): 370.
21. Ibid., 375.
22. Suvin, "P. K. Dick's Opus," 9.
23. Philip K. Dick, *The Man Who Japed* (New York: Vintage, 2002), 120.
24. Ibid., 15.

25. Ibid., 133.
26. Ibid., 119.
27. Douglas A. Mackey, *Philip K. Dick* (Boston: Twayne, 1988), 26.
28. "Satire," *EBSCO Literary Glossary*, 2019, ebscohost.com.
29. Dennis Weiss and Justin Nicholas, "Dick Doesn't Do Heroes," *Philip K. Dick and Philosophy*, ed. D. E. Wittkower (Chicago: Open Court, 2011), 37.
30. Ibid.
31. Philip K. Dick, "How to Build a Universe That Doesn't Fall Apart Two Days Later." *The Shifting Realities of Philip K. Dick: Selected Literary and Philosophical Writings*, ed. Lawrence Sutin (New York: Vintage, 1996), 279.
32. Suvin, *Metamorphoses*, 10. This novum, or "new thing," distinguishes science fiction stories from other genres and makes possible their speculative nature, setting up imaginative thought experiments that present reader and writer alike with questions of "what if."

Chapter 10

Many thanks to Greg Bassham, Michael S. Jones, and especially Dean Kowalski and Steve Patterson for helpful comments on earlier drafts of this essay. We attribute any remaining weaknesses to them, thereby absolving ourselves of all responsibility.

1. "Special Features," *Amistad*, DVD (Glendale, CA: DreamWorks, 1999).
2. There is a third type of right that we will just mention here called "conventional" rights. These are claims grounded by the rules and principles adopted within certain conventional relationships. Examples would be the relationship between a lawyer and his client or between a priest and his confessor. There are also employee right and even conventional rights in organized sports. Such rights need be neither morally nor legally based.
3. We also need to make a distinction between what are referred to as "negative" rights and "positive" rights. This language is not used in an evaluative sense; negative rights are not bad and positive ones good. A negative right entails an obligation to refrain from doing something. It is a right to be free from an action taken by others. Negative rights are often called rights of noninterference. The U.S. Bill of Rights is a good example of negative rights: freedom of worship, free speech, free press. These all say that the government cannot interfere with our exercising these rights without just cause. A positive right entails a right to expect another to do something. It means that someone is obligated to provide a particular good or service. Your right to an attorney is a positive right; the government must provide one for you if you cannot do so yourself. This distinction is an important one that is often confused.
4. Mill was the protégé of Jeremy Bentham, well known for his utilitarianism. Bentham was not the first to advance this principle of ethics, by any means, but he is one of its best-known advocates. Utilitarianism says that morality is a matter of maximizing utility, of generating the greatest happiness for the greatest number of people in a society. Mill would later modify and further develop this theory. We mention Bentham at this point because he was notorious for denying the existence of natural rights. Questions of rights and duties for him were to be answered by appeal to what he called the two "sovereign masters" of pain and pleasure, governing us in all we do. According to utilitarians, for moral guidance we must look to pleasure and pain rather than anything more abstract or metaphysical. Rights described as

natural or intrinsic violate utilitarian's consequentialism; to the extent that we have rights, according to utilitarianism, they would be ways of protecting people's interests with an eye on maximizing overall utility.

Utilitarianism and other "interest theory" accounts of rights typically ground rights in morally important interests that we believe all persons who fit into the class of rights bearers have. There are important variations here, from Richard Brandt's subtle rule utilitarian reading of moral rights to Alan Gewirth's view that the universality of a particular interest across the class of rights bearers presents a grounding for the right. Most theories of legal rights typically begin from some version of interest theory. In fairness to utilitarianism, it should be stressed that, in a great many cases, maximizing utility and treating people *as if* they possessed basic and essential human rights lead to identical results. But in cases where doing the latter produces severe disutility, utilitarianism, with the theoretical resources at its disposal, would find it hard to justify upholding such rights. In *Amistad*, we hear Calhoun (Arliss Howard) make an essentially utilitarian appeal in favor of maintaining slavery, warning of the prohibitively high price to be paid for abolition. Although such problems riddling utilitarianism have led the majority of political philosophers to see utilitarianism as inadequate in providing an account of rights, it is a view that still has its defenders. We do not explore a utilitarian account of rights here, although we wanted to mention that not everyone is convinced natural rights exist in the same way or even at all.

5. See especially Locke's *Essay Concerning Human Understanding* (1690), *Two Treatises of Government* (1689), and *Letter Concerning Toleration* (1689).
6. John Locke, *Two Treatises of Government* and *A Letter Concerning Toleration*, ed. Ian Shapiro (New Haven: Yale University Press, 2003), section 87, 136. In Locke's context of seventeenth-century England, the protection of property was one of his biggest motivations for arguing against the unchecked powers of kings and in favor of the need for an autonomous parliament. Property in fact was said by Locke to be a prerequisite for there to be any violation of justice at all, but this cryptic saying of Locke's from his *Essay* has often been analyzed in terms of a broader understanding of property, by which it means more than just ownership of land and possessions. Most expansively, it denotes something like the human quest for fulfillment and happiness, which requires more than just basic needs to be met. It also requires incentives to create and engage in meaningful work. It is by work, Locke thought, that we become entitled to the fruit of our labor. By mixing our labor with the world, we acquire the right to property.
7. For reasons of space we cannot delve into the matter of biblical exegesis to see in what, if any, sense the Bible sanctioned or allowed slavery. Suffice it to say we agree with those, from William Wilberforce to Dr. Martin Luther King, Jr., who affirm that slavery, especially the American version that treated humans as chattel, is antithetical to the normative force of biblical revelation rightly understood. A distinction between kinds of slavery, incidentally, is also at play in *Amistad*, when the prosecutor asks Cinque questions about the practices of slavery in his own country, refusing to acknowledge any potential moral distinction between kinds of slavery and indentured servitude. For insightful commentary on the Christan church's historical stance on slavery and relevant disanalogies between activities called "slavery," see Oliver

O'Donovan's *The Desire of the Nations* (New York: Cambridge University Press, 1998), especially pages 184-86 and 263-66.

8. Locke, *Two Treatises*, ed. Shapiro, 311. Although in recent decades there have been some very intelligent modified versions of voluntarism articulated, such as that by Robert Adams (see *Finite and Infinite Goods* [Oxford: Oxford University Press, 1999]), voluntarism in its starkest forms, like we find in Ockham (see Janine Idziak [ed.], *Divine Command Morality: Historical and Contemporary Readings* [New York: Mellen Press, 1979]), has raised notorious arbitrariness objections. For what if God were a despot? Even if not an evil despot, but rather a benevolent one, can God do just anything with us simply because he created us? Does God, for example, have the prerogative not to give us freedom and equality? On the other hand, if God did not have such a prerogative, does that mean God is bound by a moral code that exists independently of himself? Is God, for example, bound by the principle that making entails ownership, or was such a principle a function of his will? The way Locke hinted that divine moral authority gives God very wide prerogatives leaves many readers convinced that his theistic account, as it stands, needs further explication and defense.

9. Richard John Neuhaus, *The Naked Public Square: Religion and Democracy in America* (Grand Rapids, MI: Eerdmans, 1984), 164.

10. See Gary Rosen, "'Amistad' and the Abuse of History," in *The Films of Steven Spielberg: Critical Essays*, ed. Charles L. P. Silet (Lanham, MD: Scarecrow, 2002), 239-48.

11. Thomas Jefferson, *Notes on the State of Virginia* (New York: Harper and Row, 1964 [1861]), Query 18.

12. A fascinating issue in political philosophy introduced by this issue of religious motivation is the relevance to public discourse of religious conviction and reasons, particularly when it comes to coercive legislation. One of the admittedly vexed questions in political philosophy pertains to the legitimacy of bringing to bear one's religious convictions in the context of political discourse. On one side of the debate are thinkers like Robert Audi, who insist that religion, because of its all-encompassing scope, ambitious metaphysics, and perceived unquestionable authority, ought not to be able to provide compelling public reasons for legislation. (On this issue we might remind readers that the excesses and abuses of the French Revolution show that when a society rejects the idea of divine authority, it tends to transcendentalist alternatives, such as secular values, that themselves can come to be seen as authorities that none are permitted to challenge.) Richard Rorty and the early John Rawls were even stronger advocates for the privatization of religion. On the other side of the debate are thinkers like Christopher Eberle and Nicholas Wolterstorff, who insist that the exclusion of religious reasons from public discourse is antithetical and ultimately detrimental to the democratic enterprise; see Christopher J. Eberle, *Religious Conviction in Liberal Politics* (New York: Cambridge University Press, 2002), and Robert Audi and Nicholas Wolterstorff, *Religion in the Public Square* (New York: Rowman and Littlefield, 1997).

13. A defender of slavery like Calhoun in *Amistad* could try to turn the tables here and offer an argument for the naturalness of slavery based on its ubiquity in history, as we saw before. Would not a natural law theorist have good empirical grounds for claiming that slavery itself is a natural process of human

behavior? If so, then is not the natural law theorist committed to the claim that slavery is obligatory? It is not clear that an appeal to natural law provides anything like an airtight case against slavery. (Then again, moral arguments are rarely airtight, so this might not be too great a concern.)

14. Again, Locke's empiricism perhaps served as too great a constraint on his theorizing, because the way he had to cash out God's authority was in terms of rewards and punishments. We violate another human's freedom at the risk of divine punishment. Although this is a powerful prudential reason for respecting rights, it strikes most of us as lacking authoritative force. Locke's empiricism may have hampered his ability to construct the deeper theistic theory really needed to make sense of divine authority here, rather than mere divine power alone.

15. What perhaps justifies this modest revision of Locke is that it is far less radical a revision of Locke than those interpreters who, perhaps projecting, would try expunging all religious elements from Locke's account completely. We do not deny a case can be made for engaging in such radical revisionism. In Locke's own day he was denounced as a crypto-atheist for his elevation of human reason as a proper instrument for discerning the natural law and applying its principles to evaluations of justice. Locke's contemporary critics also complained that he made God irrelevant to political morality, largely by uncoupling God's will from judgments of legitimacy. The monarchical order had long rested on a presupposition that monarchy was the preferred form of government because it mirrored on earth the divine order of one lawgiver at the pinnacle of an expanding pyramid of progressively less powerful beings, each kept in place by a divine order that she live out her place in society as given to her by God, in his infinite wisdom, and sustained by divinely imposed caste-based obligations of each class to the others. Only kings could be sovereign—never the people, who were divinely commanded to play the role appointed to them by God in virtue of their having been born into their particular station. Rebellion against the king was therefore tantamount to rebellion against God.

When Locke in effect puts dominion over civil society in the hands of the people, and when he argues that it is not divine will but human contracting that brings a political order into being, he substantially secularizes the business of evaluating the justice of political arrangements. His saying that our rights come from God has looked to some like a feeble add-on meant to keep the ecclesiastical courts away. Add to this his staunch empiricism, and it is little wonder that even in his own day he was sometimes thought to be as "godless" as the arch-materialist Hobbes. It is easy to miss the force of this argument if one reads the *Second Treatise* outside of the light of the *First*.

We do not think this argument is without merit. Locke's work marked an important move toward secularism, and his rejection of a divine right to rule was decisive. He may well have been perceived by many in his generation as a thoroughgoing secularist in a religious disguise. Nonetheless, we would suggest that this sort of radical revision simply does too much violence to Locke's intentions and convictions. It strains credulity to think that Locke was not a sincere theist who believed that our rights were rooted somehow in God. This does not make it true, of course, but the point we are making here is merely a historical one. This is not to deny that secular counterparts of Locke's view can be identified, and perhaps many readers of Locke will suggest that, since his work moved us toward secularism, there should be no end to this process until we follow secularism all the way, cutting all references to God as the extraneous remnants of an earlier age they are. However, this requires argument, and we remain skeptical that a thoroughly secular account of rights can prove adequate.

16. John Adams, letter to Evans, June 8, 1819, in Adrienne Kock and William Peden (eds.), *Selected Writings of John and John Quincy Adams* (New York: Knopf, 1946), 209.
17. Lester J. Cappon, editor, *The Adams-Jefferson Letters* (Chapel Hill: University of North Carolina Press, 1959), 551.
18. Spielberg, a big admirer of Lincoln, has signed on to direct an upcoming film of Lincoln's life as depicted in Doris Kearns Goodwin's wonderful *Team of Rivals: The Political Genius of Abraham Lincoln* (New York: Simon and Schuster, 2006).
19. Attributed to John Stuart Mill; see "The Contest in America," *Dissertations and Discussions, Vol. 1* (1868), 26 (first published in *Fraser's Magazine*, February 1862).

Chapter 11

1. Charles Dickens, *A Tale of Two Cities* (Mineola, NY: Dover, 1998).
2. George Orwell, "Charles Dickens."
3. Arthur C. Clarke, *Profiles of the Future: An Inquiry into the Limits of the Possible* [1973] (London: Orion, 2000).
4. Neil Postman, *Technopoly* (New York: Vintage, 1993).
5. Ibid.
6. Edmund Burke, Letter to a Member of the National Assembly, 1791.
7. Mother Teresa, *In the Heart of the World: Thoughts, Stories, and Prayers* (Novato, CA: New World Library, 2010).
8. C. S. Lewis, *The Screwtape Letters* (San Francisco: HarperOne, 2015).
9. William James, *The Principles of Psychology* (Mineola, NY: Dover, 1950).

Chapter 12

1. See Immanuel Kant, *Critique of Practical Reason and Other Writings in Moral Philosophy*, translated and edited with an introduction by Lewis White Beck (Chicago, IL: The University of Chicago Press, 1949), 258.
2. See John Stuart Mill, *Utilitarianism* (Indianapolis, IN: Hackett Publishing Company, 2002).
3. Blaise Pascal, *Pensées* (trans. Honor Levi) (Oxford: Oxford University Press, 1995), 143.
4. John Locke, *The Reasonableness of Christianity*, ed I. T. Ramsey (Stanford: Stanford University Press, 1958), 70.
5. Thomas Reid, *Essays on the Active Powers of the Human Mind*, intr. by B. Brody (Cambridge, MA: M.I.T. Press, 1969), 256.
6. ---, *Practical Ethics, Being Lectures and Papers on Natural Religion, Self-Government, Natural Jurisprudence, and the Law of Nations*, ed. K. Haakonnssen (Princeton: Princeton University Press, 1990), 120.
7. Kant gave this argument in the *Dialectic of the Critique of Practical Reason* and also at the beginning of *Religion within the Boundaries of Mere Reason*, translated by George Di Giovanni (Cambridge: Cambridge University Press, 1998), and the end of the first and third Critiques.

8. Terrence Cuneo, "Duty, Goodness, and God in Reid's Moral Philosophy," in Sabine Roeser ed., *Reid on Ethics* (New York: Palgrave Macmillan, 2010), 256.
9. Simon Critchley, *Tragedy, the Greeks, and Us* (New York: Pantheon, 2019), 267.
10. Ernest Becker, *The Denial of Death* (New York: Free Press Paperbacks, 1997), 166. For further discussion on this, see Alan Noble's *Disruptive Witness* (Downer's Grove, IL: IVPBooks, 2018), chapter 3.

Chapter 13

1. Christopher Luu, "*The Handmaid's Tale* Is Doing a Great Job of Freaking Everyone Out at SXSW." *Refinery29*. March 11, 2017, https://www.refinery29.com/en-us/2017/03/144808/handmaids-tale-sxsw.
2. Emily Crockett, "Why women wore Handmaid's Tale robes in the Texas Senate." *Vox*. March 21, 2017. https://www.vox.com/identities/2017/3/21/15000098/handmaids-tale-texas-abortion-ban.
3. Dominic Patten, "'The Handmaid's Tale' Review: Elisabeth Moss-Led Adaptation Is Gripping, Chilling." *Deadline*, April 25, 2017. https://deadline.com/2017/04/the-handmaids-tale-review-elisabeth-moss-margaret-atwood-hulu-video-1202072550/.
4. Hank Stuever, "'The Handmaid's Tale' isn't just timely, it's essential viewing for our fractured culture." *The Washington Post*, April 20, 2017.
5. Jen Chaney, "'The Handmaid's Tale' on Hulu, Reviewed." *Vulture*, April 13, 2017. https://www.vulture.com/2017/04/the-handmaids-tale-hulu-review.html.
6. Emily Temple, "*The Handmaid's Tale* Adapts More than the Novel: Here Is America." *LitHub*, April 17, 2017, https://lithub.com/the-handmaids-tale-adapts-more-than-the-novel-here-is-america/.
7. Margaret Atwood, "Margaret Atwood on What *The Handmaid's Tale* Means in the Age of Trump." *New York Times,* March 10, 2017, https://www.nytimes.com/2017/03/10/books/review/margaret-atwood-handmaids-tale-age-of-trump.html.

Chapter 14

1. Roland H. Bainton, *Christian Attitudes toward War and Peace* (Nashville, TN: Abingdon, 1960), 66-84.
2. Hans Küng, *On Being a Christian*, translated by Edward Quinn (Syracuse, NY: Image, 1976), 245.
3. Martin Luther, *The Sermon on the Mount* and *The Magnificat* (Nashville: Abington Press, 1956).
4. John Howard Yoder, *The Politics of Jesus*, 2nd ed. (Grand Rapids, MI: Eerdmans, 1994).
5. Ibid., 43.
6. Leo Tolstoy, *A Confession, The Gospel in Brief and What I Believe*, translated by Aylmer Maude (London: Oxford University Press, 1940), 323.
7. Jan Narveson, "Morality and Violence: War, Revolution, Terrorism," in Tom Regan, ed., *Matters of Life and Death: New Introductory Essays in Moral Philosophy* (New York: McGraw-Hill, 1990), 139.

8. Originally published as "Resist Not Evil! Jesus and Nonviolence" in *Mel Gibson's Passion and Philosophy*, edited by Jorge Gracia (Chicago: Open Court, 2004)

Chapter 15

1. Gennady Stolyarov II, *Death Is Wrong* (Carson City, NV: Rational Argumentator Press, 2013).

Chapter 16

1. Flannery O'Connor, "A Good Man Is Hard to Find," *The Complete Short Stories* (New York: Farrar, Strauss, and Giroux, 1973), 117-133.

Chapter 17

1. Manohla Dargis, "Up from Rubble to Lead a Revolution." *The New York Times*, November 20, 2014.

Chapter 18

1. Whedon, Joss, DVD Commentary on "The Body." *Buffy the Vampire Slayer: The Complete Fifth Season*. 20th Century Fox, 2008. DVD.

Chapter 19

1. *Variety*, March 15, 2018.
2. *The Wrap*, July 21, 2018.
3. Darko Suvin, *Metamorphoses of Science Fiction: On the Poetics and History of a Literary Genre* (Yale University Press, 1979).
4. Ibid., 10.
5. Robert Adams, "Moral Faith," *The Journal of Philosophy* 92, no. 2.
6. Ibid., 81.
7. Ibid.

Chapter 22

1. Lloyd N. Dendinger, "Mark Twain," *Critical Survey of Long Fiction*, 4th ed. (Ipswich, MA: Salem, 2010), 1–7. Twain first used this famous pen name in 1862, drawing it from the riverboat cry marking a safe depth of two fathoms of water.
2. *Mark Twain*, produced by Noah Morowitz (Bronx, NY: Greystone Communications, 1995), Biography, https://www.biography.com/video/mark-twain-full-episode-2074654020.
3. Harold K. Bush, "Mark Twain's American Adam: Humor as Hope and Apocalypse," *Christianity and Literature* 53, 3 (2004): 305.
4. Gabriel Brahm and Forrest Robinson, "The Jester and the Sage," *Nineteenth-Century Literature* 60, 2 (2005): 139.
5. These writings from the early twentieth century, primarily centered on issues of social injustice, have been collected in *Mark Twain on the Damned Human Race*, ed. Janet Smith (New York: Sterling, 1994).
6. Two representative examples of arguments made by critics who arrive at antithetical conclusions about the question of Twain's faith are Dwayne Eutsey's "Mark Twain's Attitudes toward Religion: Sympathy for the Devil or Radical Christianity?" *Religion and Literature* 31, 2 (1999), 45–64 and Lawrence Berkove and Joseph Csicsila's *Heretical Fictions: Religion in the Literature of Mark Twain* (Iowa City: University of Iowa Press, 2010).
7. Berkove and Csicsila, *Heretical Fictions*, 1.

8. Sherwood Cummings, "Mark Twain's Social Darwinism," *Huntington Library Quarterly* 20, 2 (1957), 165.
9. Nathaniel Hawthorne, "November 20th, Thursday," *Journals of Herman Melville*, ed. Howard C. Horsford and Lynn Horth (Evanston, IL: Northwestern University Press, 1989): 628.
10. Jeanne Campbell Reesman, "Mark Twain vs. God: The Story of a Relationship," *Mark Twain Journal* 52, 2 (2014): 120.
11. David Shapiro-Zysk, "The Separation of Church and Twain: Deist Philosophy in The Innocents Abroad," *The Mark Twain Annual* 4 (2006): 25–32, http://www.jstor.org/stable/41582221.
12. Bush, "Mark Twain's American Adam," 311.
13. Reesman, "Mark Twain vs. God," 120.
14. *Mark Twain*.
15. Brahm and Robinson, "The Jester and the Sage," 145.
16. Reesman, "Mark Twain vs. God," 114.
17. Bush, "Mark Twain's American Adam," 55.
18. Jennifer Rafferty, "Clergy," *The Routledge Encyclopedia of Mark Twain*, ed. J. R. LeMaster and James D. Wilson (New York: Routledge, 2011).
19. Bush, "Mark Twain's American Adam," 310.
20. For a fuller treatment of this discussion, see *The Morals of the Story* by David and Marybeth Baggett (Downers Grove, IL: IVP Academic, 2018), 207.
21. Jerry Walls, "The Wisdom of Hope in a Despairing World," *The Wisdom of the Christian Faith*, ed. Paul Moser and Michael McFall (Cambridge: Cambridge University Press, 2012), 249.
22. Cummings, "Mark Twain's Social Darwinism," 166.
23. Bush, "Mark Twain's American Adam," 305.
24. C. S. Lewis, *Mere Christianity* (Grand Rapids: Zondervan, 2001), 136.

Chapter 23

Thanks to Mark Foreman, Laura Jones, and Noah Levin for their insightful comments on an earlier draft.

1. Rowling, J. K. *Harry Potter and the Half Blood Prince* (New York: Scholastic, 2005), 120-121.
2. Ibid., 185.
3. Ibid., 186. One wonders why, in Harry's world, love potions remain legal if they're so dangerous and potentially manipulative. They aren't allowed at Hogwarts, but they can be lawfully bought, sold, and used, apparently even by the underaged. This is an example of how dangerous things are permitted in the wizarding world that would never be allowed in our own. (Of course, wizards might well say decry our dangerous firearms, automobiles, and nuclear weapons.)
4. Ibid., 213.
5. Ibid.
6. Ibid., 214.
7. Ibid.
8. In *The Tale of Beedle the Bard* (New York: Scholastic, 2008), 56-57, Dumbledore's commentary on "The Warlock's Hairy Heart" includes this reference to love potions:

   To hurt is as human as to breathe. Nevertheless, we wizards seem particularly prone to the idea that we can bend the nature of existence to our will. . . . Of course, the centuries-old trade in love potions shows that our fictional wizard is hardly alone in seeking to control the unpredictable course of love. The search for a true love potion continues to this day, but no such elixir has yet been created, and leading potioneers doubt that it is possible.

Dumbledore even adds this footnote "Hector Dagworth-Granger, founder of the Most Extraordinary Society of Potioneers, explains, 'Powerful infatuations can be induced by the skillful potioneer, but never yet has anyone managed to create the truly unbreakable, eternal, unconditional attachment that alone can be called Love."

9. Here's an analogy: Sometimes people need medication for psychological struggles. Imagine a case in which a depressed patient has a chance to become medicated to deal with the problem, when what he really needs is to work through issues of anger or resentment. How tempting it would be for such a patient simply to pop a pill rather than to deal with the underlying causes. The pill would certainly be easier, but it wouldn't offer the real solution required. It would deal only with the symptoms, not with the real cause. Pulling out weeds at their roots may be harder than simply spraying them to make them temporarily go away, but, ultimately, it's more effective and enduring.
10. William Hasker, *The Triumph of God over Evil: Theodicy for a World of Suffering* (Downers Grove, IL: InterVarsity Press, 2008), 156. Hasker continues, "For that matter, individuals without free will would not, in the true sense, be human being at all, at least this is the case if, as seems highly plausible, the capacity for free choice is an essential characteristic of human beings as such. If so, then to say that free will should not exist is to say that we humans should not exist It may be possible to say that, and perhaps even to mean it, but the cost of doing so is very high." Ibid.
11. Merope, Dumbledore says, gave up, leaving her child behind. Surely, it would have been better had she not given up but rather persevered, at least for the child's sake. Perhaps Voldemort wouldn't have emerged if she had. Although this is true, Merope's giving up was likely not enough in Rowling's universe to ensure that Voldemort would emerge. Presumably, he had a choice in the matter and could have chosen a different path, despite the loss of his mother. So even if Merope's death was a contributing factor, it was only one among others. The nature of how Merope gave up is also an interesting question. If she committed suicide, for example, then our speculative argument in this chapter for her redemption, admittedly a redemption only partial and imperfect, would be undermined. But she may have simply been tired; having lost the will to live, she may have done the best she could. And in contrast to Voldemort's doing all in his power to avoid death, Merope's willingness to accept it seems practically virtuous. She's not responsible for doing more than the best she could, and it does good to remember that Dumbledore himself says not to judge her too harshly.
12. For more on this theme, see Greg Bassham on abilities versus choices in *The Ultimate Harry Potter and Philosophy* (Hoboken, NJ: Wiley Blackwell, 2010).
13. It's a function of literature, the philosopher Noël Carroll reminds us, to magnify and thereby clarify the patterns that shape human affairs in order that we may discern such regularities when they appear less diagrammatically in the flesh. See Noël Carroll, "*Vertigo* and the Pathologies of Romantic Love,"

in *Hitchcock and Philosophy: Dial M for Metaphysics*, edited by David Baggett and William Drumin (Chicago: Open Court, 2007), 112.
14. In the final book, Snape casts Harry in negative terms, concluding, "He is his father over again." To which Dumbledore replies, "In looks, perhaps, but his deepest nature is much more like his mother's." *Deathly Hallows*, 684.

Chapter 24

1. Rudolf Otto, *The Idea of the Holy* (New York: Oxford University Press, 1958).
2. Syamal K. Sen and Ravi P. Agarwal, *Zero: A Landmark Discovery, the Dreadful Void, and the Ultimate Mind* (Cambridge, MA: Academic Press, 2015), 74.

Chapter 25

1. "J. K. Rowling and Emma Watson discuss Ron, Hermoine, and Harry: The full interview." *Hypable*, February 7, 2014.
2. "Our Mrs. Reynolds." *Firefly*.

Chapter 26

Many thanks to Rose Alaimo, Greg Bassham, Kimberly Blessing, Elton Higgs, Stuart Noell, and Jerry Walls for feedback on this essay.
1. Nicolas Wolterstorff, *Lament for a Son* (Grand Rapids: Eerdmans, 1990), 90.
2. Originally published in *Movies and the Meaning of Life*, edited by Kim Blessing (Chicago: Open Court, 2005).

Chapter 28

1. In another sense, the love the Williams sisters have for each other goes beyond friendship, of course. As sisters who seem genuinely close, they probably have a much deeper bond than many friends do. This, however, is not always the case. Siblings are not necessarily friends, and, not uncommonly, friends can be far closer emotionally than siblings. Sibling relationship is (typically) rooted in a biological deliverance, not a volitional preference the way friendship is (although volition may have much to do with loving a sibling); thus the saying, "We can choose our friends, but we're stuck with our relatives." It seems more likely that a "mere friendship between rivals would cool or snap than that a sibling rivalry would ruin the relationship, since clear thinking immediately reveals the primacy of, say, a sibling relationship over even, say, a Grand Slam; but stranger things have been known to happen. Family relationships ideally feature *agape* (unconditional) love, not merely friendship, or *phileo* love, but hopefully *phileo* love as well. A third type of love is *eros*, romantic love; *agape*, *eros*, and *phileo* love are not mutually exclusive. Hopefully a marriage features all three. We need not settle here whether they are collectively exhaustive.
2. It's probably attributable to the erosion of the notion of friendship that "friendly" has come to mean niceness, affability, rather than the thicker and richer traits associated with genuine friendship: but if we were to defer to such watered-down and common colloquialisms, we could say that part of the goal of this chapter is, more minimally, to ask how rivals (opponents, conflicting partisans, et cetera) can remain at least on "friendly" terms despite the conflict.
3. Alasdair MacIntyre criticizes Aristotle's analysis of friendship on this ground: "His catalogue of types of friendship presupposes that we can always ask the

questions, 'On what is this friendship based? For the sake of what does it exist?' There is therefore no room left for the type of human relationship of which it would miss the point totally to ask on what it is based, for the sake of which it existed. Such relationships can be very different." Alasdair Macintyre, *A Short History of Ethics* (Notre Dame, IN: Notre Dame University Press, 2007), 80.
4. A friend once told us of an old hitting partner of his, Paul Koscielski, who was ranked #1 at the University of Texas, Austin, and also played professionally. Our friend recounts that their friendly matches were good for Paul's game, but that Paul never really found him either friend or enemy.
5. Mark Ryan, *Justine Henin: From Tragedy to Triumph* (New York: St. Martin's, 2008).
6. Mark Foreman, "Stabbing Seles: Fans and Fair Play," *Tennis and Philosophy*, edited by David Baggett (Louisville, KY: University of Kentucky Press, 2010), 164-181.
7. Arthur Ashe and Arnold Rampersad, *Days of Grace* (New York: Ballantine, 1994).
8. Ibid., 88.
9. Ibid., 89.
10. Ibid., 89-90.
11. For an eminently useful resource on Aristotle and friendship, see Lorraine Smith Pangle's *Aristotle and the Philosophy of Friendship* (Cambridge: Cambridge University Press, 2003).
12. Johnette Howard, *The Rivals: Chris Evert vs. Martina Navratilova, Their Epic Duel and Extraordinary Friendship* (New York: Broadway, 2005), 263.
13. Ibid., 271.
14. Ashe and Rampersad, *Days of Grace*, 260.
15. Ibid.
16. Ibid., 263.
17. C. S. Lewis clarifies: "Friendship arises out of mere Companionship when two or more of the companions discover that they have in common some insight or interest or even taste which the others do not share and which, till that moment, each believed to be his own unique treasure (or burden), The typical expression of opening Friendship would be something like, 'What? You too? I thought I was the only one.' We can imagine that among those early hunters and warriors single individuals—one in a century? One in a thousand years—saw what others did not; saw that the deer was beautiful as well as edible, that hunting was fun as well as necessary, dreamed that his gods might be not only powerful but holy. But as long as each of these percipient persons dies without finding a kindred soul, nothing (I suspect) will come of it; art or sport or spiritual religion will not be born. It is when two such persons discover one another . . . they share their vision—it is then that Friendship is born. And instantly they stand together in an immense solitude." C. S. Lewis, *The Four Loves* (New York: Harcourt Brace Jovanovich, 1960), 96-97.
18. Ibid., 104. Lewis's observation that friends look at projects side by side as opposed to pure romantic lovers, who may gaze at each other, seems especially useful when considering a doubles partnership like that of Mac and Peter Fleming. One can only imagine the almost martial solidarity those two felt playing Davis Cup in front of hostile crowds. Indeed, they did to some extent

resemble comrades in arms, which seems to be a friendly amendment to the basic Lewisian model.
19. Pete Sampras, with Peter Bodo, *A Champion's Mind: Lessons from a Life in Tennis* (New York: Random House, 2008), 273.
20. René Stauffer, *The Roger Federer Story: Quest for Perfection* (New York: New Chapter, 2006), 169-74.
21. Lewis, *Four Loves*, 117, 122.
22. For powerful resources on Nietzsche and friendship, read Ruth Abbey "Circles, Ladders and Stars: Nietzsche on Friendship," in *The Challenge to Friendship in Modernity*, ed. Preston King and Heather Devere (London: Frank Cass, 2000), 50-72. In addition, we would direct you to Peter Berkowitz's *Nietzsche: The Ethics of an Immoralist* (Cambridge: Harvard University Press, 1995), especially 171-75. Also see Daniel Conway's *Nietzsche's* On the Genealogy of Morals (London: Continuum, 2008) and Brian Leiter's *Routledge Philosophy Guidebook to Nietzsche on Morality* (New York: Routledge, 2002).
23. Ashe and Rampersad, *Days of Grace*, 82.
24. See Friedrich Nietzsche, *The Gay Science* (New York: Random House, 1974), section 279.
25. ---, *Thus Spake Zarathustra* (New York: Dover, 1999), I, chap. 14.

Chapter 29

1. Horace makes this same point regarding the poet in his classic *Ars Poetica*: "It has been made a question, whether good poetry be derived from nature or from art. For my part, I can neither conceive what study can do without a rich [natural] vein, nor what rude genius can avail of itself: so much does the one require the assistance of the other, and so amicably do they conspire [to produce the same effect]."
2. "What we have here is an intrinsic good in a slightly odd sense; not that we have value, each of us, all by ourselves ... since we have our value in relation. But the value is not reducible to the valuing by someone outside us, on this account, but resides in what each of us can uniquely be in relation to God." Hare, *God's Command* (New York: Oxford University Press, 2015), 29.

General Index

A
Abanes, Richard, 30–34, 36
About Time, 188
Adams, John Quincy, 72, 74, 82–86
Adams, Marilyn, 59
Adams, Robert, 142–144, 241
afterlife, 10, 62, 99, 104, 107–108
agnosticism, 7
Amistad, 72–76, 78–82
analytic philosophy, 19–20
Aquinas, Thomas, 48, 79, 84
  see also Thomism
Aristotle, 99
  on character, 33, 152, 166
  on friendship, 193–195, 199–200, 205
  on moral education, 37
  on moral judgment, 216
  on metaphysics, 49
  on virtue, 39
art
  Sherlock Holmes as artist, 22
  mathematics as art, 171
  Nietzsche's appreciation of art, 204
Ashe, Arthur, 196–202, 205
atheism, 7, 44, 157, 179
Auden, W. H., 57
authority
  God's authority, 78–79, 82
  human authority, 144
  moral authority, 51–53, 104–105, 124

B
beauty
  evidence of divinity, 170–171
  experience, 43–44, 62, 114
  transcendental, 2–3
Becker, Ernest, 108
belief,
  actions revealing belief, 142
  nature of belief, 25–26
  religious belief, 81–82, 112
Bonhoeffer, Dietrich, 125
Bradbury, Ray
  Fahrenheit 451, 135, 145–148
Burke, Edmund, 91

C
Camus, Albert, 41, 44, 63
Christ and Pop Culture, 1
coming-of-age story, 175, 189
compatibilism, 165
competition, 192–193, 201–204, 206
Connors, Jimmy, 205–206
consequentialism, 101, 122
correlativity thesis, 75
Creel, Richard, 157
Critchley, Simon, 107, 173
crucifixion, 115, 121, 123

D
Darwin, Charles, 157
Dick, Philip K., 65–71, 140–142
  The Man in the High Castle, 67, 71, 140–142, 144
  see also, science fiction
Dickens, Charles, 36, 87–88
divine command theory, 51
Dostoevsky, Fyodor, 15, 44
  The Brothers Karamazov, 15

E
education, 87–96
  moral education, 37, 96
egoism, 30, 32, 100
empiricism, 82
epistemology, 11–13, 19, 82–83
  feminist epistemology, 19
eternal life, 64, 127–128
ethical subjectivism, 32
eudaimonists, 107
Euthyphro Dilemma, 46, 50, 52
Evert, Chris, 200
evil, 115–125, 149–153

and Voldemort, 33
  moral evil, 180
  natural evil, 180
  systemic evil, 60
  see also, Problem of Evil
existentialism, 43, 46–47, 51

F
facticity, 45, 50
faith, 114, 156, 172, 183
  consolations of faith, 186
  imagination and faith, 38
  loss of faith, 44, 179
  moral faith, 122, 140–144
  precursive faith, 26
  religious faith, 38
fantasy, 29–30, 35, 65–66, 137
feminism, 206
forgiveness, 25, 114, 116, 120–121, 167
free will, 50–51, 165–166
freedom, 40–53, 58–59
  metaphysical freedom, 40–43
  political (or legal) freedom, 73–86
  requirement of love, 165
friendship
  between Ginsburg and Scalia, 56
  between Ramanujan and Hardy, 171, 174–175
  in *Harry Potter*, 91–92
  of pleasure, 194
  of usefulness, 194, 196
  of virtue, 199

G
Gibson, Mel, 115–116, 120
  The Passion of the Christ, 115
Ginsburg, Ruth Bader, 54–56
God's authority, deficient arguments
  divine retribution theory, 84
  divine workmanship theory, 84
  see also, authority, God
Green, John, 11, 61–64, 170
Gresham, Joy, 178, 181
grief, 185–187

H
The Handmaid's Tale, 110–113
Hardy, G. H., 170–174
Hare, John, 210, 217

Harry Potter
  Chamber of Secrets, 31–32, 34, 90–91, 161
  Goblet of Fire, 31
  Half-Blood Prince, 161, 163
  Prisoner of Azkaban, 161
  Sorcerer's Stone, 31, 89, 92, 94
  see also, Rowling, J. K.
Hitchcock, Alfred, 45, 211–212
  Rear Window, 211–213
Hobbes, Thomas, 73, 83
hope
  as theological virtue, 26
  for redemption, 113–114
  in death, 139
  obligation to hope, 157–158
Horace, 88
human artifacts, 48
humanism
  exclusive humanism, 2
  secular humanism, 127
  transhumanism, 126–128
humanities, 90
Hume, David, 82, 179
Hunger Games, 133, 135

I
identity
  natural kinds, 48
  human artifacts, 48
imagination, 175–177
  and faith, 38
  as means of understanding, 22
  educative function, 90
  moral imagination, 56, 95
imago Dei, 210
Interstellar, 215–217
intuition, 21, 171–172
Irwin, William, 1, 45

J
James, William, 16, 26, 39, 96
  Principles of Psychology, 22–23, 213
  Talks to Teachers, 153
Jesus, theories on teaching of nonviolence
  two-class ethics interpretation, 117

interim ethics interpretation, 117–118
Lutheran penitential ethic interpretation, 118
absolute pacificism interpretation, 119
implicit qualifier interpretation, 119–120
justice, 110–114
  and rights, 76
  essential to reality, 104
  social justice, 58–60
  lex talionis, 59

K
Kant, Immanuel
  argument from grace, 106
  argument from rationality, 105–106
  categorical imperative, 216
  deontology, 34–35, 101–105, 125
karma, 107
Kierkegaard, Søren, 44, 99, 139
King, Martin Luther, Jr., 58–60
Kinlaw, Dennis, 127
knowledge, 10–23,
  accessed by intuition, 172
  book (or propositional) knowledge, 180, 212
  difficulty of obtaining, 31
  experiential knowledge, 180, 213
  pursuit of knowledge, 38

L
law, 72–86
  letter of law, 120
  natural law, 78–79, 82–84
  moral law, 101
  Old Testament law, 118
  spirit of law, 120
  universal laws, 216
  see also, Ginsburg, Ruth
legalism, 120
Lewis, C. S.
  The Four Loves, 190
  The Great Divorce, 217
  A Grief Observed, 185, 190
  on courage, 94, 151
  on friendship, 202–203
  on tyranny, 135

The Problem of Pain, 180–181
The Screwtape Letters, 176
Till We Have Faces, 171–172
Lincoln, Abraham, 85–86
Locke, John, 72–85, 104
logic
  abduction, 14
  deduction, 11–12
  induction, 14
love, 94–96, 222
  and partiality, 217
  as foundation of community, 135
  Golden Rule, 37
  Greatest Commandment, 117
  love potion, 161–169
  love story, 62, 188–191
  of enemies, 116, 121
  of neighbor, 54–57
  risks of love, 178–187
  see also, suffering

M
magic, 30, 36, 89, 150–151
mathematics, 82, 170, 173–174
McEnroe, John, 196–199, 204–205
Mill, John Stuart, 35, 73, 75–76, 86, 101–102
Miller, Walter, 65–66
moral relativism, 28, 30
moral transformation, 185–186
Morris, Tom, 37
Mother Teresa, 91

N
Navratilova, Martina, 200
Newman, John Henry, 139
Nietzsche, Friedrich
  on human inequality, 51–52
  nihilism, 100
  overman, 92, 203–206
nonviolence, 115–120, 122–125
  see also, pacifism
Nussbaum, Martha, 37

O
O'Connor, Flannery, 92, 129–130
obligations, 1, 8, 75, 142, 145, 215–216, 218
occult, 28–30, 35–36
Once Upon a Time, 149

Otto, Rudolph, 171

P
pacifism, 118–119, 123–124
  see also, nonviolence
partiality, 215–218
Pascal, Blaise, 104, 108
passion, models of
  character model of the passion, 124
  duty model of the passion, 123
  freedom model of the passion, 123
Philosophy and Pop Culture, 1
Plantinga, Alvin, 172–173
Plato, 23, 48, 94, 99, 193, 212
  Platonism, 173
Postman, Neil, 90
  End of Education, 90
Problem of Evil, 179–184, 187
  see also, evil

R
Ramanujan, Srivivasa, 170–174
Reid, Thomas, 105–106
  coincidence thesis, 104–106
religion, 38, 80–82, 155–156
resurrection, 127–129, 139
rights
  civil rights, 58–60, 72
  human (or natural) rights, 59, 73, 84–85
  legal rights, 74
rivalries, 96, 195–196, 204
Rogers, Fred, 25, 95, 219–222
Rowling, J. K., 28–39, 175–177
  see also, *Harry Potter*
Ryken, Leland, 176

S
sacred, 2, 7, 188, 190, 209–210
Sartre, Jean Paul, 40–53
satire, 68, 70, 113
Schweitzer, Albert, 117
science fiction
  alternate history, 66, 141–142
  cognitive estrangement, 141
  novum, 71, 141
  space western, 41
  time travel, 66, 188–190
  tropes of science fiction, 65–67

  see also, Suvin, Darko and Dick, Philip K.
Seinfeld, Jerry, 208–210
Sermon on the Mount, 116
Shadowlands, 178–181, 184–186
Sherlock Holmes, 10–12, 18, 20, 23, 172
skepticism, 13, 16, 38, 152, 212
slavery, 72–86, 156–157
Socrates, 86, 104, 107, 121
Solzhenitsyn, Alexander, 33, 80
spectatorship, 211–213
Spielberg, Steven, 72–73, 80–81, 83
Stolyarov, Gennady II, 126–127
Suffering, 178–187
  Christ suffering with and for us, 64, 115
  co-suffering with Christ, 59, 125
  redemption of suffering, 157
  see also, love
Suvin, Darko, 65–68, 71, 141
  see also, science fiction
Swift, Jonathan, 70, 113

T
Taylor, Charles, 2, 108
  immanent frame, 2, 108
  A Secular Age, 2
technology, 65–71, 90
teleology, 52–53
tennis, 189, 192–196, 198–207
theism, 1, 7, 107, 148, 183
Thomism, 79
Three Billboards, 129–130, 132
Tikkun Olam, 222
Tolkien, J. R. R., 36–37, 178
Tolstoy, Leo, 118–119
transcendence, 2, 62, 177
Trump, Donald, 55, 111–112
Twain, Mark, 155, 157
  Huckleberry Finn, 37, 154–156
  Pudd'nhead Wilson, 156
tyranny, 41, 53, 135, 168

U
utilitarianism, 101, 122–123
  act utilitarianism, 122–123
  rule utilitarianism, 122–123

V
vocation, 12, 22
Volf, Miroslav, 189
voluntarism, 84–85
Vonnegut, Kurt, 7–9
voyeurism, 211–212

W
Warren, Tish Harrison, 114

Whedon, Joss
   Firefly, 40–52
   Buffy the Vampire Slayer, 136–139
wisdom, 38, 95–96
Wolterstorff, Nicholas, 187

Y
Yoder, John Howard, 118

SCRIPTURE INDEX

Exodus
20:8, 120

Ecclesiastes
12:5, 143
12:9-10, 176

Matthew
5:11-12, 121
5:39-41, 116
5:40, 117
5:48, 117
6:35, 121
8:22, 117
10:17-22, 116
10:28, 121
10:38-39, 116
16:25, 121
25:31f, 121

Mark
2:23-28, 120
12:31, 119

Luke
6:6-11, 120
6:20-21, 121
6:27-28, 116
6:30, 117
6:31, 119
6:35-36, 121
14:5, 120
14:26, 120
18:9-14, 118
22:49, 119

John
1:1, 9
2:14-16, 119
10:18, 125
11:50, 122
17:3, 127

Romans
12:17-19, 119
13:1-5, 119

I Corinthians
13:5-7, 135
15:26, 139

Ephesians
6:12, 60

I Thessalonians
4:13, 139

I Peter
3:13, 121

Revelation
2:17, 210
21:4, 64

PERMISSIONS

All essays in this volume were originally published elsewhere. They are reprinted here with kind permission from the initial publishers.

Published at ChristAndPopCulture.com:

"*About Time*: A Romantic Comedy That's Actually About Love," originally published December 4, 2013

"Refusing Counterfeits: *Rear Window* and Our Struggle as Spectators," originally published January 4, 2014 (original title: "You're the Voyeur: *Rear Window* and Our Struggle as Spectators")

"Kurt Vonnegut: Unlikely Apologist," originally published February 5, 2014

"J. K. Rowling: In Praise of Imagination," originally published February 27, 2014

"'And Death Shall Be No More': Going beyond Transhumanism for Kids," originally published April 1, 2014

"The Fault in Green's Story," originally published June 24, 2014

"Living in the Not Yet: *Mockingjay – Part 1* as Microcosm of the Fall," originally published November 26, 2014

"His Truth Is Marching On: *Selma*'s Clarion Call," originally published January 28, 2015

"*The Handmaid's Tale* Evokes a Longing for Peace and Justice, originally published May 4, 2017

"*Three Billboards Outside Ebbing, Missouri* Shows Us a World Full of Meanness," originally published January 23, 2018

"*RBG* Invites Us to Love Our Political Neighbors," originally published June 21, 2018

Published with Open Court Press:

"How to Resist Evil: Nonviolence in *The Passion of the Christ*," in *Mel Gibson's Passion and Philosophy*, edited by Jorge Gracia, 2004 (originally titled "Resist Not Evil! Jesus and Nonviolence")

"Magic, Muggles, and Moral Imagination," in *Harry Potter and Philosophy*, edited by David Baggett and Shawn Klein, 2004

"Rats in God's Laboratory: *Shadowlands* and The Problem of Evil," in *Movies and the Meaning of Life*, edited by Kim Blessing, 2005

Published at *AndPhilosophy.com*:

"*Once Upon a Time* and Philosophy: Rumpel's Redemption," originally published June 6, 2014

"Risking Belief: *Ted Lasso* and Faith," originally published February 12, 2021 (titled "Why We Need *Ted Lasso* and Philosophy")

Published through *Christian Research Journal*:

"*The Man in the High Castle* and the Necessity of Moral Faith," published on September 18, 2018

"Mark Twain's Tightrope Walk: Caught between Despair and Hope," published December 2018

"More Than Mere Machine: The Indomitable Human Spirit of Philip K. Dick," published December 2019

Published at *MoralApologetics.com*:

"*Interstellar* and Partiality," originally published December 10, 2014

"Intuiting the Beauty of the Infinite: Ramanujan and Hardy's Partnership," originally published November 5, 2016

"*Jerry before Seinfeld*: Delightfully Distinct," originally published November 29, 2017

"Hold Fast to the Good: *Fahrenheit 451*, the Love of Books, and the Value of People," originally published June 22, 2018

"The Faithful Witness of Fred Rogers," originally published July 13, 2018

"Train Up Your Wizards in the Way They Should Go," originally published October 24, 2018

Published through University of Kentucky Press:

"Human Rights, Human Nature, and *Amistad*," in *Steven Spielberg and Philosophy: We're Gonna Need a Bigger Book*, edited by Dean Kowalski, 2008

"Friendship, Rivalry, and Excellence," in *Tennis and Philosophy: What the Racket Is All About*," edited by David Baggett, 2010

"*Firefly* and Freedom," in *The Philosophy of Joss Whedon*, edited by Dean Kowalski, 2011

"Sherlock Holmes as Epistemologist," in *The Philosophy of Sherlock Holmes*, edited by David Baggett and Phil Tallon, 2012

Published through *The Worldview Bulletin*:

"Weighing Death in *Buffy the Vampire Slayer*," originally appeared March 8, 2020

Published through Wiley-Blackwell; Wiley-Blackwell's copyright notice applies and is reprinted here at the publisher's request: No part of this publication may be reproduced, store in a retrieval system, or transmitted in any form or by any means, electronic, mechanical, photocopying, recording, scanning, or otherwise, except as permitted under Section 107 or 108 of the 1976 United States Copyright Act, without either the prior written permission of the Publisher, or authorization through payment of the appropriate per-copy fee to the Copyright Clearance Center, 222 Rosewood Drive, Danvers, MA 01923, (978) 750-8400, fax (98=78) 646-8600, or on the web at www.copyright.com. Requests to the Publisher for permission should be addressed to the Permissions Department, John Wiley & Sons, Inc., 111 River Street, Hoboken, NJ 07030, (201) 748-6011, fax (201) 748-6008, or online at http://www.wiley.com/go/permissions.

"Love Potion No. 9 ¾," in *The Ultimate Harry Potter*, edited by Greg Bassham, 2010

"How Do You Like Them Ethics?" in *The Good Place and Philosophy*, edited by Kimberly Engels, 2020

www.ingramcontent.com/pod-product-compliance
Lightning Source LLC
LaVergne TN
LVHW051546070426
835507LV00021B/2439